# The Best Guide to
# MEDITATION

# The Best Guide to
# MEDITATION

## VICTOR N. DAVICH

Additional Material by Jean Marie Stine

Series Editor Richard F. X. O'Connor

ST. MARTIN'S GRIFFIN ♠ NEW YORK

www.stmartins.com

Design by Susan Shankin

Library of Congress Cataloging-in-Publication Data

Davich, Victor N.
    The best guide to meditation / Victor N. Davich
        p. cm.
    Includes bibliographical references (pp. 325–340) and index (pp. 341–350)
    ISBN 1-58063-010-3 (pbk)
    1. Meditation. I. Title.
BL627.D38  1998
158.1'2—dc21                                                                97-36555

First published in the United States by Renaissance Books

10   9   8

**To Mom and Dad**

I finally finished my homework.

The publisher gratefully acknowledges the use of cartoons from *Tricycle, The Buddhist Review,* copyright © by Neal Crosbie.

Special acknowledgment for contributions is made to Arthur Morey, Jean Marie Stine, Brenda Burke, Frankie Hill, and Scott Gerdes.

Portions of chapter 3 are reprinted by permission of Jeremy P. Tarcher, Inc., a division of The Putnam Publishing Group from CHOP WOOD CARRY WATER by Rick Fields, Rex Weyler, Rick Ingrasci, and Peggy Taylor. Copyright © 1984 by Rick Fields, Rex Weyler, Rick Ingrasci, and Peggy Taylor.

The author expresses his gratitude to Shinzen Young, whose body of work assisted greatly in some portions of this book.

## Note to the reader

# Contents

**Foreword**  *xv*

**Your Guided Tour of Meditation**  *xvii*

**Introduction**  *xix*

**Part 1: The First Steps**  23

**1. It's Easier than You Think**  25
Beginner's Mind
Meditation and Science
What is Meditation?
The Roots of Meditation
Approaching Meditation Practice

**2. Jump into Meditation**  43
Start Meditation Now
The Power of Breathing
Understanding the Breath
Focus: The Object of Meditation

**3. Bridging the Barriers to Meditation**  59
Doubt
Misconceptions
Pitfalls
Avoiding the Pitfalls

## 4. Developing Your Meditation Practice  73

Meditation Posture
What to Sit on
How to Sit
Sitting Positions
Space and Time to Meditate
Am I Doing it Right?

## Part 2. The Varieties of Meditation Practice  105

Many traditions
Mantra
Visualization

## 5. Eastern Meditation Traditions  115

Hinduism
    *Yoga*
    *Kundalini*
Buddhism
    *Zen*
    *Insight*
    *Tibetan*

## 6. Western Meditation Traditions  143

Meditative Prayer
Gnostic Meditation
Jewish Meditation
    *The Kabbalah*
Christian Meditation
    *The Prayter of Jesus*
    *Walking Meditation*
    *Gregorian Chant*
    *Canonical Hours*
Islamic Meditation
    *Sufism*

## 7. Meditation among Traditional Peoples 175

African Meditation
Native American Meditation

## 8. Contemporary Meditation Traditions 187

Gurdjieff and Ouspensky
Visualization of the Positive
Transcendental Meditation
Edgar Cayce
The Goddess and Women's Spirituality
Trying Different Techniques

# Part 3. The Meditative Life 219

## 9. Meditation in Action 221

Being Present
Karma Yoga
The Work Day
Recreation and Sports
Sleep

## 10. Meditative Home 237

Mindful Chores
Mindful Eating
Watching Your Words
Children
Intimate Relations

## 11. Pain to Ecstasy 255

Happiness as a Goal
Reducing Stress
Reducing Pain
Patience
The Way to Happiness
Your Summation

## 12. Lovingkindness and Compassion  273

The Goal of Lovingkindness
Tonglen
Approaches to Lovingkindness

## Appendix. Deepening Your Practice 293

Teachers
Cult or Consciousness Raising?
Meditation Retreats
Finding the Right Meditation Retreat for You
Getting Your Feet Wet
Etiquette
Costs

## Glossary  315

## Resource Section  325

## Index  341

# Meditation Exercises

**Beyond Words**  38

**Meditation with the Breath**  45

**Counting Exhalations**  56

**Counting Inhalations and Exhalations**  57

**Banishing Doubts**  61

**First Mantra Exercise**  111

**Developing the Breath**  120

**Koan Exercise--"Who Am I?"**  129

**Expansion and Contraction of Breath**  131

**Noting Body Sensations #1**  135

**Noting Body Sensations #2**  136

**Body Scan**  138

**Visualization**  141

**Power of Silence**  146

Reconciling Creative Opposites   148

The Shema Meditation   149

Lighting the Tree   154

Prayer of Jesus   159

Centering Prayer   160

Walking Exercise #1   162

Walking Exercise #2   164

Observing the Divine Offices...   168

Your Holy Pilgrimage   171

Sufi Stories and the Spiritual Path   173

Meditating on the Oracle   179

An Altar Meditation   180

The Medicine Wheel   183

Seeking the Totems   185

Self-Observation   193

Tarot Meditation   194

Imaginary Calisthenics   197

Answers from the Unconscious   199

Two Kriya Visualizations   200

**Meditation on Your Ideal   209**

**In the Arms of the Maternal Universe   211**

**Seven Goddess Meditations   213**

**Gaia Meditation   215**

**Taking on the Day   226**

**Meditating at Meetings   228**

**Mindful Dreaming   234**

**Mindful Eating   241**

**Minding Your Words   244**

**Mindful Lovemaking   252**

**Managing Stress   258**

**Expansion and Contraction   264**

**Locating Your Inner Ecstasy   269**

**Tonglen Exercise for One Who Suffers   282**

**Sending to a Loved One   283**

**The Lighthouse   284**

**Lovingkindness Exercise   286**

**...Lovingkindness to
Your Object of Hatred   289**

**Loving Yourself   290**

# Foreword

Taking a cue from the United Nations, the author of this book notes that more people on the planet meditate than those who don't.

Why is that?

Most people in the West have heard of meditation. Many have wondered how meditation might benefit their daily lives. And some have actually developed a meditative practice.

It would be fair to say that millions of us are seekers, people striving to be happier, more well-balanced human beings who endeavor to connect with our very self in a conscious attempt to get in touch with what we call the soul.

Through *Chicken Soup for the Soul* and its companion works my co-author, Mark Victor Hansen, and I have devoted our fullest efforts to help readers through the problems of daily existence by inspiring them with experiences of others that point toward living life to the fullest.

So too does meditation enrich daily life.

For many in both East and West, meditation is a way of life. It is an eons-old practice with roots in the major religious traditions of the world, joining hands as it does to help humankind in the quest for connection with something greater than itself—with the goal of becoming enlightened.

Whatever your goal—happiness, stress reduction, peace of mind, serenity, finding meaning, achieving connection—meditation, with its many faces and forms, is something that each of us is capable of.

And this book will serve as your personal guided tour to meditation through its easy to comprehend explanations of mantras, koans, retreats, karma, and even the various schools or belief systems surrounding meditation.

From the author's definition of meditation as "opening to each moment with calm awareness," to explanations of spiritual enlightenment, to showing the way of mindfulness in daily activity, *The Best Guide to Meditation* takes the reader one baby step at a time in developing a meditation practice of his or her own.

And each step—from the simple breath meditation which gets the reader meditating right away, to intermediate and advanced techniques culled from the masters—is accompanied by clearly delineated exercises to improve the practice.

It is a compliment to the author and a benefit to the reader that the essence of meditation is captured on these pages. For certainly no one would dispute that learning to live life with lovingkindness and compassion is a worthy goal. Therein lies the key to the best in all of us.

JACK CANFIELD
*Santa Barbara, California*

# *Your Guided Tour of Meditation*

When you go on a trip you use a guidebook, usually because you don't have the time to see everything, don't know what to see, or know what you want to see and want to know how to get there the fastest. A good guidebook:

- gives you choices of where you want to go,

- highlights what is generally agreed to be "don't miss" places,

- anticipates and answers frequently asked questions, and

- points you in the right direction for more in-depth study.

When the tour is over, you come away feeling that, although you may not have seen an entire city or country, you have a sense of the place. And you know that if you ever return you can really focus on particular aspects that interested you.

Along these lines, consider this your guidebook to a new, intriguing and exciting place—the world of meditation. If you read this book and follow its instructions, you will, by tour's end:

- already be meditating, using an elegant, easy to understand meditation technique based on working with your breath,

- understand how meditation came about,
- understand what meditation is about,
- have explored a variety of different meditative techniques,
- have started to make meditation part of your life,
- know how meditation can help you suffer less and therefore be happier,
- have tried a form of meditation that can transform your relationship your family, your friends, even your enemies, and
- know how to go further and where to look to deepen your practice.

To give you direct experience of meditation, this book includes over fifty exercises, set off from the main text by gray rules.

# Introduction

What you have heard about meditation is simple and true: this centuries-old technique can make your life today happier, richer, calmer, and fuller.

Meditation can help you:

- relieve stress,
- relax,
- learn to go with the flow,
- get in touch with your emotions,
- reduce acute and chronic pain levels,
- become more compassionate,
- live a fuller, richer life, and
- be a better golfer, jogger, or cook.

The list is endless. It includes everything that is important in your life. And learning meditation does not require you to learn countless skills and techniques or to change your religious convictions.

The practice of meditation does require that you make a commitment, starting with just a few minutes a day, to learn more about who you are through the practice of calm awareness. That's it. There are no big treatises to read, no secret societies to join, no large sums of money to pay.

Meditation is simply the art of opening to each moment of life with calm awareness.

You may be skeptical that something as simple and ancient as meditation can bring such amazing benefits to modern life. That's fine. It's good to approach meditation with healthy skepticism. The truth of the matter is that you will only know if meditation can change your life for the better by meditating. This book is here to help you do just that.

## Who meditates?

When you decide to become a meditator, you're in very good company. Around the globe, hundreds of thousands of people meditate every day. People you thought did, like the Dalai Lama and The Beatles. And people you'd never think would, like Richard Gere, Pamela Lee, Oliver Stone, Arnold Palmer...and believe it or not.... America's top radio host:

"[Howard] Stern wakes at 4 a.m. A car and chauffeur waits outside in the suburban dark. On the ride into Manhattan (and on the ride back to Long Island), he sits in the back seat and meditates. Stern has been practicing transcendental meditation for twenty years."

DAVID REMNICK
"The Accidental Anarchist,"
*The New Yorker*, March 10, 1997

The goal of this book is to demystify, clarify, and teach you the process, or art, of meditation. It is designed for beginners and experienced students alike—anyone who wants to start and develop a meditation practice. This book is designed for you.

This book assumes that you:

- are a regular person who naturally wants to be happier, and thinks meditation might be rewarding,

- have little or no prior experience reading about or actually meditating, and/or

- want to cut to the chase and try meditation today.

There are many books, tapes, and other programs already available about meditation. Usually, like Goldilocks's porridge, they fall into three categories:

- too hard,

- too easy, or

- just right.

This book falls into the "just right" category, which puts it in the minority. Meditation is not too easy, and not too hard. If somebody tells you meditation's a snap, or, on the other hand, it means renouncing your life, job, family and going to a monastery in Kyoto for the next ten years, they're not leveling with you.

This book is designed to make the practice of meditation:

- simple to learn,

- manageable within your daily life,

- attainable, something you can become proficient in, and

- rewarding to you and the people around you.

To put it in terms used by the Buddha, the first meditation teacher, this book will take you on *the middle way* to meditation. And that is the best way.

# Why You Don't Want To Say You're A Meditator

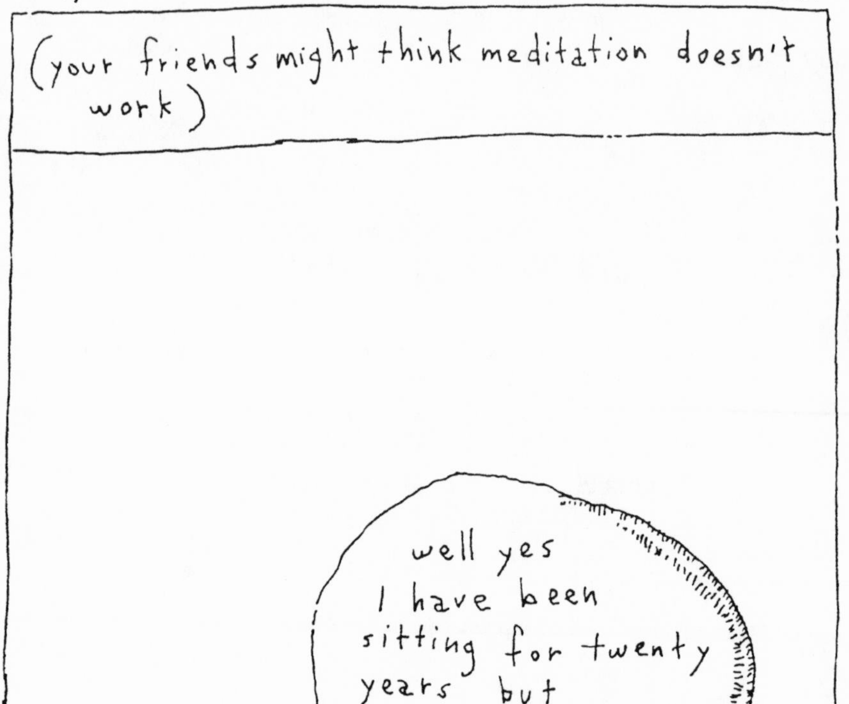

# P A R T  1

# *The First Steps*

In *It's All in your Head*, Jean Marie Stine puts meditation in perspective: "What's older than the dawn of history—and as modern as today's neuroscientific researchers? Need a hint? It cures mental and physical illness and provides solutions to your most pressing problems. Give up? Meditation.

"Mediation quiets our usually busy consciousness. Through physically and mentally stilling the mind, we achieve heightened mental clarity. Multiple experiments, writes physician-researcher Harold Bloomfield, prove meditation produces 'positive feelings that...promote emotional health...add noticeably to self-esteem [and] sociability...reduce anxiety, tension, irritability, chronic fatigue, and depression,' while doubts and insecurities fade.

"The mental quiet and relaxation produced by meditation confers profound benefits on body as well as mind. 'Inner silence is crucial to health,' Bloomfield claims. 'One experiences a state of deep rest, marked by decreases in heartbeat rate, oxygen consumption, perspiration, muscle tension, blood pressure, and levels of stress hormones.'

"No wonder it's still around after ten thousand years."

It's difficult to imagine how anyone could resist dropping everything to learn meditation practice. Many of us have friends who meditate daily and announce that their lives have been changed for the good by doing so. They have become serene, more efficient, more successful. Their relationships

**23**

with loved ones and with people at work have improved.

Why do we resist learning meditation? Many of us feel we don't have time. And when we try to make time we're put off by the fear that we won't, somehow, do well. The exotic background of some meditation practice is a little frightening, even off-putting. We think we may not understand. And when we actually try to meditate we're overcome by fear of failure. And so we make excuses—no time, no money for classes, no available teachers, etc.

Reading a book is only a beginning. No book on meditation can give the reader a complete picture of the practice. (Though there are very good books on gardening, tennis, personal relationships, for example, which promise radical improvement, none of them can guarantee success either.) Reading about a profound experience cannot reproduce the experience. In order to know about meditation, you have to begin.

In the next chapters you will be encouraged to move as quickly as possible into meditation practice. Theory, history, ramifications can come later. For now, you will be encouraged to take a leap of faith. Part I will clear the ground and give you a foundation. Possible objections or doubts will be dealt with. Fears of ignorance will be dispelled. You will be shown how to prepare yourself—what you need, how to start meditating even before you've found a class or teacher.

If, in your reading, you come across an unfamiliar word or concept, look it up in the word list at the front of the book. If you want more information, check the more detailed glossary at the end. The appendix will give you suggestions that can help you continue your research.

But for now, just go ahead. You are about to begin a practice that is older than organized religion, common to virtually every culture on the planet. Once you've taken a few steps along this path you may become convinced, as many have, that your brain and body were built and wired for meditation. You won't be starting something new and foreign, you'll be uncovering resources, skills, and insights you never realized you possessed.

*Many of us have friends who meditate daily.... They have become serene, more efficient, more successful. Their relationships with loved ones and with people at work have improved.*

# It's Easier than You Think

**1**

**S**hunryu Suzuki Roshi (*roshi* means teacher or elder) was the Japanese Zen master instrumental in bringing *Zen meditation* to America in the 1960s. In his classic book *Zen Mind, Beginner's Mind,* he said: "In the beginner's mind there are many possibilities, in the expert's there are few." The great traditions of meditation have welcomed beginners with open arms. Suzuki Roshi advised all his students, even the most advanced, always to keep their beginner's mind. For a true beginner, as you may be, this is a wonderful thing. Coming to meditation without preconceived notions, not locked into any particular idea of what is right or wrong, is like learning to play golf without any bad habits.

## BEGINNER'S MIND, GOAL-ORIENTED MIND

While it's good to approach meditation with an open mind, there's no need to beat yourself up for having some preconceptions. We're all human, and we rarely do anything without preconceptions. Beginner or not, if you are reading this book, you probably have some goal or expectation in mind of what meditation is like and what it will do for you. You may have read something on the cover that

*   **The connection between meditation, goals, and happiness**

*   **The origins of meditative practice**

*   **Definitions of meditation**

*   **Changes in the body and mind with meditation**

*   **First steps**

intrigued you, or heard something of meditation's benefits and rewards—from peace of mind to improved health to creative insights to spiritual development—that sounded intriguing, or made it worthwhile to give meditation a try.

It's good to have goals and expectations, they'll help motivate you to give the suggested meditations in this book a try, and to clear aside the twenty minutes a day needed to sit and meditate. Before going farther it may even be helpful to review the rewards that first stirred your interest in meditation. The following are goals that people typically bring to meditation practice. Check off any that apply to you. Which do you hope to find through meditation?

*"Nevertheless, the flowers fall with our attachment.*

*"And the weeds spring up with our aversion."*

DOGEN
*noted Zen monk*

\_\_\_ Inner happiness and/or peace of mind.

\_\_\_ Relief from high-blood pressure, stress, a heart condition, asthma, or other medical condition.

\_\_\_ A spiritual experience.

\_\_\_ Self-discovery or greater self-knowledge.

\_\_\_ A solution to a personal or professional dilemma.

\_\_\_ Creative insights.

\_\_\_ Healing from the stress and pain of traumatic life events, such as death of a loved one, abuse, war, accident, divorce.

\_\_\_ Relief from anxiety, confusion, depression.

\_\_\_ Aid in recovery from alcoholism, substance abuse, sex-addiction, or other obsessive-compulsive behaviors.

\_\_\_ Boosted memory and intelligence.

\_\_\_ Reduced or eliminated chronic physical pain.

\_\_\_ Communion with God.

\_\_\_ A better handle on your weight, temper, passivity, anger, or other unbalanced areas of your life.

Meditation can help you achieve these goals in a natural, simple, and permanent way.

Meditation works at a deep, intuitive level and results in real, not superficial or cosmetic, changes. Meditation is not a form of wishing for something. When you meditate, you don't meditate to lose twenty pounds. You simply meditate.

### *"No thank you"*

Using diet as an example, however, meditation could help you lose that twenty pounds. The more meditation you do, the more you get in touch with yourself naturally. You become more aware of what you are doing on a moment-by-moment basis. And that includes the moments when you are eating.

One seemingly normal day, you've finished dinner and are ready for one of those fattening desserts you love. It is put in front of you. It looks great. You pick up your spoon. And then you do something you haven't done before: You really look at that dessert.

What happens next surprises everyone, including you. You politely say, "No, thank you," and you pass on it.

The next morning at breakfast, you find yourself really looking at the usual plate of sausage, waffles, and syrup in front of you. You are naturally—for the first time perhaps—totally aware that this is not something that someone who needs to lose weight eats for breakfast. Calmly, you push away the waffles and reach for the cereal.

That's how it starts. No books, no starvation diets, no complex food balancing charts—just an increased awareness of what you are doing and a sense of being that much closer to your body's desire to be healthy. The result is real and lasting change. You're happier and healthier.

*The more meditation you do, the more you get in touch with yourself naturally. You become more aware of what you are doing on a moment-by-moment basis.*

## HOW SCIENCE SAYS MEDITATION CAN HELP YOU

Meditation research increased dramatically during the past three decades, particularly in the United States. Since the early 1970s, more than a thousand laboratory studies of meditation have been reported in scientific journals, books, and graduate theses in the English language alone. These tests—involving EEGs, brain scans, blood and hormonal

**Detailed analysis showed meditation produced important cardiovascular, cortical, hormonal, and metabolic benefits...and significant beneficial alterations of interior experience, perception, and self-image.**

samplings, and a host of other cutting-edge scientific research methodologies—provided incontestable evidence of meditation's benefits. Detailed analysis showed meditation produced important cardiovascular, cortical, hormonal, and metabolic benefits, along with several positive behavioral effects and significant beneficial alterations of interior experience, perception, and self-image. These studies, says Michael Murphy, co-founder of California's famed Esalen Institute, are "gradually improving our scientific understanding of meditation in ways that complement the insights contained in the traditional contemplative literature." Everyone seemed to benefit from these improvements—regardless of gender, race, or the type of pain they suffer.

## Psychological benefits

Hundreds of laboratory tests show that practicing meditation for as little as twenty minutes once a day promotes improved psychological well-being and mental performance. Among the other beneficial effects, meditation results in:

- improved mental health,
- greater emotional stability,
- outgoingness,
- independence,
- spontaneity,
- lessened anxiety and depression,
- reduced dependence on licit and illicit drugs,
- greater sense of and interest in the spiritual,
- more accurate judgment,
- creative thoughts,
- increased concentration,
- empathy, and
- improved memory and intelligence.

## *Physical benefits*

Hundreds of other research studies indicate that meditating only twenty minutes a day improves health and can ameliorate the symptoms of even some serious illnesses. For instance, it:

- boosts energy,

- increases stamina,

- speeds recovery,

- lessens the frequency and severity of asthmatic attacks, and other allergic reactions,

- lowers blood pressure significantly,

- materially reduces stress and stress-related illnesses like heart disease, hypertension, and insomnia,

- significantly alleviates present-moment and chronic physical pain from arthritis, back injury, and most other causes,

- improves response time, motor skills, coordination, and other physical responses.

> **The purpose of meditation is to help you wake up.**

## WHAT IS MEDITATION?

Meditation may seem mysterious and difficult. But it's easier than you think. In fact, it's as easy as falling off a log, says Herbert Benson, M.D. Benson has successfully taught thousands to meditate in the laboratory. It may take a few tries to get the hang of meditation, Benson warns. But he promises that you'll soon notice its physical and mental benefits.

Benson's research shows that four things are necessary to produce a state of deep meditation:

1. a quiet environment to eliminate distractions;

2. a comfortable posture that allows complete relaxation;

3. a few moments spent relaxing; and

4. a "mental device" (traditionally called a *mantra* or prayer) to help block the endless flow of thoughts generated by our waking mind.

Begin by slowly relaxing all your muscles, Benson advises, starting at your feet and ending with your neck, head, and face. Then for the next ten to twenty minutes, while keeping the muscles relaxed, breath in and out easily and naturally, mentally saying "one" (or the mental device of your choice) with each breath.

> *"...Meditation seems to produce a physiological state of deep relaxation coupled with a wakeful and highly alert mental state....The physiological state brought about by meditation appears to be the opposite one from the state brought about by anxiety or anger."*
>
> LAWRENCE LeSHAN
> *How to Meditate*

Why do meditation? Why not just sit quietly and relax? Because simple relaxation doesn't produce the same mental and physical benefits as meditation. One joint Oxford University and University of London research project found meditation-like programs are far more effective at reducing stress than just relaxing.

## Defining meditation

There are many definitions of meditation. The truth is, any attempt to define meditation with words falls short of truly explaining this practice.

There is a famous Zen saying, "Zen is not the moon, but only a finger pointing at the moon." This means that the word is not the reality. In the words of Alfred Korzybski, "The map is not the territory."

Just as looking at a map of Kansas is not the same as being in Kansas, reading definitions of meditation or books on meditation technique is not meditation. *The only way to understand what meditation means is to meditate.*

One of the most famous and wisest books in the world is the Chinese *Tao Te Ching*, The Book of the Way. It is attributed to the eighth-century Chinese master Lao-tzu. Its subject is the *Tao*, the great flow of life and death.

In one passage Lao-tzu says:

But words that point to the Tao
seem monotonous and without flavor.
When you look for it, there is nothing to see.
When you listen for it, there is nothing to hear.
When you use it, it is inexhaustible.

Meditation, like the Tao, is beyond words. You can read about it forever and still come up scratching your head. But when you use it, meditation is an inexhaustible, continual source of energy, insight, and true wisdom.

*Awake* as used by the Buddha does not simply mean alert. Awake means a new, more joyous, enriching, and happier way of being. As the powerful sun of clarity burns off our individual fog of delusion, we find ourselves in a new, bright, happier place where the sun always shines. Moreover, meditation helps us to connect to the universe in a whole new way.

## Buddha on the road

*Stories have been a way of conveying wisdom in every human culture. Here is a classical story from the Buddhist tradition that points at what meditation is. This version is from the book* Seeking the Heart of Wisdom, *by Joseph Goldstein and Jack Kornfield:*

*It is said that soon after his enlightenment, the Buddha passed a man on the road who was struck by the extraordinary radiance and peacefulness of his presence. The man stopped and asked, "My friend, what are you? Are you a celestial being or a god?"*

*"No," said the Buddha.*

*"Well then, are you some kind of magician or wizard?" Again the Buddha answered, "No."*

*"Are you a man?"*

*"No."*

*"Well, my friend, what then are you?" The Buddha replied, "I am awake."*

## A simple definition

Work with this definition as you begin your practice:

Meditation is the art of opening to each moment with calm awareness.

You might want to place copies of this sentence wherever you post memos—over the kitchen sink, on your computer monitor, on your bathroom mirror, on the sun visor of your car, on your dining room placemat, on the refrigerator door.

As you continue your meditation practice, you will come across many definitions of meditation. You may also come to formulate your own. Remember that whatever they are, and wherever they come from, definitions are merely words, and as such can only point at meditation. The only way to understand what meditation means is to meditate.

## Quieting the mind

The meditative state is different from being high, asleep, or hypnotized. It is a unique physiological state. The writer and psychologist Lawrence LeShan, in *How To Meditate*, says that the singularity of the meditative state is connected with a dramatic reduction in the number of signals that our body and brain are called upon to process.

Normally, our senses are bombarded with a wide variety of stimuli that urgently demand responses from the brain. They can be physical, such as hunger; mental, such as thinking; or emotional, such as fright. When too many messages are sent at once, the brain can overheat like an overloaded electrical system. The manifestations on a conscious level include being anxious, overwhelmed, confused, and stressed.

In the meditative state, on the other hand, the meditator ideally brings total awareness, concentration, and attention to only one thing, such as the breath, which is called the object of awareness. This becomes an anchor in the sea of thoughts and feelings that we call consciousness. When focused on breath we let go of thoughts and sensations as we become aware of them and immediately return to the breath.

By focusing the mind on just one object, the number of signals sent to our brain is greatly reduced, allowing the mind to settle down into a deeply relaxed, yet highly alert state.

## Suzuki Roshi and the animals

In *Zen Mind, Beginner's Mind*, the great Zen Master Suzuki Roshi used farmyard animals as an analogy for our limited thoughts and ideas:

To give your sheep or cow a large, spacious meadow is the way to control him. The same way works for you as well. If you want to obtain perfect calmness in your zazen (meditation practice), you should not be bothered by the various images you find in your mind. Let them come and let them go.

## THE ROOTS OF MEDITATION

Meditation is a tradition with roots in the major religions of the world. Meditation joins company with devotion and prayer to help humanity in its quest for connection with something greater than itself.

Prayer is like talking to God, meditation is a way of listening to God.

EDGAR CAYCE
*The Divine Within*

# *Some classical descriptions of meditation*

*1. Act of meditating; deep, continued thought; reflection. 2. Solemn reflection on sacred matters as a devotional act.*                                      WEBSTER'S NEW WORLD DICTIONARY

*The art of suspending verbal and symbolic thinking for a time, somewhat as a courteous audience will stop talking when a concert is about to begin.*                                 ALAN WATTS

*Thoughtful action to establish order. Meditation is nothing other than a relaxation technique with various larger purposes.*                                 ANDREW WEIL

*...bringing the mind home.*                                 SOGYAL RINPOCHE

*...attention, attention, attention.*                                 ZEN MASTER IKKYU

*...like great scuba gear. You can see, hear, touch and taste your thoughts without drowning in them.*                                 LAURIE FISHER HUCK

*Meditation must be used as a tool to come to the freedom beyond tools.*          JACK KORNFIELD

*...calm abiding.*                                 TIBETAN TRADITION

*...not a means to an end. It is both the means and the end.*                                 KRISHNAMURTI

*The development of awareness, using concentration as a tool.*

VEN. H. GUNARATANA MAHATHERA

*A way of practice that can open us to see clearly our bodies, our hearts, our minds, and the world around us and develop a wise and compassionate way to relate to and understand them all.*

JOSEPH GOLDSTEIN AND JACK KORNFIELD

*Brain and consciousness become pure. It is exactly like muddy water left to stand in a glass. Little by little, the sediment sinks to the bottom and the water becomes pure.*          TAISEN DESHIMARU

*One is one's present self, what one was, and what one will be, all at once.*          PETER MATTHIESSEN

*When thine eye is single thy whole body also is full of light.*          JESUS OF NAZARETH

All of the great traditions, including Judaism, Hinduism, Christianity, and Buddhism, developed, along with their devotional side, a wisdom, or meditative aspect.

In *Coming Home*, Lex Hixon gives this analogy:

> Imagine you are wandering through a vast cathedral. Countless stained-glass windows, radiant in the darkness, represent the modes of worship and ways of understanding that humanity has evolved throughout its history. Some windows picture Divine Presence through personal forms or attributes, and seekers worship before these windows with devotion. Other seekers, preferring the way of wisdom, contemplate stained-glass windows that present nothing personal, simply esoteric patterns evoking harmony and unity. Devotion and wisdom are alternate ways to Enlightenment. Some sacred traditions interweave both ways.

*Devotional prayer embraces meditation in the search of humankind to name that thing that has no name but goes by many. This is the ground of the great religious traditions.*

Thus, devotional prayer embraces meditation in the search of humankind to name that thing that has no name but goes by many. This is the ground of the great religious traditions, which the Hindu scripture, the Bhagavad-Gita or the Song of God, describes as "that one-pointed concentration of the will which leads a man to absorption in God." God goes by many other names including: The Dharma, Christ Nature, Higher Power, Tao, Divine Presence, Godhead, Allah, Yahweh, Original Mind.

Paralleling the many names for God are the varied practices of chanting, affirming, and meditating, all focused on a similar end. Thus, one might find a follower of the Jewish faith in Ohio meditating on Psalm 77:

> I remember the deeds of God.
>
> I remember Your wonders from days long ago.
>
> I meditate on all Your work, Your actions....

One might find a devotee of Buddhism in New York continuously chanting *Om*, or Zen Buddhist monks in California, in *zazen* (sitting meditation), watching their breath with pure attention and calm.

These people all share mind talk, using meditation in the practice of their own particular religious faith.

Many meditators combine their religious beliefs with meditation from another tradition, sometimes with synergistic results. Phil Jackson, coach of the Chicago Bulls basketball team, was raised in the Pentecostal tradition. In *Sacred Hoops*, Jackson mentions that his discovery of Zen Buddhist meditation enhanced his Christian beliefs.

However, religious beliefs are not a precondition for a valid, strong, meditation practice. Meditation can be religion-based or not.

## The Dalai Lama and the Gospels

Nowhere was the coming together of Eastern and Western religious traditions more evident than in September 1994, at the Tenth Annual John Main Seminar in England, when the World Community for Christian Meditation convened a four-day symposium. Religious leaders from around the world gathered to hear the Dalai Lama, winner of the Nobel Prize for Peace, give a discourse, from a Buddhist perspective, on the Sermon on the Mount, the Resurrection of Christ, and the Christian Gospels.

In *The Good Heart*, a transcript of the seminar, the Dalai Lama explained how the two principal types of Tibetan meditation, one contemplative and the other focused, can be applied to Christian worship to yield a deep and powerful experience of compassion:

> Let us take the example of meditation on love and compassion in the Christian

### Diversity in mindfulness

"In my early retreat experience I was part of a large group, perhaps a hundred people, doing intensive mindfulness practice in a monastery in Massachusetts.

...I saw Theravadan [Southern Asian] monks in orange robes, Zen people in traditional Zen clothing, and Tibetan monks and nuns. Some people wore red clothes and beads, which meant they were followers of a certain Hindu teacher. One man wore a Franciscan habit...the long beads and crucifix that hung from his belt made a pleasant clicking sound.... On Friday evening, I entered the dining room and saw that someone had lit two candles.... A sign said 'These are Sabbath candles. Please do not blow them out.'

I looked around and thought 'Here we all are! Each of us, in whatever religious context we live our lives, is trying to wake up.'"

SYLVIA BOORSTEIN
*It's Easier Than You Think*

context. In an analytical [thinking] aspect of that meditation, we would be thinking along specific lines, such as...to truly love God one must demonstrate that love through the action of loving fellow human beings in a genuine way, loving one's neighbor.... This type of thought process is the analytical aspect of meditation on compassion.

Once you feel totally convinced of the preciousness of and need for compassion and tolerance, you will experience a sense of being touched, a sense of being transformed from within. At this point, place your mind single-pointedly in that conviction. Thus, both types of (Tibetan) meditation are applied in one meditation session.

## APPROACHING MEDITATION PRACTICE

These days there is a tendency to plunge into new activities with a gung-ho, take-no-prisoners attitude. The result of our impatience often leads to frustration and finally abandonment of the activity as too hard or not worth it. That's why you should approach your practice gradually.

At one time matchbook covers were a fertile ground for companies to advertise their wares. One such advertisement that appeared in the 1950s promoted a course in speedwriting, a simplified kind of shorthand. The ad read: "IF U CN RD THIS YOU CN LRN SPDWRTNG." Well, the same is true of meditation: IF U CN BRTHE, U CN MEDT8.

Like speedwriting, meditation is a skill that requires effort and cannot be mastered overnight. At the same time, meditation is not complex, arcane, or beyond your comprehension. Meditation is not hard to learn and is accessible to everyone.

In chapter 2: *Jump Into Meditation*. you'll be introduced to a simple, elegant, and effective way to meditate, based on an ever-present, simple yet powerful meditation tool—your own breath.

> *Once you feel totally convinced of the preciousness of and need for compassion and tolerance, you will experience a sense of being touched, a sense of being transformed from within.*

## Start slowly

When you first start to meditate, be aware that what might be called your meditation muscles may be a bit weak. The same logic that says not to take your first nature walk up Mount Everest should tell you to be gentle, and not push or overwhelm yourself by over-meditating.

In the beginning, a minute of meditation may seem as overwhelming as Mount Everest. This is natural and to be expected. Take it easy and be kind to yourself. Start out slowly and work your way up.

When you first begin your practice, one ten-minute meditation a day is totally adequate. Start with this and build slowly, adding time in increments that won't overwhelm or frustrate you.

## The feel of meditation

The following exercise (indicated by a gray rule) has been designed to help you get a taste of what meditation can be. But if you are like most beginners, you probably want to know what meditation will feel like for you mentally and physically before you begin. You may even have heard something that made it sound scary—though the truth is there is nothing scary about meditation, especially for first timers and beginners. In fact, there is no way to guarantee in advance what meditation will feel like for you—only that it will be a positive experience.

One reason it's so hard to predict how meditation will affect you, is that meditation is as individual as you are. It feels different to different people. Sensations afterward range across a broad spectrum of reactions and feelings.

*Jack Kornfield, a meditation teacher, says in* **Living Buddhist Masters** *that a Thai meditation teacher was once asked if meditation was like self-hypnosis. The teacher replied, "No, it's de-hypnosis."*

### Spiritual first aid

*All of the meditations in this book have been carefully selected for beginners. They are very unlikely to create any kind of strong energy surge. But should you experience difficulty with them or any meditations you learn subsequently, here's a spiritual first aid tip: Merely continue sitting and focus on your breath. Try to see and feel the energy inside you as a glowing mass in your chest. Then each time you exhale picture and feel that energy flowing out from you with your breath. When you body feels emptied of the energy, stop, and end your meditation.*

Among the reactions first timers report are:

- nothing at all (rare),

- peaceful and relaxed (very typical),

- quietly positive and energized (very typical),

- ecstatic and tingling (not as common, but not uncommon), and

- surging mental and/or physical energy that feels difficult to control (extremely rare, easily dealt with).

But, again, the feelings you are most likely to have at the end of the exercise below are peace, tranquility, relaxation, calm.

In chapter 4 you'll find instructions for building a daily meditation schedule that you can use to move yourself along without turning yourself off.

The following statements can help pinpoint your optimum ten minutes for beginning your practice:

- The quietest time of the day for me is _____.

- I am least likely to be disturbed for ten minutes at ____ o'clock.

- The place where I have the fewest outside stimuli and demands made on me is _____.

## BEYOND WORDS

1. Set aside the next ten minutes. Find a comfortable, quiet place where you will feel safe and are not likely to be disturbed. Take the phone off the hook, take off your shoes. Begin to relax.

2. Sit or lie down in a comfortable position. Gently close your eyes but remain alert.

3. Tell yourself that you would like to begin to remember certain life experiences, those particular times when your senses were so deeply involved in an activity or event that:

- It seemed timeless. There was only the present moment.

- You felt unencumbered by the past memories and future anticipation.

- You were being instead of doing.

You may even call them peak experiences. Your experiences could be visual ones—that unforgettable sunset at Yosemite, the time a pod of dolphins skirted your fishing boat, your child's first step. Your experiences might have been auditory—that incredible performance by Pavarotti, the sound of wind on a downhill ski run at Sun Valley, your child's first word.

4. As your mind sifts, sorts, and categorizes these peak memories, one in particular will assert itself strongly. Focus on it. Now, holding that memory in your mind, begin to examine it closely, minutely. Let the memory resonate throughout your entire body and being. Can you sense the overall feeling of being present in that experience? Can you recall the timeless quality of just being in an event that you were not trying to control, shape, fiddle with, or judge?

5. Let yourself go and once again relive this timeless moment of presentness. Do not interfere with it. Do not edit it into something more than it was. Gently work with the moment—opening to it with calm awareness.

And when you have finished reliving the moment, gently stop and open your eyes. Take a pause to feel the experience of the body and mind.

---

In the beginning, you will start with one meditation session each day. As you continue to practice, you can gradually extend that period and add a second sitting. Most meditators meditate twice a day, usually on arising and just before bed. Try to meditate at the same time every day. It's a positive habit and makes for a more consistent practice.

At first, try to follow the guidelines in this book. But also be flexible and sensitive to your personal life and schedule. Meditation is a reflection of real life—everything changes. So if you start out meditating in the morning at the office but later find that it's more convenient during your lunch hour, feel free to make the adjustment.

Most meditators meditate at home where they can exercise some degree of control over their immediate environment, but only you know the best time and place for you.

Remember, your goal is to establish a daily meditation practice that will last for a lifetime. It is better to meditate a few minutes a day, every day, than an hour once a week.

## Before you begin

When you sit down to meditate, you are most likely at the start of a busy day. You might be puzzling over the dream you woke with, or already checking the laundry list of must do's for the day ahead.

If you immediately sit down to meditate with your mind going at high speed, it may not slow down until the end of the session, if at all. That's why it's good to take a minute or so before you begin to meditate to slow down.

Follow this checklist:

- Take your sitting posture. Become very still.

- Rock back and forth gently. Feel your body in your posture.

- Say to yourself, "For the next ____ minutes, I will be doing my meditation practice. There is nowhere to go, nothing to do, no place to be. No one I have to be."

- Begin your meditation period.

## After you meditate

You will usually feel more relaxed, calmer, and have a greater sense of well-being at the conclusion of your meditation period; to leap out of your chair or up from your cushion could be a jarring experience. It is important to your well-being to take several minutes after you finish meditating to adjust back to your activities.

Taking one or two minutes for transitioning after the conclusion of your session gives you interest on your investment. Here's a finishing checklist:

- Sit still and quietly survey your body and mind. Does anything feel different from before you started? Better or worse? Positive or negative?

- Realize that you have done something good for yourself by meditating. No matter what you may think happened, it was positive.

- Tell yourself that you are going to take the benefits of mindfulness with you wherever you go from here.

- Slowly rub your knees and elbows, bringing fresh circulation to those areas.

- Mindfully, rise from your meditation posture. Be aware of the whole body as it moves from a sitting to an upright position.

*"Each day human life contains joy and anger, pain and pleasure, darkness and light, growth and decay. Each moment is etched with nature's grand design—do not try to deny or oppose the cosmic order of things."*

MORIHEI UESHIBA
founder of the Japanese martial art Aikido
*The Art of Peace*

## CHAPTER RECAP

- Meditation is simple and easy.

- Always keep your mind open.

- Meditation produces scientifically proven physical and mental benefits.

- The only way to understand meditation is to meditate.

- Meditation stems from the great religious traditions of the world.

- Meditation produces a physiological state of deep relaxation coupled with a wakeful and highly alert mental attitude.

- Twenty minutes once a day is all it takes to benefit from meditation.

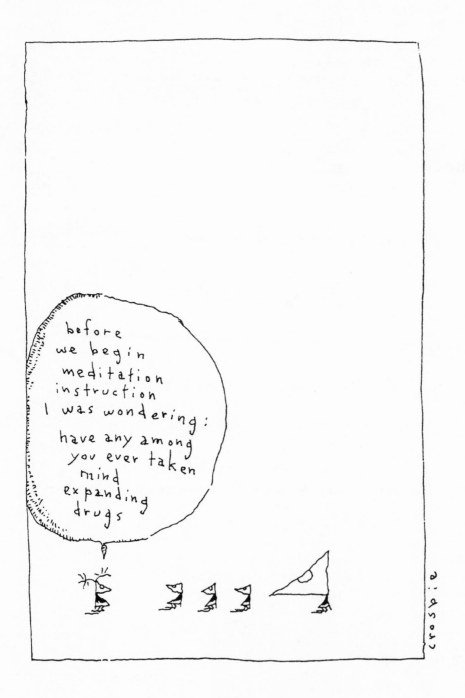

# *Jump into Meditation*

# 2

As we've already said, meditation goes beyond words; the only way to understand what meditation means is to meditate.

This section enables you to begin meditating right now. Simply sit down, in a relaxed yet alert posture, and follow the instructions. After you've meditated, read the rest of the chapter.

## START NOW

This is the start of your first meditation session. For the next ten minutes you are going to practice the art of opening to each moment of life with calm awareness. Without any preconceived notions, without any discussion of what to sit on, how to sit, where to put your hands, what to do with your eyes, you are simply going to meditate.

If you did the exercise in the last chapter, you got an inkling of what it is like to focus on an image or experience without getting sidetracked by other sensations or thoughts. Now, for the next ten minutes, you are again going to do just that. Your focal point, or object of meditation, will simply be your breath.

For this short period of time, create a peaceful, undisturbed environment for yourself. Shut the door and let the answering machine take your calls.

- **Meditation and the breath**

- **Ways of looking at the breath**

- **The object of meditation and meditative practice**

- **Strategies for dealing with distraction and your wandering mind**

Many people initially feel that making time to meditate is, in fact, an excuse to goof off or waste time. However, when you meditate, you are doing something very important for yourself; every moment of meditation is a golden opportunity for a full, happier life. Let yourself feel totally entitled to your meditation period. Try not to think about what you need to do, should be doing, or must do. Remember, this is only for the next ten minutes. After you meditate, you can go back and pick up exactly where you left off.

For your initial meditation, you can sit on anything and in any position that you find comfortable. If you are not feeling well, are sick or injured, you can lie down. If you are in a wheelchair, you do not have to change your seat unless you want to.

You should feel relaxed in your posture, but not so relaxed that your body is confused into thinking it's going to go to sleep. Remember, our definition of meditation is the art of opening to each moment of life with calm awareness. This does not allow for snoozing.

Once you have found a comfortable spot, just sit there for a moment. Take several deep breaths and feel your entire body. You have begun to meditate.

### Looks can be deceiving

*"Breathing, which seems so mundane and uninteresting at first glance, is actually an enormously complex and fascinating procedure. It is full of delicate variations, if you look. There is inhalation and exhalation, long breath and short breath, deep breath, shallow breath, smooth breath and ragged breath. These categories combine with one another in subtle and intricate ways.... It is like a symphony.... The depth and speed of your breathing changes according to your emotional state, the thought that flows through your mind and the sounds you hear. Study these phenomena. You will find them fascinating."*

VEN. H. GUNARATANA MAHATHERA
*Mindfulness in Plain English*

While you do this or any meditation exercise, put the book aside. The only method by which one can do exercises is to read about them first and ingest their meaning, to make mental notes for use when actually going through the exercise. When you are in meditation, it would be counter-productive to take this book and flip it open. Digest the content of the exercise, committing as much to memory as is feasible, and proceed comfortably. If you prefer, you can make a tape of the instructions and follow the words of the tape.

## MEDITATION WITH THE BREATH

1. Take a posture that you can hold comfortably. Seated in this posture, awake and alert, take four deep, slow breaths. Notice that you are in control of your breath at this point. Realize this as you settle into position.

2. Become aware of your breathing. No matter what you think of it, no matter what judgments you have about it, do not try to control it. Just be aware of it.

3. Continue to settle into your breath. At the same time, let go of it. Allow the breath to dance its dance. Try not to criticize, or identify with it. Perhaps you noticed that your breath, when you first began, came in short bursts. Now it seems to be settling down into a longer, more fluid, undulating movement. That is the wisdom of your breath. It knows what it is doing. There is no need to worry about it. Your breath is wise. It knows where it is going, how quickly and how slowly. It will, of its own accord, settle into whatever pace, rhythm, exhalation, and inhalation that is right.

4. Become aware of the pauses, the gaps between the exhalations and inhalations—one at the end of each exhalation and one at the end of each inhalation. These are called *stillpoints*.

5. Become a neutral observer of these stillpoints as the breath ebbs and flows, moving of its own accord. It's an endless sea of life. You are the shore, caressed by this ceaseless tide. Observe each moment of breath with calm awareness. There is nothing to do, nothing to be, nowhere to go. Sit like this for several minutes.

6. Now, bring your attention to the contact point, the place where you feel the stillpoints meet. It may be just inside the rim of your nostrils, perhaps directly under them. Or it could be in your chest or abdomen. Watch the breath as it effortlessly glides over your stillpoint.

7. Make your stillpoint an observation tower, the place to watch your breath. Watch the inhalation as air flows in. Notice the moment of stillness, the moment between inhalation and exhalation. Watch the exhalation as air exits.

8. When thoughts arise, simply notice them without the need to do anything about them. Try not to get emotionally involved with thoughts or take a ride with them. Just receive them as thought. Keep the awareness on the breath.

9. Now flood the breath with peaceful awareness. Do not make any value judgments, just continue to watch your contact point. A long breath is not worth more than a short one. Both are both the same—breathing.

10. Now, move your focus of concentration to the diaphragm. Watch as it undulates with the rise and fall of the breath.

11. Move slowly outside your body. Can you see where your exhalation ends? Is it two feet away? Three? Now watch the inhalation. How far into your body does it go? To your very center?

12. For the next few minutes, watch the breath wherever it is most pronounced in your body. It may be your nostrils, your diaphragm, chest, or abdomen. Or it may fluctuate. Don't think about the movement. Just let it be. Thoughts come and go and they don't have to be named, conceptualized, or held onto.

13. Continue to watch your breath. Whenever thoughts, feelings, or sensations appear, note them, let them go, and return to your breath. Meditation teacher Sharon Salzberg says, "This act of beginning again is the essential art of meditation practice. Over and over…we begin again."

14. Now, slowly, gently, open your eyes. Take an inventory of how you are feeling, right at this moment. As you move onto your next activity, try to bring this quality of calm awareness to it. And to the next, and the next.

Congratulate yourself: You have just meditated!

## THE POWER OF BREATHING

Meditation with the breath has various names: watching the breath, following the breath, *pranic* breathing. Whatever name it goes by, observing the breath is universally recognized as one of the most powerful methods of meditation and is probably the most accessible, direct, and fundamental technique for a beginner.

Don't be deceived, however, by the simplicity of the name or the instructions. This method is not something you do for a few weeks, master, and then discard as you move up to the next plateau. Following the breath is a technique used not only by beginners, but also by seasoned meditators, even Zen masters. You could center a lifelong meditation practice around it.

Perhaps you thought meditation would be much more exciting than merely an exercise in breathing. You were expecting fireworks—and all you got was a sparkler. Boredom and disappointment can be normal reactions at this point. Nevertheless, your breath supplies power for perhaps the most fantastic voyage you will embark on: a veritable journey to your own center and the outer reaches of the universe. Your breath is a microcosm of the life force, the Tao. Like the sun, it rises and sets; like the tide, it ebbs and flows. Your breath is your doorway to increased presence, aliveness, and happiness.

So just give meditation the benefit of the doubt. After all, there must be a reason this practice has survived the centuries.

## METAPHORS FOR THE BREATH

Many meditators find it helps to take visual snapshots along with them when they meditate. Images can help you stay grounded in your breath. Here are several ways to look at your breath in meditation:

### Breath as trust

You may remember the Greyhound Bus slogan that invited you to "Take the bus, and leave the driving to us." What a great feeling to relax, lean back in a comfortable seat, and let your silver-haired, reliable-looking, uniformed driver take you to your destination. It's a wonderful feeling to let someone else do the driving—someone you trust to do it right.

Imagine your breath to be that smiling, trustworthy, dependable Greyhound driver. Just as he always knows what he is doing, so does your breath. It is right by definition. Trusting your breath permits you the freedom to accept experience, without the need to constantly monitor whether everything is okay. You don't have to drive, control the driver, or be a backseat driver.

### Breath as frame of reference

Another way to view your breath is as a landmark. Let's say that you are in Paris, and suddenly find yourself lost. To get your bearings, all you have to do is look around until you see the Eiffel Tower. Now you know exactly where you are.

*Trusting your breath permits you the freedom to accept experience, without the need to constantly monitor whether everything is okay.*

*Your breath is...a spiritual lighthouse to guide you back to the present moment.*

It's the same with your breath. As your mind meanders through a foreign landscape of thoughts, feelings, and sensations, it has, just like a tourist, a tendency to become lost. That's when your breath comes to the rescue. Your breath towers over the landscape of delusion, thought, and distraction that you are lost in, as the Eiffel Tower does over Paris rooftops. It is your landmark, guiding you back to your meditation practice.

## Breath as a visitor

Achaan Chah, a Theravadan Buddhist monk and meditation teacher in Thailand, makes an analogy between developing mindfulness of the breath and watching a close relative departing after a visit to your home:

> When a relative leaves, we follow him out and see him off. We watch until he's walked or driven out of sight, and then we go back indoors. We watch the breath in the same way. If the breath is coarse, we know that it's coarse. If it's subtle, we know that it is subtle. As it becomes increasingly fine, we keep following it, while simultaneously awakening the mind. Eventually the breath disappears altogether and all that remains is the feeling of wakefulness. This is called meeting the Buddha.

## Breath as a guide

Another way of looking at your breath is as a spiritual lighthouse to guide you back to the present moment. Although we think we are living in the present, it is really rare when we do so. Instead, we spend most of our lives in memories of the past or projections of the future, wishing a pleasant experience had lasted longer, or hoping that an upcoming negative one will be shorter. In the words of St. Augustine:

> These days are like nothing. They go almost sooner than they come. And since they came, they cannot be lasting. They intertwine, run into one another, and do not stop. Nothing can be called back from the past. What is future, is awaited. One cannot yet have it, while it has not come. One cannot keep it, since it came.

Being rooted in a past that no longer exists and anticipating a future that has not yet arrived is probably the greatest cause for unhappiness on this planet. The goal of meditation is to allow you to spend as much of your life in the present as possible, instead of the future or the past; staying on the path of the now is the road that leads to happiness.

In the words of Vietnamese monk and teacher Thich Nhat Hanh:

Breathing in, I calm my body. Breathing out, I smile.

Dwelling in the present moment,

I know this is a wonderful moment.

To consistently achieve that wonderful moment of peace and happiness requires a beacon powerful enough to cut through the darkness of delusion we create—a beam that directly illuminates an unmistakable, omnipresent path to reality, which is the present moment. Your breath is powerful enough to provide this illumination.

The scope of the present is vast, clear, and open, like a clear sky on a summer day. There is nothing more present, right now, than your breath. It is a symbol of your aliveness and connectedness. It is fresh and alive and has none of the otherworldly distortions of the past and future.

Breath is a common gift that each of us shares with all other living beings.

Some of the most beautiful and profound words were written by the great Sufi poet, Kabir, in *The Breath of God:*

> **There is nothing more present, right now, than your breath.**

## Spiritual aspects of breath

*For at least 2,500 years, the breath has been used as a way to strengthen our connection to that which is beyond the self: God, the cosmos, the dharma. Here are some ways that breath is acknowledged as the gift of gifts:*

- *In Christianity, the Holy Spirit inspires—breathes into. In the Book of Ezekiel it is written, "Behold, I will cause breath to enter into you, and you shall live." St. Francis DeSales said, "If at times we are stunned by the tempest, never fear. Let us take breath, and go on afresh."*
- *In Judaism, the word for breath is ruah, which means the spirit of God.*
- *In Sanskrit, the language the Buddha taught in, breath is called prana, which is intuitive wisdom that goes beyond intellect.*
- *In The Tibetan Book of Living and Dying, Sogyal Rinpoche calls the breath "the vehicle of the mind."*

Are you looking for me?...
You will not find me...
in Indian shrine rooms,
nor in synagogues, nor in cathedrals....
When you really look for me, you will see me instantly—
you will find me in the tiniest house of time.
Kabir says: Student, tell me, what is God?
He is the breath
inside the breath.

*"Zen teaches that the past and future are illusions; the present is eternally real."*
ALAN WATTS
*The Way of Zen*

## FOCUS

The activity that you choose to make the focal point of your attention during a meditation period is called your *object of meditation*. There may be only one object of meditation, or more than one. For example, in the breathing exercise you just practiced, the object of meditation was your breath. Objects of meditation can take many forms:

- a physical object, such as a burning candle,
- a phenomenon in the body, such as breathing, hearing, or seeing,
- a phenomenon in the mind, such as thinking,
- a particular movement, such as walking,
- a process, such as eating, or
- a phrase, a sound, or a chant.

Some techniques have multiple objects of meditation. For example, in the bare awareness practices of Insight meditation, the object of meditation is whatever happens to be the most prominent phenomenon in the body, moment by moment. Thus, for example, as the meditator sits, he or she may experience pressure in his or her leg changing to a thought about bicycle riding, then changing to a feeling of pleasure. Each of these, during its moment of prominence, is the object of meditation.

*As you continue to meditate, you'll find that your mind constantly wanders from the object of meditation. This is totally natural.*

As you continue to meditate, you'll find that your mind constantly wanders from the object of meditation. This is totally natural and to be expected. Training the mind to stay focused is akin to the work of Sigfried and Roy: You've got to be constantly aware of this beautiful, playful, yet very independent Siberian tiger, and keep her from straying. Without a whip.

Bringing calm awareness to the mind and staying with the object of meditation enables you to develop concentration, mindfulness, and focus, which will greatly enrich your quality of life.

*Keep in mind, "The map is not the territory."*

## Working with distractions

Although meditation instructions seem extremely simple, you'll probably find that executing them is not.

Keep in mind, "The map is not the territory." In the beginning, training the mind will make you confused, frustrated, and even downright angry. This is normal. What follows are two typical predicaments that every meditator—beginner as well as seasoned veteran—has had or will have:

### Where was I?

You've just begun to follow your breath. There is nothing. No thought. You are just following your breath. And then, suddenly, out of nowhere, it comes to you—the perfect birthday gift for your close friend Richard. It's that beautiful jade green vase you saw at that crafts fair last weekend. You now proceed to have the following dialogue—with yourself:

> Wait a sec, isn't the crafts fair over? Let's see, today is Wednesday, and the flyer said...but so what, I remember the name of the artist who was selling the vases. Wait...wow, am I smart...I've got his card on my desk! But was the phone number on it? Hey...so what? I'll just call the crafts fair office, they'll have his number...but will he take a phone order? Is he set up to take VISA? Which reminds me, I've got to call them about that mistake on my bill last month. I'm not going to pay for someone else's meal. What was the name of that restaurant anyway?...

And suddenly you wake up, thinking about a restaurant. You wonder, "Where was I?"

### Your Niagara of Thoughts

You've just begun to follow your breath. There is nothing. No thought. You are just following your breath. And then, somewhere in your mind, out of nowhere:

> Hey, I'm doing it. I'm meditating! Look Ma, no thoughts! Wait a sec...wasn't that a thought? Damn, it was...I'm thinking about not thinking!! Maybe I'm going crazy? Let's see, what was the instruction?... Oh yeah, object of meditation, my breath. Right...where is it...OK, I'm back...found the breath. Oh no, I'm thinking again! Boy, this is confusing. Guess I wasn't doing it right. Or was I? Let's see....

And on and on and on....

Sigmund Freud called it free association. Marcel Proust called it *Remembrance of Things Past*. No matter. After ten minutes of watching your mind carom like a ball in some cosmic pinball machine, you'll be calling it the most annoying and frustrating experience of your life.

Let us assure you that you are not alone, nor are you going crazy. In fact, what you are is on the verge of a huge revelation that could change your whole life: *This is what your mind has always been doing!* The only difference is that you've finally noticed it. This is the beginning of wisdom. Congratulate yourself.

What distracted you and took you for this ride on your thoughts is simple: It was your mind, just doing its job, which is to think. It will always be thinking, up until your last thought. As Yogi Berra said, "It ain't over until it's over."

Many people think that meditation is the art of blocking out all thoughts, making the mind go blank. Then they begin to meditate and almost immediately realize that blocking out all thoughts is like trying to dam Niagara Falls with a sink stopper. And so they do what mankind has been doing, in one way or another, since time immemorial: They kill the messenger, which in this case is meditation.

*After ten minutes of watching your mind carom like a ball in some cosmic pinball machine, you'll be calling it the most annoying and frustrating experience of your life.*

*Blocking out all thoughts is like trying to dam Niagara Falls with a sink stopper.*

As German Zen Master Wolfgang Kopp notes in *Free Yourself of Everything,* "Many are of the opinion that once the evil intellect is suppressed, the ardently desired Nirvana will automatically reveal itself. It cannot be stressed enough that this belief has not the least to do with the true practice of Zen. The point is not to suppress thought, but rather to surpass it."

Bernard Spinoza, the great philosopher, once said, "All noble things are as difficult as they are rare." Meditation is one of those noble things. Be patient with yourself and the process.

## Distraction—an opportunity in disguise

Homespun philosopher Elbert Hubbard said, "Life is just one damned thing after another." Meditation is the art of opening to each damned thing, allowing it its time, and then letting it disappear. This is the key to meditation.

When you look at thoughts and distractions mindfully, which is what meditation teaches, you live your life in a new, more joyful way. Imagine being able to see things as they truly are, not masked by a fog of opinions, ideas, and emotions, but drenched in brilliant sunlight. This is the key to happiness.

Distraction is not your enemy. Treat it with the same kindness you would a six-year-old child you've taken to the aquarium, who has innocently wandered off on her own while you were looking at the jellyfish exhibit. Simply find the dear thing, take her hand, and gently lead her back to where she should be.

There are many strategies for bringing your wandering mind back to where it should be. These techniques are applicable both in formal meditation and in all of your daily activities. A few follow:

### Swinging Door Strategy

Zen Master Shunryu Suzuki Roshi, in his book Zen Mind, Beginner's Mind, advised students to treat their breath as a swinging door:

*Imagine being able to see things as they truly are, not masked by a fog of opinions, ideas, and emotions, but drenched in brilliant sunlight.*

*The point is not to suppress thought, but rather to surpass it.*

*Be the door.*
*Not the*
*doorman.*

When we practice zazen [meditation] our mind always follows our breathing.... In this limitless world, our mind is like a swinging door. The air comes in and goes out like someone passing through a swinging door...which moves when we inhale and when we exhale.

In the swinging door technique, you regard a phenomenon not as something happening to you, but just something happening. It's as if you're not taking anything in this world personally.

Imagine that your mind is the entrance to the Waldorf Astoria Hotel and all the doormen are on strike. There's no one to scrutinize the steady stream of visitors going through the doors, no one to judge whether they are guests or don't belong. It's just a constant flow of people coming and going.

Imagine that steady stream as your thoughts, feelings, and emotions. Be the door. Not the doorman.

### Stillness Strategy

In *A Still Forest Pool*, Jack Kornfield and Paul Breiter quote Achaan Chah, the Thai meditation teacher, who gives this guidance for dealing with distraction:

Try to be mindful, and let things take their natural course. Then your mind will become still in any surroundings, like a still forest pool. All kinds of wonderful, rare animals will come to drink at the pool, and you will clearly see the nature of all things. You will see many strange and wonderful things come and go, but you will be still. This is the happiness of the Buddha.

Be still and sit. This is the best kind of advice in dealing with distractions.

### Markers and Counting

*Markers* and counting are support strategies for awareness. Markers are techniques that you can use to keep the mind from straying.

Before you begin to meditate, you can designate a marker. For instance, you might say, "For the next ten minutes, I am going to mindfully count my breath inhalations up to ten. And then begin over again." During your meditation period, whenever you realize that you have become lost in thoughts or sensations other than your breath, immediately return to your marker, which, in this example, is counting inhalations up to ten.

Counting is frequently used in Zen and other meditation traditions as a way of focusing the mind on the breath when the mind wanders. Counting techniques are helpful supports for your breath meditation.

You usually count silently, but if you are alone, there is nothing wrong with softly counting out loud. You can also switch back and forth.

Your instructions are basically the same as those you received for observing the breath. The only difference is that once your breath settles down, instead of watching stillpoints and contact points, just count inhalations, exhalations, or both.

There are many ways to count the breath. Detailed exercises appear on the following pages. The basic technique is outlined below.

*Counting is frequently used in Zen and other meditation traditions as a way of focusing the mind.*

- Count each exhalation up to ten. If you are interrupted by thought, or lose count, begin over at one. If you are just beginning to meditate, start with counting to four.

- Silently repeat, "One, one, one, one," as you inhale and your lungs are full. As you exhale, count, "Two, two, two, two," until all the air is expelled. On the next inhale, it's, "Three, three, three, three," as you inhale and your lungs are full. As you exhale, count, "Four, four, four, four," until all the air is expelled. On the next inhale, it's, "Five, five, five, five." Use succeeding numbers on each breath until you reach ten. Then start all over again.

- Count a full breath as "one." This is the cycle of the lungs totally filling and expelling the breath. Count up to four or ten. Restart if you lose count.

## COUNTING EXHALATIONS

1. Take a seated posture that you can hold comfortably. Begin by taking several deep breaths. Notice that you are in control of your breath at this point.

2. Become aware of your breathing. Now, no matter what you think of it, no matter what judgments you have about it, do not try to control it. Just let it be.

3. You are settling into your breath, just letting it do its thing, its dance. It is not important that you judge, criticize, or approve the breath's dance. The breath is wise. It knows where it is going, how quickly and how slowly. It will, of its own accord, settle into whatever pace, rhythm, exhalation, and inhalation that is right.

4. Now, watching the breath, label the next exhalation with the number "one." The breath and the number are bound together, not separate. As the breath dissipates, so does the number. They both disappear together.

5. Without getting caught up in where the breath went, watch as it begins to return to the body with the inhalation. Let go of thoughts and judgments.

6. Now, as this breath becomes an exhalation, label it with the number "two." Again, watch it merge with the exhalation as both move out into space. Watch the breath and the number until they both disappear.

7. Continue following this process until you have watched and labeled four consecutive exhalations. If you lose track, or if thoughts or sensations pull you away from the counting, gently return the awareness back to the breath, and begin again, starting at one. You may become caught in the phenomenon and forget the number. You may be fixated on the number and forget the phenomenon. Fine. Just be aware of that, and gently, without judgment, come back to the breath. Continue this process for your timed period of meditation.

# INHALATIONS AND EXHALATIONS

1. Take a posture that you can hold comfortably. Seated in position, awake and alert, begin by taking several deep breaths. Notice that you are in control of your breath at this point. Let the body settle into position.

2. Become aware of your breathing. No matter what you think of it, no matter what judgments you have about it, do not try to control it. Just let it be.

3. You are settling into your breath. You're letting it do its thing, its dance. It is not important that you approve of the way it is dancing. Your breath is wise. It knows where it is going, how quickly and how slowly. It will, of its own accord, settle into whatever pace, rhythm, exhalation, and inhalation that is right.

4. Watching the exhalation, continuously repeat the number "one." You may do this once, several times, many times, depending on how long the exhalation takes.

5. When the exhalation starts changing into an inhalation, watch the breath make its journey back to the body of its own accord. And as it does, continue to repeat, "One...one...one," until it ends. Most people repeat the number fewer times following the exhalation. For some it may be more.

6. As this inhalation comes to its natural conclusion, it becomes the next exhalation. As the breath leaves the body, number this breath "two." And gently repeat, out loud or to yourself, "Two...two...two," until it ceases.

7. Continue following this process until you have watched and continuously labeled four sets of consecutive inhalations/exhalations. If you lose track because of other thoughts, sounds, or feelings, gently bring the awareness back to the breath, and label the next inhalation, "One...one...one." You may become caught in the phenomenon and forget your number sequence on either an exhalation, an inhalation, or both. You may be fixated on the repetitive nature of the numbers and forget the breathing phenomenon. Fine. Just be aware of that, and gently, without judgment, come back to the breath.

8. Continue this process for your timed period of meditation. When you are done, gently open your eyes. Take a relaxed survey of your body and mind. How does it feel? More relaxed, yet more aware? Take this feeling of calm awareness with you throughout all the events of your day.

# CHAPTER RECAP

- The only way to understand meditation is to meditate.

- Every moment of meditation is a golden opportunity for a fuller, happier life. Let yourself feel totally entitled to your meditation period.

- Remember the definition of meditation: the art of opening to each moment of life with calm awareness.

- Observing the breath is the most accessible, direct, and fundamental meditation technique.

- Trusting your breath permits you to allow experience, without the need to monitor it.

- The object of meditation is the focal point of your attention during a meditation period.

- The goal of meditation is to help you spend as much of your life in the present as possible.

- Meditation teaches us to deal skillfully with the constant distractions that life presents. Markers and counting are support strategies for awareness.

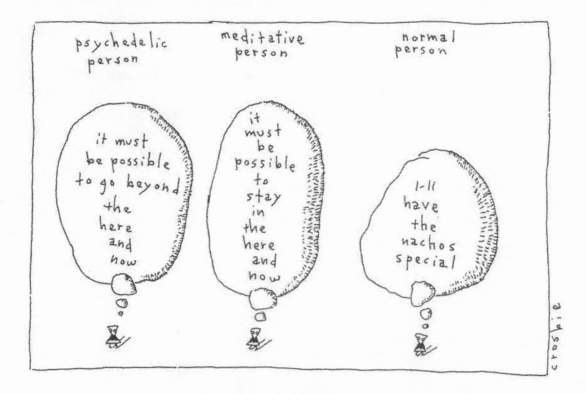

# Bridging the Barriers to Meditation

**M**editating sounds easy. Sitting. Breathing. Focusing in a relaxed kind of way. So why isn't everyone doing it? For that matter why do so many who start meditating, or open a book on the subject, fail to carry through and make meditation a part of their daily lives?

The answer is that both our inner and outer worlds raise barriers between us and meditation. The greatest of these are the doubts about meditation raised by our own minds and by Western society. There are also certain spiritual/psychological pitfalls that mediators can fall prey to if they fail to pay attention to their practice.

Without guidance, these barriers can seem insurmountable. But, with the aid of a little guidance, they can easily be bridged. As meditation teacher Ram Dass says in *Journey of Awakening*, "There are certain guidelines—some from great masters and others from psychologists and other outside observers—that can help you hone your intelligence and keep your balance."

## DOUBT

You have had your first experiences of meditation, and they produced positive results in the way of relaxation,

- *11 misconceptions that keep people from meditating*

- *9 pitfalls of the meditation path*

- *4 strategies for avoiding them*

59

revitalization, and spiritual deepening. But you still find yourself resisting the idea of regular meditation practice. This almost unconscious reluctance to meditate is natural.

Our minds and deepest selves always resist change in some way, whether it's a move to a new town, a new social circle, or a new job. As Ram Dass warns, "One of the ego's favorite paths of resistance is to fill you with doubt." This resistance usually takes the form of fears or anxiety that undermine our commitment to meditation.

You have probably experienced doubts of your own. On the list below, check off any that have haunted you.

> "When you want to sleep late, you'll find reasons not to get up to do your sadhana. You won't see the usefulness of meditation any more. You'll doubt your teacher, yourself, and the Spirit. You'll doubt God."
>
> RAM DASS
> *Journey of Awakening*

\_\_\_ Meditation is too easy or too hard.

\_\_\_ Meditation is a religion and will conflict with yours.

\_\_\_ Meditation means giving up things you like.

\_\_\_ Meditation is like being hypnotized.

\_\_\_ Meditation is a way of escaping reality.

\_\_\_ Meditation means shutting out the world.

\_\_\_ Meditation means you have to go to a monastery.

\_\_\_ Meditation is weird.

\_\_\_ Meditation means you need a teacher.

\_\_\_ Meditation has a right way and wrong way.

**Our minds and deepest selves always resist change.**

## Why we fear meditation

The doubts and fears that plague us are often the echos of misconceptions we learned at society's knee as we grew up. These negative myths, widely prevalent in the Americas and Europe, are the spawn of cultural ignorance, prejudicial misconceptions generated by rational, left-brain Western society's antithetical attitude toward anything Eastern, intuitive, and right-brain.

They are, doubtless, the very concerns that plague you when you think about meditating. Do you find yourself thinking meditation will be too hard or that it is a religion (and therefore in conflict with yours) or is it a kind of hypnosis? If so, the best anodyne is the truth. As it says in the Bible, "The truth shall make you free."

## BANISHING DOUBTS

Don't resist these concerns. Our egos are healthy enough and strong enough to protect us from any of the supposed negative effects of meditation. Resisting these doubts means giving them power over you. They will seize control and bring your meditation to a halt. Instead, Ram Dass suggests an approach that has inspired the following exercise:

1. Sit someplace free of distraction.

2. Focus on any doubts or worries you might have about meditation.

3. Be completely open to them, do not censor any out. Examine each carefully—the absurdity of most will suggest itself instantly.

4. Consciously let go of each—imagine it as a balloon that sails away and then vanishes out of sight.

## ELEVEN MISCONCEPTIONS

The best bridge across these barriers to meditation is replacing ignorance and misconception with knowledge and fact.

### I. Meditation is either too easy or too hard.

Meditation is simpler than you think. And, paradoxically, harder than you might think. The directions on how to meditate are deceptively simple. For instance, what could be clearer than instructions that merely direct you to watch your breath?

Try it for yourself. Right now. Close your eyes. And for the next inhalation and exhalation, just observe your breath. That's all.

**Meditation practice is gently returning, without judgment, over and over again to the object of your meditation.**

If you were able to take one full breath, and not think, daydream, fidget, wonder what the heck you were doing, you have done incredibly well. If you are like the rest of us, however, you probably had a lot going on in that breath. It's amazing how many thoughts you can pack into just one breath when you take the time to actually examine the process of your mind.

Although the directions may be simple, what your mind does while you try to follow those directions is an entirely different thing.

Focusing on your breath or any object of meditation requires persistence and commitment. And it requires the kind of patience a parent has for a constantly straying six-year-old child at the zoo.

When you stray from the object of meditation and find yourself waking up, as you do on the highway, ten miles down the road, clueless as to how you got there, you simply return to the object of meditation. This is what meditation practice is: gently returning, without judgment, over and over again to the object of your meditation.

The key to successful meditation practice is, in the words of the famous violinist who was asked by a stranger how to get to Carnegie Hall, "practice, practice, practice."

**2. Meditation is a religion.**

You can practice any religion or no religion, and still derive the full benefits of meditation. You may also meditate using the techniques of your tradition. Meditation is an equal opportunity practice; it treats religion just as it treats everything else: openly and with total acceptance.

**3. I'll have to give up the things I like.**

You don't have to give up anything. There are no edicts against coffee, chocolate, Haagen-Dazs, World Professional Wrestling, MTV, or even *Beavis and Butthead*.

Of course, you may naturally find yourself cutting down on things that might not be in your own best interest. If you find yourself on your meditation cushion instead of watching a *Seinfeld* rerun or a football game, you'll know that meditation is putting that deeper part of you in contact with what is best for you.

### 4. It's like being asleep or hypnotized.

Meditation is about being awake, not asleep or in a trance state. And while relaxation is a naturally occurring phenomenon of meditation, it is not the object or goal of the practice. Think of it as a wonderful by-product, or perk, like a corner office or enclosed parking.

While in meditation, you may experience states that are even more relaxing than sleep or hypnotic trance. If this happens, bring your full attention to them, watch them, then let them go. You don't chase states of mind in meditation; rather, you welcome whatever comes your way, and then let it go.

### 5. Meditators are trying to escape from reality and responsibilities.

Some hold that meditation is a selfish, narcissistic attempt to avoid responsibilities and real life. Nothing is further from the truth. The goal of meditation is to become happier by developing the ability to escape into, not away from, life. When your mind is sharp and focused, your quality of life is improved, your experience of life is richer, and you are just naturally happier.

### 6. You have to shut out the world.

Meditation is about total immersion in the experience of the present moment, both internally and externally.

There is a popular misconception that meditation can only be properly done in absolute silence, preferably on top of a mountain in Nepal, where the meditator is entirely removed from the sights and sounds of the material world.

The skillful meditator takes his world as he finds it, without sunglasses, earplugs, or nose clips. In the real world, car alarms screech, children laugh and play, planes drone overhead, telephones suddenly ring, and neighbors

> *The goal of meditation is to become happier by developing the ability to escape into, not away from, life.*

*The skillful meditator takes his world as he finds it, without sunglasses, earplugs, or nose clips.*

play U-2 albums too loudly. When you meditate, you cultivate your innate ability to deal skillfully with all arising phenomena, whatever they may be.

Meditation is not about shutting out the world. It's about letting it in.

### 7. You have to go to a monastery.

Entering the monastic life isn't necessary to get the benefits of meditation. Josh B., a former Zen monk, now a record company executive with a hot new label, says, "The zendo is everywhere." (*Zendo* is the Zen word for meditation hall.)

In the Zen tradition there is a saying: "If you want a small enlightenment go to the country. If you want a big enlightenment, go to the city." This means that the more challenging the environment, the more it has to teach you. This may make New York City the world's best meditation hall.

The eighth-century Tibetan, Shantideva, wrote that a spiritual life could be lived anywhere. He says the following in his classic text, *A Guide to the Bodhisattva's Way of Life* (a *bodhisattva* is a person who aspires to attain full enlightenment for the benefit of all beings):

> Where would I possibly find enough leather
>
> With which to cover the surface of the earth?
>
> But wearing leather on the soles of my shoes
>
> Is equivalent to covering the earth with it.

Make your world your monastery. And that includes your home, office, car, the subway, even the laundromat. Wherever you are, whatever you encounter is meant to provide you with exactly what you need to work with right now.

### 8. Meditation is weird.

Meditation is not only not weird, it's totally in keeping with the American way of life.

Our Declaration of Independence states that we have certain inalienable rights, including "life, liberty, and the pursuit of happiness." Those three rights are also the goals of meditation—to be totally present in life, to be liberated from our confined sense of self, and to be happy.

Meditation is not only not weird, it's downright patriotic.

### 9. You need a teacher.

Learning a skill is always easier when you have a good teacher. In the United States there is a scarcity of good, reputable meditation teachers. And the large followings of a few good teachers consequently make it difficult to receive training on an individual basis.

But that should not deter you. An old Buddhist proverb says, "When the student is ready, the teacher appears." It's been happening that way for thousands of years.

For now, this book is more than adequate to get you started on the path of meditation. And don't worry, when you really need your teacher, he or she will appear. Teachers will be discussed in more detail later.

### 10. There's a right way and a wrong way.

There is no one way and no best way to meditate. The ways of meditation are many, and stem from the world's rich and varied religious traditions. It is said that the Buddha alone taught eighty-four ways of mindfulness. So there's obviously room for many opinions.

Some schools and teachers of meditation insist that their way is the only correct way or system to meditate. Be skeptical of those who tell you, "It's my way or the highway." True teachers of meditation follow the middle way (a balance between a search for and a surrender to the truth). They are usually tolerant of and receptive to techniques from other disciplines.

If there is any right way to meditate, it will be the one that resonates with you, the one to which you want to apply yourself with discipline and diligence.

Chapters 5–8 contain examples of many kinds of meditation techniques that have been passed down for generations.

*Make your world your monastery.... Wherever you are, whatever you encounter is meant to provide you with exactly what you need to work with right now.*

"Monks and scholars should accept my word not out of respect, but upon analyzing it as a goldsmith analyzes gold, through cutting, melting, scraping and rubbing it."

THE BUDDHA

**11. Meditation cuts you off from the rest of life.**

Meditation is not just something you do on a cushion or in a chair for a certain amount of time and then forget about. Your goal should be to make meditation an ongoing part of your life.

Dr. Andrew Weil, the well-known author on holistic health, says, on his CD, *Eight Meditations for Optimum Health,* "On some level, you are meditating all the time. Become aware of that practice, extending this awareness to more and more areas of your daily life."

It's good advice. Try it for yourself. Stay as mindful as possible, all day long.

## NINE PITFALLS OF THE PATH

Another form of inner resistance to meditation is falling prey to one or another of the emotional or spiritual temptations that practice can bring. These temptations have collectively been called the "pitfalls of the path" or "the perils of the path" by many teachers in many books.

As Peggy Taylor and the other editors of New Age Journal write in their book *Chop Wood, Carry Water: A Guide to Finding Spiritual Fulfillment in Everyday Life,* "Every level, every step on the path seems to have its corresponding stumbling block. It is no wonder that the Upanishads, one of the oldest sacred texts in the world, describes the spiritual journey as walking on the razor's edge."

Fortunately, these snares are relatively easy to avoid, with a little prior knowledge that they might be coming. The great meditative guides—from Buddha and Jesus and Mohammed to Ram Dass and roshi Philip Kapleau—have mapped them out for us and provided advice for coping with them. In *Chop Wood, Carry Water,* Taylor and company describe the nine "most common" perils of the meditation/spiritual path as:

> *Spiritual materialism* is probably the most basic and pervasive peril of the spiritual path. [Spritual seekers can fall victim to

*If there is any right way to meditate, it will be the one that resonates with you.*

*"Paradise is the prison of the sage as the world is the prison of the believer."*
YAHIAB MU'ADH AL-RAZI

peace of mind and godliness as a single-minded paradigm, which in itself can become obsessive.]

*The Stink of Zen.* This expression refers to the odor of people who make a big deal of their having undergone particularly powerful, ego-shattering spiritual experiences—with the emphasis definitely on the fact that such a thing has happened to them.

*Being in a Hurry.* The spiritual journey is a lifelong journey at the very least. North Americans in particular expect, even demand, instant results. This may work for breakfast foods, but it is not the way the spiritual path works. "Patience" is an important quality in every spiritual tradition.

*Guru-Chasing in the Spiritual Supermarket....* At the beginning of the search it is necessary to sample a bit to know what's out there, but this can all too easily become "spiritual window-shopping"—a substitute for getting down to the real living of a spiritual life.... Window-shopping is nice, but at some point it is necessary to sit down and eat.

*Getting High.* There are lots of different states of mind that we may experience during spiritual practices. Some of them feel very good, indeed.... These states can...become a distraction; they are not the aim of spiritual practice—merely a stage along the way.

*Everything is Maya.* Or illusion. True, perhaps, on one level (the absolute) and not so true on another (the relative), where most of us live most of the time.... No matter how deep your understanding or how wide your love and compassion, you still have to pay the bills, stop at red lights, take out the garbage, and do the dishes....

*Everything is Karma.* Or destiny or fate. This belief is the source of the infamous "spiritual passivity" syndrome. In fact,...teaching of karma refers to nothing more mysterious than the law of action and reaction.... What you do today results, to some extent, in what happens tomorrow. Therefore pay attention to your actions in the present. Don't blame or focus on the past.

*Putting too great a stock in miracles.* The Buddha, it is said, met a yogi who...demonstrated he could walk on water.... It had taken him twenty-five years of hard spiritual training to obtain this power. The Buddha scratched his head and asked why he had bothered, since for a mere five rupees the yogi could have taken the ferry.

*Getting sidetracked by the Occult.* "Occult" means hidden. This is the realm of secret teachings, magic, visitations from beyond.... Paying more attention to signs and portents, rather than to the here-and-now, is a symptom that you have lost your way in this admittedly fascinating realm.

## AVOIDING THE PITFALLS

Don't let the traps along the way intimidate you. You can cut through their snares with three powerful tools, mediators have used for millennia. They are:

- listening to your heart,
- maintaining a sense of humor, and
- following the middle way.

Use them any time you feel you might be caught in one of the pitfalls—or practice them always and avoid stepping into the meditation pitfalls. They will help keep you on the path and signal you when you are headed wrong, or are becoming unbalanced, or going to extremes.

### 1. Follow your Heart

When you have a concern or doubt, listen to your inner voice, your heart. The truth is always there. The prompting of your innermost heart will guide you from your first baby steps throughout all your experiences with meditation. From addiction to spiritual highs to being in a hurry to getting sidetracked in the occult, no matter how convinced you become that you are on the right track mentally, your heart will always know—and reveal to you—the truth about your motives, beliefs, and actions.

One way to get in touch with your heart's truth, of course, is meditation. Any time your mind is filled with doubts, use this four point strategy:

*When you have a concern or doubt, listen to your inner voice, your heart.*

1. Sit quietly.

2. Allow any subject of concern or behavior to surface.

3. Ask your heart, "What is the truth?"

4. You'll feel a mental "click" when you reach the truth.

### 2. Maintain a Sense of Humor

Laughing at yourself is excellent preventive medicine. Several liberal doses a day will do for the pitfalls of the path what the proverbial apple did to the doctor. As the most famous of nineteenth-century American clergymen, Henry Ward Beecher, put it, "A person without a sense of humor is like a wagon without springs—jolted by every pebble in the road."

Failing to maintain a sense of humor is a warning sign that one is beginning to wander off the spiritual path. When people fall pray to ego and begin to think they are more spiritual than others, or to believe that whatever befalls them and others is the result of bad or good karma, they tend also to lose their sense of humor. The importance of humor in avoiding meditation temptations is underscored by lecturer/author Allen Klein in *The Healing Power of Humor,* "Once we find some comedy in our chaos, we are no longer caught up in it, and our problems become less of a burden. Humor offers a way out before we reach such desperate states."

Humor helps keep us from taking ourselves too seriously. "When you lose your sense of humor," says McMurphy in Ken Kesey's *One Flew over the Cuckoo's Nest,* "you lose your footing." "He knows," says one of the other characters, "you have to laugh at the things that hurt you just to keep yourself in balance, just to keep the world from running you plumb crazy."

Humor helps keep us balanced. When we can find some humor in our pretensions, extremes, foibles, needs, upsets, even our worse sides like anger, hostility, envy, prejudice, no longer loom so large or seems as important.

Humor provides perspective. It expands our limited picture frame and gets us to see more than just our prob-

*Failing to maintain a sense of humor is a warning sign that one is beginning to wander off the spiritual path.*

lem. As Ashleigh Brilliant says in *I May Not Be Totally Perfect, But Parts of Me Are Excellent*, "Distance doesn't really make you any smaller, but it does make you part of a larger picture."

Humor enables us to be more tolerant of the foibles of others. This is the humor of compassion symbolized by the Buddha's quiet smile. It understands and forgives everyone, for Buddha understood the universal predicament. All of us are caught in illusion, and so are prone to error and frailty. All are one day fated to awaken from that illusion and to become enlightened.

Humor is also the anodyne when we "wake up" to find we ourselves have become ensnared in one or more of the spiritual snares. To do so isn't to be "wrong" or "bad" or "stupid" or "weak" or "less pious" or "lacking in sincerity." It's the human part of ourselves that has its weaknesses, fears, needs and wounds. "None of us is perfect," Allen Klein observes. Most of our situations are far from ideal. One of the most compassionate things we can do for ourselves is not take those imperfections too seriously. When we can find some humor in our losses, in those things that we push away, then we are, as clinical psychologist Walter O'Connell points out, "honoring our imperfections and chipped edges."

### 3. The Best Advice—Follow the Middle Way

Overall, most traditions and teachers agree, the best advice for avoiding the pitfalls of meditation practice is to follow what Buddhists call middle way. Others call this principle the golden mean or the rule of moderation. The middle way, according to the Shambhala Dictionary of Buddhism and Zen, is "generally, a term for the way of the historical Buddha, which teaches avoidance of all extremes... and it leads to release from suffering."

The key to the middle way is pointed to in the opening lines of a Kabbalistic text, "This is the book of the equilibrium of balance." A centered person is a balanced person, a follower of the middle way. A centered, balanced person,

*All of us are caught in illusion, and so are prone to error and frailty.*

*"It has been said that the reason angels can fly is because they take themselves lightly."*

ALLEN KLEIN, M.A.
*The Healing Power of Humor*

following the middle way will not feel holier than one person, or spend too much time seeking the high of meditation. As Theosophist Talbot Mundy advises, "Be moderate in all things, so preserving equilibrium, which is a form of justice that the gods love."

Like riding a bicycle, discovering the trick of balance of the middle way takes practice. "Of every ten who tread the middle way to Knowledge there are nine who turn aside through avarice, though not all avarice is born of belly-hunger or the greed for gold," Mundy writes. "Some seek preeminence, such eminence as they have won corroded by insane pride. So by this mark you shall know the Middle Way, that whoso treads it truly avoids vices, having found them in himself, so that he knows their habit and is temperate in judgment, throwing no stones lest he break the windows of his own soul."

### 4. The Final Authority—You

A concluding thought from Ram Dass: "The final authority—since any spiritual path must be freely chosen—is one's own best judgment.... For, while there are many reasons to take care, there is no reason to turn back, even if that were possible. The pitfalls and perils, the stumbling blocks and obstacles, are an essential part of the journey. Indeed, how we respond to their challenge is the way we make the journey our own."

*"Buddha, the Perfect One, avoided these two extremes and found the middle path, which opens the eyes, produces knowledge and leads to peace, insight, enlightenment, and Nirvana; to wit, perfect knowledge, perfect outlook, perfect speech, perfect action, perfect livelihood, perfect effort, perfect mindfulness, and perfect concentration"*

SAMYUTTA-NIKDYA

## CHAPTER RECAP

- Why people resist meditating, even when their initial experience is positive.

- You can overcome fear of meditation with a simple exercise.

- One reason some people fear meditation is that they think it means giving up everything a person likes.

- Meditation is not a religion.

- Some people become side-tracked by the "high" of mediation.

- Some people miss the point of meditation by believing they have found it, and go around being "holier than thou" about their experiences.

- Three good ways to avoid the pitfalls of meditation are:

    listening to your heart,

    maintaining a sense of humor,

    following the middle way.

- When it comes to meditation, let your own best judgment be your guide.

# Developing Your Meditation Practice

# 4

**N**ow that you've meditated, it's time to make some decisions that will enable you to build a sound, consistent, and rewarding meditation practice. And the nuts and bolts of your practice include posture, scheduling, and the tools of the trade.

## MEDITATION POSTURE

Over the centuries, particular meditation postures have been developed to align the body and mind optimally into a stable, calm, and aware synergistic balance.

Although having to sit in a certain way may seem arbitrary, uncomfortable, and unreasonable, once you've done it for a while you will understand why taking the proper posture or attitude is important in meditation. Thus, you should approach meditation posture in the same manner that you do meditation itself—with your beginner's mind.

As you experiment with different postures, keep in mind that meditation is not about discomfort and that a position that feels painful is not for you. There is a difference between discomfort, which is to be expected, and physical pain, which definitely is not. Be aware of your body's strengths and weaknesses. And always remember: Doctors'

- **When to meditate**

- **How to sit**

- **What to sit on**

- **Building your environment**

- **Timing your session**

- **Establishing a schedule**

- **Frequently expressed feelings and fears**

- **How posture affects practice**

73

## The attributes of posture

*"The posture of meditation depends on three primary attributes: alignment, relaxation, and resilience. Each of these attributes is equally important, and each supports the others' manifestation. Appearing together in harmonious relationship to one another, they generate a powerfully catalytic effect on the process of meditation. In this posture the healing energies of the body and mind are naturally activated, and the process of transformation begins spontaneously.... Whatever personal postural habits of body and mind serve to obscure the truth of our enlightened nature are gradually dissolved through the assumption of this posture, just as the constant unimpeded flow of water gradually dissolves sandstone."*

WILL JOHNSON
*The Posture of Meditation*

## Posture reflects attitude

Making sure you take and stay in a proper meditation posture is more than merely a physical act; it is a manifestation of your current state of mind and inclination toward enlightenment and happiness.

In the opinion of Zen Master Suzuki Roshi, the act of sitting properly, in itself, is very powerful. In *Zen Mind, Beginner's Mind*, he describes the effect of correct posture on mental state:

> You should not be tilted sideways, backwards, or forwards. You should be sitting straight up as if you were supporting the sky with your head....
>
> These forms [posture] are not a means of obtaining the right state of mind. To take this posture itself is the purpose of our practice. When you have this posture, you have the right state of mind.

orders and/or physical pain take precedence over anything said in this book.

## Posture optimizes practice

A golfer will spend hundreds of hours at the practice range, working on the swing until it becomes automatic. Incorrect arm, hip, or foot alignment can result in a miss, a slice, or a hook. Correct stance and swing yields optimum performance.

It is the same for meditation posture. The correct posture is designed to align your skeletal, respiratory, nervous, and circulatory systems in the most synergistic way.

The directions in this chapter will help you achieve a strong, secure, yet relaxed meditation posture that can put you, in the current vernacular, "in the zone."

As Suzuki Roshi said, the very act of sitting in meditation means that you have, by definition, already achieved the purpose of practice. Next time you meditate, as you settle into your position, begin to notice emotional states that reflect this right state of mind.

Posture is important because it is important to be alert, accepting, and comfortable in this world, whether you're meditating in your room or sitting in a traffic jam. The more you develop awareness of your posture in meditation, the more you become aware of move-

## Sitting like a flower

*"Whether standing or sitting, think of your spine as the stem and your head as the blossoming rose. Become aware of the tail end of your spine and your chin. If either one is sticking out excessively, it is like the root or the flower being cut off from the stem."*

MICHIKO ROLEK
*Mental Fitness*

ment and position during your daily activities. This awareness can serve as a mental alarm clock that can keep you alert to your different states of mind, especially ones that might prompt you to do something you'll later regret.

The next time you interact with your boss, for example, note the way you stand. Is your jaw thrust forward, are your hands on hips? Then you may be angry, or hurt, or feeling confrontational. Watch out! You don't want to do anything foolish. Is your jaw relaxed, are your hands open? This indicates receptivity, confidence.

As you become increasingly aware of your physical attitude, you'll find yourself naturally avoiding uncomfortable positions, both physical and emotional.

*The real work of sitting is done by you, not your cushion or bench.*

## Posture at a retreat

*Meditation postures at retreats are similar to dress codes at restaurants. With as many as two hundred people meditating together, some rules are usually necessary. Thus, in a Zen meditation hall (zendo), you would only be allowed to use a cushion and a sitting mat. No chairs, back supports, beach chairs, no leaning against the wall (because you're facing it).*

*In comparison, an Insight meditation retreat allows chairs, benches, even special sitting devices with back supports. Neither way is better than the other, the two are simply different.*

## Sitting with a disability

If meditation instructions require physical movements that you can't manage, simply substitute ones that you can. For instance, in walking meditation, the phenomenon of walking is the object of meditation. If you are not able to walk but can move your arms, make the slow, fluid, upward and downward stroke of the arms your object of meditation. If you are in a wheelchair, you might use the sensations of your hands on the wheels of the chair as you slowly roll forward. Improvise your own movements.

Disabilities, whether temporary or permanent, are not impediments to establishing a strong meditation routine. Everything said in this book is meant for everyone. It doesn't matter that you are unable to sit without the aid of support, or are in a wheelchair or a hospital bed. Your practice can be as strong and effective as anyone's.

Remember that the object of meditation is not carved in stone; adapt it to your particular situation. As you bring calm awareness to your object of meditation, your meditation practice will expand and become stronger.

## WHAT TO SIT ON

Sitting equipment is intended to facilitate meditation posture, not support it. The real work of sitting is done by you, not your cushion or bench.

Finding a supplier for sitting gear can be easy or difficult, depending on where you reside. If you have the good fortune to have a spiritually oriented bookstore in your area, you can probably find a variety of cushions, benches, and pillows there. If not, there are several reputable companies that sell sitting equipment by mail; you will find some listed in the Resource section at the end of this book.

Perhaps the best place to see and try sitting accessories is at a meditation retreat. If you see something interesting, find out after the retreat where your fellow meditator got the item. You might even ask if you can test drive the item while he or she is not using it.

### Dharma pain versus real pain

From time to time, all meditators experience some discomfort while sitting, but discomfort and pain are not the same. It's very important to know the difference. In meditation practice, discomfort also goes by the name dharma pain, a by-product of meditation.

Dharma pain is what is felt as you unconsciously unravel a lifetime's store of painful physical, emotional, and mental experiences held in the body. As you sit in meditation, these knots, which you have always carried around, spontaneously start to untangle. When you open yourself to this dharma pain, it is a sign of growing meditational maturity.

Real pain, on the other hand, means that your body is sending you a distinct message: "Get me out of this!" The appropriate response is to respect the message.

In meditation, as in life, the first rule is to practice a policy of non-harming and kindness, especially toward ourselves.

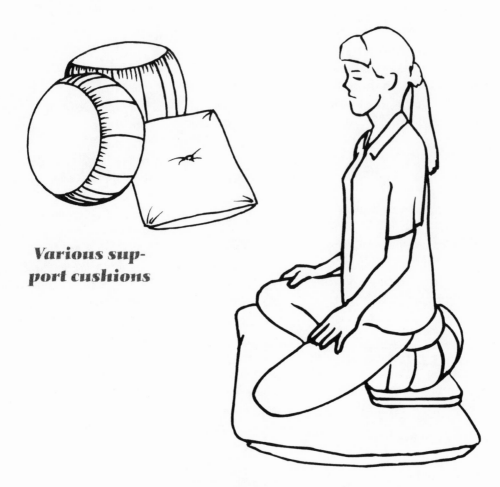

*Various sup-port cushions*

## Cushions

The simplest and most easily available sitting aid is the classic round meditation cushion, commonly called by its Japanese name, *zafu*. You may be used to sitting down on the center of a cushion but you will sit on the front third of a zafu.

Zafus come in different sizes, thickness, and materials. The best way to find which type works best for you is actually to test some. Here are some guidelines:

- Try to find a zafu that is the right size. Zafus usually come in small, medium, and large circumferences.

- Also make sure you have the right thickness. The higher your knees are off the floor, the less pressure there is on your kneecaps. If you intend to sit Burmese style (described later in this chapter), you will probably want a thick cushion which makes possible a higher sitting perch, but not one that is unstable or wobbly. Tall and long-legged meditators will probably find that a thick cushion is more comfortable. Be sure you feel stable on a thick cushion.

Meditation cushions are usually one- to six-inches thick and stuffed with kapok, the same kind of cotton batting that you'd find inside a futon. Cushions are also available filled with millet husks; these are like very small beanbag chairs, which means that they can be contoured to your buttocks.

While you can contour the husk-filled cushions, they are extremely hard and have no cushioning. Kapok is much softer, but you may find it gives you too little support. Kapok also compresses as you sit on it for long periods of time.

Millet husk cushions are usually available only by mail order. Check the Resource section for listings.

Basic black is the color of choice for meditation cushions. It will not distract you or other meditators. Some cushion makers offer products in a variety of colors. For instance, you can purchase Tibetan sitting cushions, called *gomdens*, in the traditional colors of bright red-orange and yellow.

## *Training wheels*

*Support cushions are like training wheels for meditators who may not be flexible enough to sit freely yet; they provide support and stability without discomfort. Support cushions can be used anywhere—to support your knees, under your arms, or as a platform for your hands.*

*Support cushions come in different sizes and shapes.*

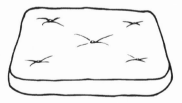

## *Meditation benches*

Some meditators find that a kneeling position takes pressure off the back, allowing them to sit straighter and for longer periods. Keep in mind that kneeling imposes a greater stress on your kneecaps, so the comfort gained in

**Kneeling
bench**

your back may be lost in your knees. Many meditators
alternate between a cushion and a kneeling bench, especially at meditation retreats. Remember: Never use a
kneeling bench without adequate knee cushioning.

The traditional sitting bench is made of plain wood,
often walnut, with seat dimensions of eight inches by
twenty. The bench seat is sloped, meaning that the back of
the bench is approximately two inches higher than the

front. The seat rests on squat wooden legs that raise the rear edge nine inches from the floor.

The seat can be upholstered or bare. Some bench designs feature folding legs or a tripod-type support for compact storing and travel. Benches are not very expensive and are good to have in reserve.

## Sitting mats

A good mat is important, especially to protect your knees and ankles. You are probably familiar with the Japanese futon bed. The futons used in meditation are exactly the same, albeit smaller. The normal size of a *zabuton*, or sitting mat, is approximately thirty-three by thirty inches and one- to two-inches thick.

You can create a makeshift mat out of folding blankets. Be sure the mat is large enough to accommodate your joints and kneecaps.

## HOW TO SIT

When you take a meditation position, you are making a statement as to who you are, right at this moment: a person endeavoring to live his or her life in a particular way. By assuming this position, you signal your intention to take your rightful place in the great continuum of all who have meditated before you and all who come after.

Your overall posture instruction is the same as the overall instruction for meditation: to sit with calm awareness—spine straight and comfortably upright, without being stiff or tense.

### Back and spine

Keep the back and spine erect, not slumped. Imagine that there's a string attached to the crown of your head. Keeping the back straight not only helps you stay awake, it allows an unimpeded circulation of your *chi*, the vital life-force energy in the body. This results in more energy, which promotes awareness, tranquillity, and mindfulness.

### Head, jaw, and tongue

Before making adjustments to your head position, it is helpful to relax your jaw. Open your mouth and let go of the jaw. Allow it to hang loosely. Slowly draw the lower jaw up until your lips touch lightly. Keep the jaw in this relaxed position.

Next, notice the position of your head on your neck. Chances are, after a day of work, driving, and stress, your jaw is jutting forward, causing you to strain the back of your neck.

Close your eyes and allow your head to float directly over the neck. If you still feel that your jaw is jutting forward and preventing your head from coming back, gently tuck in (but don't brace) the chin.

*It is important to feel grounded in meditation practice.*

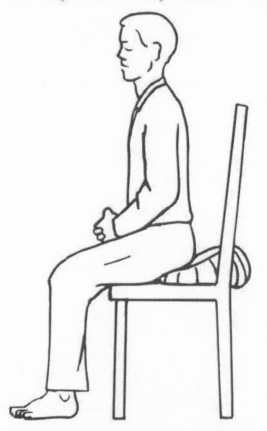

Relax your tongue. Some meditation teachers instruct students to make contact between the tongue tip and the roof of the mouth, believing that this position completes the microcosmic energy circuit that travels up the spinal cord, over the crown of the head, and descends along the front of your body. Positioning the tongue on the roof of the mouth also inhibits saliva secretion during meditation.

## Eyes

In some meditation traditions, such as the Insight tradition of Theravadan Buddhism, you are instructed to shut your eyes. In certain sects of Zen Buddhism, the eyes are either open or partially open, staring down at a forty-five degree angle to the floor. Still other traditions tell you to keep your eyes wide open.

When you first begin your practice, keep your eyes shut gently. If they open of their own accord during your meditation period, that's fine.

## It's not how you look

*If you ski, you've probably seen that fashionably attired person with state of the art equipment on the lift line. He or she looks totally together. And you feel inferior.*

*Looking like a meditator is not your goal. It's no big deal if you need to sit in a chair. People with very strong practices and even some teachers can only sit in chairs because of joint and health problems. Mindfulness is the objective, not discomfort. The Buddhist principal of "non-harming" means that you should not harm yourself.*

## Arms

Let your arms hang freely and openly; you don't want to squeeze them against your body. Imagine that you are holding an egg in each armpit. Hold the eggs firmly enough to keep them from dropping, yet loosely enough to keep them from breaking. Wherever you place your hands, it is important to keep in mind that they are not to be used as braces or supports.

## Feet

It is important to feel grounded in meditation practice. If you are sitting in a chair, plant your feet firmly with the backs of your heels touching the floor. You may support your feet with a cushion.

## Placement of hands

The hands may rest in several places relative to the body and may be held in any of several positions. They should always be relaxed.

### On the Knees

The hands may rest on top of the kneecaps. Allow them to be calm. They can be either turned down, lightly cupping the knees, or turned with palms facing upward. Some teachers believe that the turned-up position creates more openness to energy.

Be mindful of any tensing in your arms or grasping of your kneecaps with your hands.

### In the Lap

In the following positions, your hands rest between the navel and the genital area, in the energy center of the body known as the hara. Your hands should be re-laxed and supported by your legs. If you find your hands unsupported, or uncomfortably low, or pulling you towards the floor, place a small support cushion or folded towel under them.

## Hand positions

Hand position is also called *mudra*, which translates from the Sanskrit as sign or gesture. In some traditions, such as Hinduism and Buddhism, particular mudras are believed to evoke the mind states of higher beings or deities.

Try several different hand positions. You'll probably find that particular ones resonate for you at different times. From one meditation period to another there is nothing wrong with mindfully varying hand positions.

In all of the positions that follow, notice that the left hand always rests in the right palm.

## The center of the universe

In the Buddhist and Hindu meditation systems, the hara is one of the two powerful psychic centers in the body (the other is located at your solar plexus). Cosmic force is thought to flow through the hara, making it a fountain of the energy of the cosmos. When your hands are on your hara in meditation, it is thought that you are holding the center of the universe in the palms of your hands.

### The Cosmic Egg

This is a popular position in the Rinzai Zen tradition. The open left palm rests on the open right palm. The thumbs barely touch. In essence, you are creating a cosmic egg, or receptacle. Don't force the thumbs against each other to establish stability. They should be touching each other as lightly as if you were supporting a thin sheet of paper between them.

### The Fist

The left hand, curled into fist, fits inside the open right palm. The closed left fist rests against the hara area (energy core) below the navel area and above the genitals. Used in the Soto Zen tradition.

### Locked Thumbs

The left palm is open and resting on the hara. The right palm is open and on top. Thumbs are interlocked. Used in the Insight tradition.

## SITTING POSITIONS

As you take your meditation posture, remember to be kind and gentle with your limbs. If a position seems truly uncomfortable, try a different, less demanding, one. If a position is painful, it is not right for you. If a position feels too easy, perhaps you are cheating a bit.

If you are just beginning your meditation practice, meditate in a chair until you feel comfortable. Using a chair is also advisable for meditators with limited flexibility, knee problems, an injury, or any other kind of physical limitation.

Sit comfortably on the front part of your chair. Your back should be straight, head centered over the spine. Do not lean on the back of the chair. Plant your feet firmly, feeling your heels and toes flat on the floor. For support and insulation, you may use a flat pad or cushion under your feet.

## Sitting cross-legged

This is the classic sitting meditation position. Set your cushion down near the rear of your mat (do not sit on a bare floor) so that when you take your position, you will have plenty of room for your crossed legs.

When taking this sitting posture, do not simply target the center of your cushion and flop down on it. For proper weight displacement and position, slowly lower your buttocks onto the front of the cushion. The farther forward you are on the cushion, the more clearance there is for your knees to contact your sitting mat.

Once you are seated on the cushion, cross your legs in front of you in a stable and comfortable position. Both knees should make contact with the mat. If your knees don't touch the mat, try placing a support cushion or folded towel under them. If that doesn't do it, try another position.

## The Burmese posture

Many meditators find this elegant position also to be the most comfortable. When you sit in Burmese style, you sit higher on your cushion than you would in the lotus positions described below. Thus, you will probably want to raise the height of your cushion with a large support cushion, second cushion, or folded blankets.

## Switching legs

*It's always a good idea to vary leg positions from one sitting period to the next. For instance, if your legs are crisscrossed with your left foot on your right in the morning, rest the right foot on the left during your evening meditation. This is a balanced way that allows you to gradually adapt to sitting and is especially recommended at meditation retreats.*

## Flexibility

*Most discomfort in meditation positions is due to the body's lack of flexibility. Although you may feel that the problem is your knees, the area of the body that controls the ability of the knees to open up is the hip and pelvic area. The more flexibility you have there, the more the legs can open up and touch the floor.*

*There are many exercises to enhance flexibility. A minute or two of stretching prior to meditation is highly recommended.*

To sit Burmese style:

- Sit on your cushion. Cross your left or right leg in front of your body.

- Cross the other leg in front of the first leg.

- Both kneecaps should touch your meditation mat. You should feel a triangle support configuration between your contact point with the cushion, your navel, and both kneecaps.

- Rest the hands comfortably on the table formed by the crossed legs.

**Sitting Burmese posture.**

## *The quarter lotus*

This is the way you sat around the campfire, roasting marshmallows. It's basically a simple cross-legged position. Your cushion makes it even more comfortable. To sit quarter lotus do the following:

- Sitting on your cushion, cross your legs in front of you.
- Make sure your ankles are comfortably positioned.
- Sit up straight. Don't lean forward or back from your crossed legs.
- Both kneecaps should be touching the floor.
- Rest the hands comfortably, either on the table formed by the crossed legs, or on a support cushion.

*Notice the position of the foot in the quarter lotus.*

## The half lotus

The fact that this classic position is called half lotus does not mean that it is half as difficult. Half lotus requires the meditator to be exceptionally supple in the hips and legs. Again, if you feel any kind of pain sitting in this posture, you are not ready to do it:

- Cross your legs comfortably, the closer to the body the better.
- Fold either leg close and into your body.
- Gently lift the ankle of the opposite leg and slowly move it back toward the thigh of the folded leg.
- Gently lay the ankle down so it rests on the opposite thigh. Both knees should be touching the floor.
- Rest the hands comfortably, either on the table formed by the crossed legs or on a support cushion.

*Note where the foot is placed in the half lotus.*

## The full lotus

You've probably seen the pictures of Zen monks sitting in a row, legs crossed in perfect full lotus. This is the classic Eastern meditation posture and the one that comes to mind when we think about Eastern meditation practice.

Meditation is an art which allows the meditator to open to each moment of life with calm awareness. The practice should not wind up sending anyone to an orthopedist. Full lotus sitting can result in damage to your kneecaps. The posture is not recommend for a person with average flexibility. This posture is only for those who are superbly limber and flexible.

For these reasons, you won't find instructions on full lotus here. If you want to sit in full lotus, consult *The Three Pillars of Zen* by Roshi Philip Kapleau or other Zen meditation books.

## Kneeling

This position requires that you have a kneeling bench. Essentially, you will have your legs folded back and under your sitting bench. Some meditators find that this position enables them to keep their backs straighter without discomfort. If you have bad knees avoid using this posture or only do so very carefully.

If you have a sitting bench and want to use this posture, do the following:

- Place the sitting bench on your futon.
- Kneel with your back to the bench.
- Insert your legs through the opening under the bench.
- Slowly slide back until your buttocks rest comfortably on the bench.
- Your hands should rest comfortably in your lap. If your lap is too low, use a small support cushion.

Here's an alternate way to assume the kneeling posture:

- Standing on the front of your futon, grasp the bench behind your back with one hand on each end of the bench.

- Pull the bench seat under you as if you were sitting on it.

- Slowly kneel down on the futon. As you do, bring your legs together so that they fit between the legs of the sitting bench.

- Slowly sit back. Your legs are now folded behind you, between the legs of the bench.

## SPACE AND TIME TO MEDITATE

The following sections are about the where and when of your meditation practice—setting aside an area and a time of the day for you to meditate.

### *Your meditation environment*

### *Preparing for meditation*

- *Phone off the hook, or answering machine on and volume off.*

- *TV, stereo off.*

- *Nothing on the stove, in the microwave, the toaster, etc.*

- *Nothing else scheduled during the meditation period.*

- *Several minutes set aside for coming out of meditation.*

While it is not imperative that you set up a permanent meditation area, your decision to do so would be evidence of your commitment to your practice. This is yet another way for you to take your place in this ancient tradition. The very fact that you dedicate a certain amount of time every day to do something positive for yourself and others can be a source of comfort and happiness.

The meditation area in your home should contain everything you need: your cushion or chair, a timer, ceremonial gong or bell, support cushions, mat, perhaps a photo or other spiritual symbols or reminders.

Your meditation area reflects not only how you feel about your practice, but also how you feel about life in general. A sloppy, cluttered, and dusty meditation area suggests that your current state of mind is fuzzy and disoriented. An orderly, clean area indicates mindfulness and alertness.

Try to practice mindfulness when you sit down and get up from your session. If you use a meditation blanket, for example, be mindful how you fold it. Are you just going through the motions, or are you folding that blanket as carefully as if a child were tucked inside?

## Noise

A peaceful meditation environment is fine, but not mandatory. Remember, skillful meditators take their world as they find it—warts and all.

Before meditating, do whatever you can to create an optimally peaceful space. Once you take your position, however, you need to accept any distraction that arises. This includes noise.

If distracting sounds can be heard, look at the thoughts, emotions and sensations that they create. Usually it is not the sound that is bothering you, it is your judgment about it. Stop judging it and simply label the sound as noise.

Noise, when worked with in a skillful way, can be a tremendous opportunity for deepening your practice; it can lead to an entirely new perspective, not just on noise, but all the external distractions in your life.

## Timekeeping

At meditation retreats and in sitting groups, one meditator is the designated timekeeper. The timekeeper will keep track of elapsed time for the entire group and will sound the bell or gong that indicates the beginning and conclusion of each sitting period.

If you are meditating alone, you will be your own timekeeper. Here are several ways to time your sitting period without having to consult a clock repeatedly:

- Set a kitchen or microwave timer.

- Set a timer that turns on a light to signal the end of the period.

- Use a prerecorded timed tape (see Resource section), or make one of your own.

### Finding time

*Lama Zopa Rinpoche, the Tibetan Buddhist teacher, describes a foolproof method for making sure that you have time for daily meditation:*

*Life is very busy, especially for those living in the West. Many people say, therefore, that it is difficult to find the time during a busy day for a regular meditation practice. In this case, the best solution is to get up earlier each morning.*

*The best time to find peace and quiet for practice is generally after the children have gone to bed or before they awaken in the morning and demand your attention.*

## Making a schedule

Training the mind is like training the body: the idea is to make gradual progress, or as Goethe called it, "deliberate haste."

Let's say you haven't jogged in twenty years and now decide to compete in the New York City Marathon. A professional trainer would probably start you out very slowly, maybe just by stretching and walking a couple of blocks a day for the first week. Then, gradually, walking distance would be increased. Only after this would you begin jogging and running, gradually working up to marathon level.

Along the same line, if you've never meditated and you go to a good teacher, you will also start slowly and build up your practice.

### Consistency

When Ralph Waldo Emerson said, "A foolish consistency is the hobgoblin of little minds," he was not talking about meditation. Consistency is key to an optimum meditation practice, and is every bit as important as actual sitting time.

When you're in physical training, it's good to lay off one or two days a week so the body can heal. That's not the case in meditation; training your mind muscle is something you should do on a daily basis.

One daily, ten-minute meditation period is totally acceptable. If for some reason you just don't have ten minutes, meditate for five. Or two. Or one. The act of sitting down even for one minute reinforces the fact that you are committed to meditation. It's very important.

Try to meditate at the same time each day. But if it's a tossup between meditating at the same time or not meditating at all that day, meditate, no matter when.

After a time, and with consistency, you will find that your meditation practice has seamlessly become part of your daily schedule: get up, put on

> **Consistency is key to an optimum meditation practice, and is every bit as important as actual sitting time.**

*How long do people meditate? It varies with each person. Some meditators may sit for three hours a day, some for three minutes a day. Intensive meditation retreats may entail up to six hours of sitting meditation a day. If you go to a sitting group once a week, the leader or the group may decide that everyone will sit for one hour.*

slippers, brush your teeth, meditate, eat breakfast. Make it part of your daily routine—that's the whole idea.

### A Suggested Schedule

To lay out a schedule of meditation for everybody is impossible; each of us is unique, with our own lifestyles and responsibilities. The following sample schedule for establishing a meditation practice lets you work at your own pace:

- Start with one ten-minute period daily.

- After one week, add a second five-minute period.

- After four days, add five minutes to the second period. You are now sitting for two ten-minute periods each day. Follow this schedule for a week.

- Next, make three-minute additions to both periods. After each increase, sit for one week using that schedule.

- Adjust your schedule up or down, but don't fall below ten minutes twice a day.

> ## *Make your own timing tape*
>
> Purchase an inexpensive bell or gong. Gently tapping a pot with a wooden spoon gives a surprisingly gong-like sound. Turn on your tape recorder and let it run for the desired length of time. It is traditional to start a meditation period with three gongs and end it with one. Do that when you make your tape.
>
> If you are making your own tape, you can control the time periods. Start with a ten-minute interval to match your sitting time. As you begin to increase your sitting time, make new tapes.

At retreats, discussed in more detail in the Appendix, meditation periods usually run twenty-five minutes. That's a good benchmark to work toward.

## *Meditating out loud and silently*

While meditation is usually done silently, you may find in the beginning that it is helpful to use your voice to assist you. Sound is a very strong reinforcement. Some meditation forms, like mantra, are traditionally done out loud.

Count your exhalations up to four, aloud or to yourself, If you are noting expansion and contraction of the breath, simply repeat: "expansion, contraction."

> *Some meditation forms, like mantra, are traditionally done out loud.*

## AM I DOING IT RIGHT?

Many questions come up when you start to meditate. This is to be expected. Some seem profound. Some seem embarrassing. Never be afraid to ask a question of any teacher or instructor. Shinzen Young, one of America's premier meditation teachers, has an expression: "Subtle is significant." That applies not only during your meditation practice period, but also when it's over. The only stupid question is the one you don't ask.

Here's a checklist of reactions—feelings, statements, and questions—that are common when a meditator begins to practice. Check off any that seem familiar. Then read the responses that follow.

___ Why am I doing this?

___ I can't relax.

___ I'm not meditating right.

___ My back (leg, knee, arm) hurts.

___ I'm cold. I'm hot.

___ I just can't stop thinking.

___ I can't concentrate.

___ I'm bored.

___ I fell asleep.

___ I can't sit still.

___ My breathing is funny.

___ I've got this terrible itch.
Can I scratch it?

___ I have to go to the bathroom.
What do I do?

___ I've made a major discovery or breakthrough.
Can I stop to write it down?

___ I felt scared, as if I might be floating away.

___ I felt ecstatic, as if I might be floating away.

You may have checked one item, or you may have checked them all. The very fact that questions come up is a positive indication that you are developing the skill of mindfulness. Now here are the responses:

### 1. Why am I doing this?

The real question you're asking is this: "Is meditation worthwhile?" The unequivocal answer is yes.

In the beginning, almost all meditators resist the commitment to practice. The Buddha told his students that some degree of doubt, resistance, and skepticism were positive things to bring to meditation practice.

If you're ready to throw in the towel on meditation, wait a little longer. Give meditation the benefit of the doubt. Try making your object of meditation the different emotions, such as uncertainty, anger, and frustration that arise as you continue to meditate.

### 2. I can't relax.

In the beginning, it's only natural that you won't feel relaxed while meditating. Meditation is a new and strange experience. Think about the first time you had sex. Were you relaxed? Probably not. And that was also something you heard would be wonderful.

Relaxation and calm are natural by-products of meditation. Recall that this is the art of opening to each moment of life with calm awareness. Opening means acceptance, it doesn't mean effort. If you are properly centered, with your attention tuned as finely as possible to your object of meditation, then relaxation will occur naturally.

If you find yourself unable to relax, take a look at the body sensations, feelings, and emotions that make up the package you define as tension. The more you flood this package with calm awareness, the less resistance you will feel. When you totally accept what is happening in the present moment, you are, by definition, in the proper meditative state.

*The Buddha told his students that some degree of doubt, resistance, and skepticism were positive things to bring to meditation practice.*

### 3. I'm not meditating correctly.

You are in good company on this one. Virtually all students, teachers, and masters have, at one time or another, wondered if they were meditating correctly.

In our society, we are told "no pain, no gain," that everything has to be complicated, and that nothing will happen unless we make it happen. This is not the case in meditation. This practice is natural, easy, and worthwhile none the less.

In his foreword to Lex Hixon's book, *Coming Home*, Ken Wilbur has this to say about doing it right:

> This fundamental and universal consciousness you and all beings possess fully at every moment. It is your simple and bare awareness in this moment before you manipulate it, name it, judge it, or in any way fiddle with it. And therefore, ultimately, there is no path to this primary, basic, and ultimate consciousness. There is no way you can walk to your own feet.

The bottom line is this: Simply sit. You don't have to do anything.

### 4. My back (leg, knee, arm) hurts.

From time to time, some discomfort and dharma pain is normal for meditators at every level. When this happens, give yourself a break. Try a different position. If you're on a cushion, sit in a chair. Maybe you need a folded towel to give support under your right knee. Maybe you should be kneeling on a bench. Try different ways.

And *always remember:* Doctor's orders and/or unhealthy pain take precedence.

### 5. I'm cold. I'm hot.

It's normal to feel physical changes during a meditation period. If you are cold, you might try covering yourself with a blanket, as they do in the Insight tradition. If you're hot, wear lighter clothes, or open a window before you meditate.

## *Hindrances*

*In his teachings, the Buddha spoke of five primary hindrances that are obstacles to our awakening. They are:*

- *desire,*
- *aversion,*
- *sleepiness,*
- *restlessness, and*
- *doubt.*

Adjust your environment before you begin meditation. Once you begin, however, temperature should be treated as just another thing that has come up. It should be looked at and accepted mindfully. Look at being cold or hot as impermanent phenomena that, like all things, will change. Return to the object of meditation.

### 6. I just can't stop thinking.

Of course you can't. Your mind is always thinking. That's its job. As Zen Master Kopp says, "The point is not to suppress thought, but rather to surpass it."

Review the various strategies set out in chapter 2 for the mind: swinging door, lighthouse, and so forth. They can help you tame your wild mind.

### 7. I can't concentrate. I'm bored. I fell asleep. I can't sit still.

All of these reactions to meditation fall under the category of hindrances. Hindrances arise alone, in tandem, or as clusters. For example, you can't concentrate because meditation is boring—so boring that you could fall asleep on your cushion.

Meditation teacher Sharon Salzberg instructs students that "the antidote to the hindrances is mindfulness." When you distill and reduce the feelings and perceptions of hindrance down to their essence, you find they are just like everything else—temporary, insubstantial, transient experiences of body and mind.

Hindrances are guaranteed to come up. One effective way to handle them is to let them know who is in charge. Observe them mindfully, accept them, and then return, gently, to the object of meditation. Don't let hindrances push you around.

Here is some more advice on working with hindrances:

• Make the hindrance your temporary object of meditation. Fix it with the same total awareness as you would the breath. Watch as feelings like restlessness, boredom, and drowsiness

*The bottom line is this: Simply sit.*

> *Your insight didn't arise from your hard-charging analytical left brain, but from your deeply intuitive right brain.*

unravel into their components, and as with all phenomena, disappear by themselves.

- If you're sleepy, open your eyes. Stand up. It is better to stand and be awake than to sit and be asleep. Stare at a source of light: the sun, the moon, a lamp. Splash cool water on your face.

- If you're restless, do some walking meditation (see chapter 6). Stand in place and slowly raise and lower your arms.

Meditation is the ultimate in recycling; it transforms your doubts and skepticism and problems into opportunities to deepen your mindfulness. Nothing is excluded. And you're never wasting your time.

### 8. I've got this terrible itch. Can I scratch it?
### I need to go to the bathroom. Should I stop meditating?

Minor annoyances and irritants are a fact of life. Meditation affords you a great opportunity to learn how to put them into perspective, use them to accelerate your practice.

For example, an itch, on a one-to-ten scale of human discomfort and suffering, probably registers around one-tenth. But when you are sitting still, trying to meditate, it can feel like a nine. This has nothing to do with the physical sensation itself and everything to do with your response to it.

If you can notice the itch and everything about it and exercise mindful restraint by not scratching, you are developing a brand-new way to deal with irritants and annoyances on all levels of your life. The cultivation of self-discipline and restraint is an extraordinarily powerful tool that can prove invaluable in many aspects of your daily life.

But it may not be a nuisance that distracts you. When you meditate you may have some remarkable revelations about your life. These revelations strike without warning, like an earthquake.

### 9. I've made a major discovery or breakthrough.
### Can I stop and write it down?

An insight can take the form of anything from the answer to a major relationship problem to the plot for your Great

American Novel. Two things are certain: It will be big and you will want to stop everything, grab a pen and paper, and write it all down before you forget.

What you are accessing here is not mere surface, discursive *thinking*. It is profound, intuitive *wisdom*, arising from a deep, unconscious level. Your insight didn't arise from your hard-charging analytical left brain, but from your deeply intuitive right brain. That is why these discoveries, revelations, and truths seem so incredible—and ephemeral. You want to get them down before they disappear forever. But they won't.

The truth is that this insight has surfaced from an intuitive source of wisdom that always has been and always will be deep inside you. Since it has always been there, it's not going anywhere. Finish your meditation first. Then write it down.

### 10. I felt scared/I felt ecstatic, as if I might be floating away.

The goal of meditation is the art of opening to each moment of life with calm awareness. It is not to look for blissful experiences or to try to avoid negative ones. Still, it is common in meditation to experience feelings of fear, of disorientation, and on the opposite end of the spectrum, moments of bliss and ecstasy, perhaps even visions.

Lawrence LeShan, in his audiotape *How to Meditate*, says, "Sometimes I run into clusters of associations. For example, 'red' could have been followed by 'blue,' then by 'green.' If this happens, simply stay with the discipline, even if it means going around the [color] spectrum several times. Presently it will cease."

The meditative process accesses parts of human consciousness and subconsciousness in a new way, and experiences of fear and bliss are part of the territory. When these experiences arise, simply accept them with the same calm

### What really moves?

Two Zen monks watched a flag fluttering in the breeze. This was their debate:

"It is the breeze that is moving," said one.

"No. It is the flag that is moving," countered the other.

Their Master was passing just at this time and heard the conversation. He stopped and turned to his students.

"You are both wrong," he said. "It is your mind that is moving."

awareness, mindfulness, and equanimity that you accept any other thought, feeling, or sensation.

The opening verse of the Dhammapada, a collection of the Buddha's teachings, says :

*The meditative process accesses parts of human consciousness and subconsciousness in a new way.*

We are what we think.

All that we are arises with our thoughts.

With our thoughts we make the world.

Speak or act with an impure mind

And trouble will follow you

As the wheel follows the ox that draws the cart....

Speak or act with a pure mind

And happiness will follow you

As your shadow, unshakable.

Meditation enables you to watch your thoughts arise and see how they create your idea of the world. It is a tremendously liberating discovery to realize that you, not external events, create your experience of life.

## CHAPTER RECAP

- Over the centuries, particular meditation postures have been developed to align the body and mind optimally into a stable, calm, and aware synergistic balance.

- The various meditation postures are intended to relax the body and put it in harmony with itself and the universe. When one assumes a correct meditation posture, one has the right state of mind.

- Taking your place, not only in your meditation space, but also in this world, means being aligned, relaxed, and resilient.

- The overall posture allows you to practice the art of being open to each moment of life with calm awareness. If meditation physically hurts, you're in the wrong position. In this discipline, as in life, the first rule is to practice a policy of non-harming and kindness, especially toward ourselves.

- Many types of cushion and bench are used by meditators. But when you first begin to meditate, use an ordinary chair.

- It's not what you sit on that matters, but how you sit.

- Disabilities, whether temporary or permanent, are not impediments to establishing a strong meditation practice.

- It is better to stand and be awake than to sit and be asleep.

- You do not require perfect quiet to meditate. It isn't noise that is bothers you, it is your judgment about the noise.

- Consistency in meditating daily is just as important as actual sitting time. The very fact that you are setting aside a certain amount of time every day to do something positive for yourself and others should make you feel good. Enjoy it.

- Meditation is the ultimate recycler. It transforms doubts into mindfulness.

- Meditation puts us into a new relationship with our thoughts and feelings.

*"We are what we think. All that we are arises with our thoughts."*
**THE BUDDHA**

we are only
here for a
little while
and then somebody
turns the page

crosbie

# P A R T   2
# *The Varieties of Meditation Experience*

By now, you're meditating, have found a comfortable meditation posture, and have the answers to at least some of your questions. It's time to take a look at the origins of meditation and the many threads that make up the fabric of the meditative tradition. What follows is a condensed guided tour of the varieties of meditation schools, traditions, and techniques. In the following chapters, you'll find many meditative traditions. All of these traditions are at once unique unto themselves, yet alike in their commonality of purpose—to awaken us to the truth of who we are.

## MANY MANSIONS, MANY TRADITIONS

"In my Father's house there are many mansions," Jesus of Nazareth told his followers. "There are as many meditative paths as there are hairs in the beard of God," a Kabbalist might say. The number and variety of meditative traditions reaches into the thousands or tens of thousands. World religions such as Hinduism, Buddhism, Christianity, and Islam have sects and branches too numerous to count, many of which embrace meditation.

In truth, every major cultural area also has its own unique meditation practice. Africa is rife with them, most still unknown to Westerners. In the East, overlapping into Buddhism and Hinduism are many philosophical and aes-

*The medita-tion practices that have grown up in world religions are universal and may be practiced by anyone.*

thetic traditions which produced the types of meditation best known throughout the world. The West gave birth to Judaism, Christianity, Islam, and spun off numerous sects and philosophical schools many with their own meditative practices. The Americas, North and South, held and still hold a cornucopia of meditative and spiritual traditions. Modern times have brought us exciting new approaches to meditation.

Each of the world religions is universal. Each comprises a belief system intended for all humankind. Buddhism, Hinduism, Christianity, and Islam speak to everyone, their gods belong to and rule over everyone. Anyone may become a convert. (Indeed many Christians and Muslims think that everyone must believe as they do.) The meditation practices that have grown up in world religions are also universal and may be practiced by anyone.

*"Three men set forth seeking fortune. And the one found gold; another came on good land, and he tilled it. But the third saw sunlight making jewels of the dew. All three went by the same road. Each one thought himself the richer."*

TALBOT MUNDY
*Om: The Secret of Arbor Valley*

In the next chapters you'll be introduced to more than a dozen traditions, old and new, drawn from around the world. You'll also find guidance to get you begin practice in each. If any strikes a chord, you'll find guidance on how to learn more in the Resource section at the end of this book.

## Transformation of consciousness

On the surface, the variety of meditation techniques seems vast, contradictory, and irreconcilable. The good news is that when you go beneath the surface distinctions, you find a common bond, not only between sects of the same tradition, but between the major religious and meditational traditions of the world.

Once we go beyond appearance, we begin to see that there is a fundamental similarity in meditation practice that cuts across religious, regional, and traditional lines and encompasses all. Each of the great meditative traditions and its offshoots shares a common goal—the elevation of consciousness to a new, richer, higher level of awareness. The differences in these traditions are reflections of particular schools' beliefs as to the most effective method of achieving that level. Let's look at two areas where traditions commonly diverge.

## Place

Zen Buddhists and Christian Carthusians often practice meditation and religious observance in complete withdrawal from worldly affairs, which are regarded as a hindrance and a draining distraction. In Thailand, the forest monks of the Buddhist Theravadan tradition live deep in the woods, hundreds of miles and seemingly centuries removed from the mores and loose moral standards of Bangkok.

On the other side of the coin, systems such as Transcendental Meditation™ and Insight meditation, encourage complete immersion in the very real crucible of everyday life. In fact, these schools regard any forced change in the meditator's life and schedule as an unskillful attempt to manipulate the living situation. Thus, these traditions do not require any major lifestyle alterations.

## Attitude

Each meditation tradition is vibrant with its own philosophies, rituals, and etiquette. Some, like the Bhakti tradition in Hinduism, demand prior purification by the meditator before commencement of serious practice. Others, like Zen Buddhism and TM, do not require prior purification, believing instead that refinement of consciousness arises in the course of meditation itself.

*There is a fundamental similarity in meditation practice that cuts across religious, regional, and traditional lines and encompasses all.*

### Practice

*"We may start by practicing meditation much like practicing piano. Eventually, when we become proficient, we will not need to practice anymore. Just as playing becomes practice, everything we do will become meditation.*

*…[Meditation] is a tool to develop clarity, an awareness and acceptance of the flow of events whatever they may be. In the end, meditation techniques transcend even themselves. Then, there will be neither meditation or non-meditation. Just what is."*

JACK KORNFIELD
*Living Buddhist Masters*

Certain meditation traditions include complex rituals. The difference in ritual between Tibetan and Zen Buddhists, for example, is readily apparent at their respective monasteries. In the Tibetan tradition, monks clad in orange robes chant and beat gongs in lengthy prayer. They are surrounded by *mandalas* and depictions of Buddhist gods and goddesses. In the Zen tradition, black robed monks practice silently, facing a wall of the formal meditation hall (the zendo). The setting is austere: There are no statues of deities, no furnishings other than a dais, on which a single stick of incense glows in the half-light.

But meditation traditions have more in common than shared purpose. They also employ similar techniques. Almost all schools, for example, use spoken words and syllables to focus consciousness. And almost all use visualization to take the meditator's mind away from petty, everyday concerns.

## MANTRA

Mantra is a very popular meditation method in the Tibetan Buddhist, Sufi, Hindu, and Orthodox Christian traditions. It has become important in contemporary practice as well through Transcendental Meditation and in Christian centering prayer.

### Why is mantra so powerful?

*Mantra is the essence of sound and the embodiment of the truth in the form of sound. Each syllable is impregnated with spiritual power, condenses a spiritual truth and vibrates with the blessing of the speech of the buddhas.... So when you chant a mantra you are charging your breath and energy with the energy of the mantra....*

SOGYAL RINPOCHE
*The Tibetan Book of Living and Dying*

## Yankee Stadium mantra

*Interestingly, mantra as prayer can be found at sporting event, although the fans engaged in it might be clueless as to what they were doing. The constant repetition of a player's name at a baseball stadium when he comes to bat could be looked upon as a form of mantra: a repeated sound, phrase, or expression. Perhaps 60,000 fans chanting LOU, LOU, LOU LOU, LOU, LOU, when the great Yankee Lou Pinella came to bat believed that their collective energy would put Lou on base. Many times it did.*

Mantra as meditation is the continued repetition of a sound, prayer, or phrase that is considered to bestow certain meditational benefits on the chanter. Mantra can be recited as meditation or prayer or both. Some mantra expressions have certain meanings. For example, in the Sanskrit mantra *Om ah hum,* the sound "Om" stands for body, "ah" for speech, and "hum" for the mind. The chanting of these words is believed to purify negativity produced by the body, speech, and mind, as well as to invoke a blessing upon the chanter.

Alan Watts, on his audiotape, *How to Meditate,* suggests that Westerners who have difficulty chanting foreign words might repeat Western invocations, such as the word Hallelujah.

Some traditions believe that the sound waves emanating from the repetition of a syllable or series of syllables in the mantra contain inherent powers that manifest particular cosmic forces. Thus, for the Hindu Saiva Upanishads, each letter in the fifty-letter Sanskrit alphabet is believed to carry its own unique strength. The letter *kumkara,* for instance, is thought to be an antidote for poison. In Tibetan Buddhism, certain sounds are thought to evoke the presence of particular deities.

Other schools believe that the syllables have no intrinsic power and the effects of mantra derive from constant repetition. Thus, one could repeat any sound and achieve the benefits.

Many people became aware of the word "mantra" because it was associated with the Hare Krishna movement, which employs the words "hare krishna" in a chant—a mantra—from the Hindi: *Hare Krishna, O Krishna!* Hare Krishnas are members of a religious group, a Hindu sect, that is not a major tradition.

In mantra practice, your object of meditation is the mantra itself. When you find your mind engaged in discursive thinking, the instruction is as it always is: Gently take your mind by the hand and lead it back to the object of meditation—your mantra.

You may actually work up a good sweat if you are chanting out loud. And you will also be exercising parts of your diaphragm and larynx with a new dimension of depth.

## *Mantras*

Amen. Shalom. Peace.

So ham. *(Represents the sound of breath, so being that of the inhale, ham the exhale.)*

Om ah hum vajra guru padma siddhi hum, *and* Om ah hung bedzar guru pema siddhi hung. *(Two versions of the mantra of Padmasambhava, the mantra of all the buddhas, masters, and realized beings. The first is in Tibetanized Sanskrit, the second in Sanskrit. Loose translation, "I invoke you the Vajra Guru, Padmasambhava, by your blessing, may you grant us supreme blessings.")*

Om mani padme hung sarva shanting kuruye soha. ("O Buddha of Compassion and Wisdom, may all these sicknesses be pacified.")

Om namah shivaya. *(Used to correct imbalance of consciousness, Hindu.)*

Shri ram jay ram. *(Refers to the great king Rama, who was said to be in tune with the Divine Will, Hindu.)*

Gatay, gatay, paragatay. Parasamgatay, bodhi svaha. *(The Heart Sutra, Buddhist.)*

Alleluia! Adoramus te Domine. *(Used in France by Taizé monks. The single word or phrase is divided into four parts, Christian Latin.)*

Maranantha. *(In Aramaic, "Come to Lord, Come to Jesus," Christian. From Dom John Main, a Benedictine monk who died in 1982. Chant the word in four parts.)*

Let go. Let God. *(Alcoholics Anonymous.)*

Om swasti jampal yang sog kun gye pai lam. *("You radiate as manifestations of profound and vast dharma," Tibetan Buddhist.)*

Om mani padme hum. *(Mantra of compassion, Hindu.)*

## A FIRST MANTRA

Do the following for ten minutes:

1. Settle down in a comfortable posture with your eyes closed.

2. Bring a mantra such as "Om ah hum" into your consciousness. Then begin repeating it. Start slowly, speaking as distinctly as possible. You will naturally and gradually increase the speed of repetitions. If you are chanting out loud, you may run out of breath. This is natural.

3. Stop as needed. Gradually, you will seamlessly be able to incorporate your breathing with the repetitions. Don't try, just allow it to happen naturally. As you recite your mantra, you may find that you relax into the sound, your breath and your attention joining in a natural and powerful way. As with all techniques, this combination of alertness and relaxation is a sign of awareness.

4. Repeat your mantra for five minutes.

5. As you reach the end of your mantra period, it is good practice to exert a sort of "braking action" on the repetitions. This helps brings you to a more natural, gradual conclusion.

After you have ceased repetitions, sit quietly and attentively. Make note of the feelings in your body and mind. Some people report a feeling of cleansing, healing.

## VISUALIZATION

All schools of meditation emphasize visualization—using a word or image to focus the mind.

There is a reason: when meditators visualize something they touch on one of the greatest strengths of the human race. Vision is the dominant means of perception in our species. Examination of the fossil record indicates that long before the anatomical apparatus for spoken language evolved, the organs of vision were already highly developed, and visual communication was an important tool of the evolving human species. Gestures and postures

*When meditators visualize something they touch on one of the greatest strengths of the human race.*

conveyed such messages as peaceful intent, transactions and trade, hunger, personal desires, and so forth. Survival depended on perceiving and recognizing them. As a result, a major portion of the brain is devoted to the this sense. Anything that stimulates this part of the brain has a proportionately large affect on us and our behavior

We've all had the experience of recognizing friends at a distance just by their shape. We've all also ducked instinctively, without even realizing it, when an object whizzed by our heads. This kind of quick response is a sign that the large portion of the brain dedicated to seeing can deduce things visually and seize control of the body instantaneously—overriding our conscious minds—long before our conscious minds can register or resist.

The eye makes inferences about objects and what they are merely from shape or outline. In the same way, the brain, without ever bothering to examine the distinguishing characteristics very closely, tends to perceive ideas, concepts, and feelings as being similar if their general shapes and outlines seem to be similar.

Pause for a moment. Clear your mind with a few deep breaths. Now meditate on the following image: A bright yellow lemon cut in half, the pulp glistening. Now meditate on what it would feel like if the intensely sharp, sour juice of the lemon were to be squeezed out on your tongue.

If you actually seemed to taste the lemon for a moment, and your mouth flooded with saliva, or if you shuddered, don't feel alarmed. That's how most people respond to the above exercise. And if lemon doesn't do it for you, it's likely there's a taste that does—perhaps licorice or aniseed. In any case, now you know the power of a special form of meditation called visualization.

Thus, the mere recreation of a mental image (like the taste of a lemon, or the memory of a humiliation) will cause the brain to react as if faced by the real object. This phenomenon might furnish at least part of the explanation for the effectiveness of active imagery and affirmation, because if one is able to imagine something to be true, part of the mind appears to accept that imagined outcome as reality. As Dr. Roger N. Shepard wrote in a recent issue of the American Psychologist, "Mental imagery is remarkably able to substitute for actual perception: Subjects make the same judgments about objects in their absence as in their presence...."

Visualization may be the oldest form of meditation, long predating silent, mandala, and mantra mediations. Visualization is a fundamental tool of meditation, and most meditations and meditative traditions draw upon it. Examples in this book are in the Tibetan Buddhist meditation, the African altar exercise, and the Goddess meditation.

## Visualizing God

Meditating on the deity is the basis of the oldest and most universal form of mediation. It's at the core of Buddhist, Christian, Moslem, and Jewish meditational practices. Members of the earliest known societies, like the Babylonians and Egyptians meditated on the image of goddess Ishtar/Isis in all her glory. Protestants meditate on Christ. Catholics add Mary. Buddhists visualize the Enlightened One. Moslems meditate on Allah. Zoroastrians on Zoroaster. Native Americans on the Great Spirit. Modern hermeticists and practitioners of Magick meditate on the forms of Egyptian gods and goddesses. Many contemporary women are reconnecting with their ancient roots by meditating on the Great Mother or the Goddess. Africans are rediscovering Shango and other *orisha*.

"Perhaps the most dramatic example among religious traditions," Roger Walsh, Ph.D., professor of psychiatry and philosophy at the University of California, Irvine, writes in the Spirit of Shamanism, "is the so-called deity *yoga* of Tibetan Buddhism. Here the *yogi* visualizes himself first creating and then merging with a godlike figure who embodies virtue upon virtue—unconditional love, boundless compassion, profound wisdom, and more. After merging, just like the *shaman* and her power-animal dance, the yogi attempts to move, speak, and act as the deity. In other

*Tibetans... claim that with deity yoga a practitioner can become a Buddha in a single lifetime rather than in the "three countless eons" it would otherwise take.*

words, after merging with their allies, both shaman and yogi embody, experience, and express their allies' qualities. The potential power of these visualizations is suggested by the fact that the Tibetans regard deity yoga as one of the most powerful and advanced of their vast array of practices. In what may be the world's most dramatic claim for effectiveness, they claim that with deity yoga a practitioner can become a Buddha in a single lifetime rather than in the "three countless eons" it would otherwise take. Whatever the mechanism, it is clear that visualizing oneself merging with a powerful benevolent figure can be surprisingly empowering.

However, in the rationalist eighteenth, nineteenth, and twentieth centuries, visualizing oneself uniting with God or a deity was relegated to religious practice and rarely discussed, even among friends. It remained for science to rediscover and authenticate the potency of this visualization for deity yoga to regain the place it deserves in the meditational pantheon.

As you read the following chapters you will discover meditators time and again focusing on their gods or aspects of their gods. Clearly in many traditions, in addition to the personal benefit acquired through practice, meditation is seen also as a sort of prayer, a means to connect the everyday world with the eternal. And in the modern world, many people meditate on other images in order to make contact with what the images represent. Deepak Chopra advises meditating on images of health and prosperity. Shakti Gawain's *Creative Visualization* has taught many to achieve health, truth, and beauty through visualization. As you read about the origins of meditation, note how the practice isn't so inward-looking as it may seem at first. Meditation is also a form of communication, putting us in touch with the universe and with, as Gawain says, "our higher selves."

# Eastern Meditation Traditions

**5**

Perhaps no area of the world is so closely associated with meditation and meditative traditions as that which lies to the East of Europe, encompassing many diverse cultures in India, Greater Russia, Mongolia, Tibet, China, Southeast Asia, and Japan. Asia has produced a number of vital meditative traditions within the sects of Buddhism and Hinduism and associated with the philosophical traditions of Taoism and Confucianism.

## HINDUISM AND MEDITATION

Among the world religions, Hinduism is the most difficult to outline simply. Hinduism lacks a central historical figure (like Jesus, Muhammad, or the Buddha) whose life sets an example of right action. Hindu scriptures which are vast, imaginative poems do not easily lend themselves to interpretation.

As Hinduism evolved, its adherents did not eradicate earlier belief systems. It made room in its pantheon for everyone. (It has been estimated that there are more than 300,000 Hindu deities.) Hinduism has been described as an encyclopedia of religion which accepts the validity of simple nature gods (a god for rain, for the sun, for earth-

*• Many famous meditational traditions*

*• Various Eastern techniques embraced by the West.*

*• A sample of Eastern traditions:*

*Yoga*

*Zen*

*Tibetan Buddhism*

**115**

quakes) and of ancient religious practices. Overlaid is a complex, profound, and poetic theology and cosmology.

At the heart of Hinduism is the idea that the entire physical and spiritual world is one. Each of us is a part of the universe and a part of God.

*In the Bhagavad-Gita, Krishna, the great Hindu deity serves as charioteer of the prince Arjuna. The prince is heartsick because he has to do battle with his kinsmen; he resists the yoga of action which is his destiny. Krishna tells him:*

*"…the mind is restless, no doubt, and hard to subdue. But it can be brought under control by constant practice and by the exercise of dispassion. Certainly, if a man has no control over his ego, he will find this yoga difficult to master….*

*"…Therefore you must remember me at all times, and do your duty. If your mind and heart are set upon me constantly, you will come to me. Never doubt this.*

*"Make a habit of practicing meditation, and do not let your mind be distracted. In this way you will come finally to the Lord who is the light-giver, the highest of the high…. I am the beginning, the lifespan, and the end of all ….*
*Whatever in this world is powerful, beautiful or glorious, that you may know to have come forth from a fraction of my power and glory."*
SWAMI PRABHAVANANDA AND CHRISTOPHER ISHERWOOD
*Translators*

Meditation does more than offer insight into the self. It promises that we will better understand the nature of the universe. It is not surprising that meditation techniques, so far as we know, first flourished in the Hindu world.

## *Yogic meditation*

The mastery of *kundalini* is the basis of many, perhaps all, forms of the Indian system of physical and mental meditational disciplines called *yoga*. Many scholars believe yoga is one of the oldest of all meditational paths. Certainly it is one of the most widespread, and is practiced in one form or another in virtually every nation of the world. Yoga is often associated with India and the spiritual practices of Hinduism, particularly as elucidated in the Bhagavad Gita. However, its origins predate India's settling by the Indo-Aryan races, and are finally lost in the mists of antiquity.

There are a number of branches of yoga. Some students of meditation feel drawn to one branch of yoga, some to another branch, some to sampling or including all in their own practice. Some important ones are:

### Bhakti Yoga

The path of achieving realization solely through meditating continuously on love and devotion.

### Karma Yoga

Meditating on living life so purely that you perform no hurtful or sinful actions.

### Hatha Yoga

Focusing the mind and meditation through a rigorous system of physical exercises that also promote health, healing, and vigor.

### Tantra Yoga

Mastery of kundalini, a powerful spiritual energy that resides within everyone.

## Kundalini—the serpent power

Tantric Yoga focuses on arousing and harnessing kundalini, the tremendous physical, chemical, and electrical energies of the body, particularly those concentrated in certain nerve plexuses located in specific parts of the body called *chakras* (wheels of light), and in the nerve trunks transmitting signals up and down the spinal column. At the base of the spine is the mightiest repository of kundalini, considered to rest tightly-coiled, serpent-like, until aroused by meditation (hence kundalini is also known as "the serpent power"). Once released, it shoots up from the base of the spine toward the brain, producing a form of self-illumination or enlightenment.

As the kundalini energy passes through each chakra, it energizes and purifies, releasing its energies. When it reaches the *sashasrara* (the highest center of the body), just above the top of the head, it joins with one's divine will and causes the polarization of every cell in the body (much like the Lighting of the Tree in Kabbalistic meditations, discussed later). The resulting mental and spiritual state has been described as "luminous as lightening, shining in the hollow of this lotus like a chain of brilliant lights." Yogi Kundali Upanishad said of this kundalini arousal, "Kundalini awakens from her sleep as a serpent, struck by a stick, hisses and straightens itself."

*At the heart of Hinduism is the idea that the entire physical and spiritual world is one. Each of us is a part of the universe and a part of God.*

## Hindu medicine and the chakras

According to Tantric belief, there are seven chakras running up the spinal column. Each chakra bestows certain abilities and benefits when its energy is activated, and meditating on a chakra will activate its power. When all seven are activated, peak physical and mental states result. The seven vital energy centers are:

Muladhara. The first and lowest chakra is situated at the base of the spine. It is said to be the repository of kundalini. Omar Garrison calls Muladhara energy "the electrical force of creation, the cohesive power of matter." Meditation upon this center leads to the mastery of desire, envy, anger, and passion.

Svadisthana. The second chakra is situated at the root of the genitals. Meditation on this center confers ability to see and to communicate with entities who inhabit the astral worlds.

Manipura. The third chakra is located near the navel. Meditation on this center is said to heal illness, fulfill secret desires, and confer insight into the deepest consciousness of other minds.

Anahata. The fourth chakra is situated in the chest, near the heart. It is the core of our individual being, the very spark of the divine, which glows "like the steady tapering flame of a lamp." Meditation upon this center strengthens the "psychic" faculties, generates the ability to hear and see at great distances, and ensures material fortune.

Vishuddha. The fifth chakra is located at the base of the throat, and is considered the doorway to the plane of eternal wisdom. "Whoever will concentrate upon this center," an old saying goes, "Becomes a sage in the sacred knowledge, a prince among yogis."

Ajna. The sixth chakra is situated between the eyebrows at the site of "the third eye." It is the seat of our mental faculties, the abode of the individual consciousness—and our meeting point with the divine. Meditating on this center brings us into contact with our spiritual guru, and initiates us into the secret knowledge of Tantra.

Sashasrara. The final chakra lies just above the crown of the head, where the principal arteries of the spiritual body come together. Here, the final goal of Tantric meditation is achieved: the union of the opposite polarities, the wedding of Shiva and Shakti; solar and lunar. The sashasrara controls the six centers below it.

## Sun breath and moon breath

As in all yoga and mediation practice, breathing techniques are essential to the kindling of kundalini. However, tantric yogis have developed the science of breathing to a level of sophistication unknown in any other traditions of meditation. They believe that breathing through the left nostril (moon breath) activates the sympathetic nervous system, nourishing and regulating body functions, heightening intuition and creativity. Breathing through the right nostril (sun breath), activates the vasomotor system, releasing intense physical energy for activities that require it. Tantric meditators also believe that breathing through both nostrils simultaneously (*sushuma* breath) controls destiny, death, time, and greatly expands longevity.

Tantric literature enumerates in some detail the kind of human endeavors sun breath is said to augment and confer success upon. It is said that while the breath is flowing through the right nostril one should undertake activities that require physical exertion or passion, such as:

- building a home or boat,
- selling,
- holding parties,
- participating in contests,
- lovemaking,
- using weapons,
- eating and drinking,
- engaging in mystical or occult endeavors, or
- bathing.

Tantric writings also tell us that those times when we are breathing through the left nostril (moon breath) it is very propitious to perform activities of a calm, gentle, steady nature, such as:

- artistic undertakings,

- business,

- studying and learning,

- dealing with authorities,

- travel, journeys, pilgrimages,

- devotions and worship,

- planting and sowing,

- earning money,

- cooking,

- buying,

- celebrating weddings, and

- visiting friends and relatives.

## DEVELOPING THE BREATH

To develop your control of breathing and prepare for use of the sun and moon breaths, Omar Garrison recommends a seven week course. Practice each of the techniques below for one full week, longer if you don't feel you have completely mastered it.

Before beginning each day's meditation, relax and empty your mind by letting out all of the air in your lungs, pulling in your stomach muscles to forcefully release all residual air. Then count to seven while you slowly inhale deeply. Once you've reached seven, pause for a count of one and again exhale slowly, counting to seven again. Repeat this technique at least a dozen times to clear the nasal passages. Make sure to breath out of both nostrils. Then begin the appropriate technique.

- *Week 1, Om Breath.* Inhale, silently saying "Om." Mentally see that the oxygen coming into your body is filled with life-force energy and hold the breath in your mouth. As you force the air against your cheeks, let them fill to capacity and bulge out. Keep pressing the air into your cheeks as long as you can, without creating discomfort. Then discharge your breath quickly and forcefully through the mouth. As you do this, further imagine that your breath is revitalizing every cell in your body and awakening your psychic channels.

- *Week 2, Power Breath.* After the first breath is mastered, you may practice the second breath. This technique begins by going for a walk, preferably alone and outside the polluted confines of the inner city. A park, the beach, or the woods are the ideal kinds of places to go. This breathing exercise is the same as in the first technique. This time, however, hold your breath for a count of two, instead of one. Then exhale to the count of seven once again. Repeat this twelve times. Practice this twice a day for three days, gradually increasing the exhalation to the count of ten. Hold your breath for five counts, exhale for ten counts, then hold your breath outside for five counts.

- *Week 3, Spoon Breath.* Form the syllable "oo" with your lips as you inhale through your mouth in seven small bursts. Swallow the seven breaths. Exhale through both nostrils, counting to seven. Repeat this exercise twenty-four times in the morning and evening over a week's time.

- *Week 4, Lion Breath.* Inhale through both nostrils to the count of four. While holding in the breath, curl your tongue backwards until it hits the roof of your mouth, and let out a deep growl.

- *Week 5, Whistle Breath.* Perform this next to a window or outside. Purse your lips as though you are going to whistle, then inhale slowly through your mouth for a seven count. Pause for one count, then softly exhale through both nostrils to the count of seven. Repeat this six times. Practice this in the morning and at noon.

- *Week 6, Serpent Breath.* This exercise somewhat mimics a snake's hiss, hence the name. Put your tongue between your lips and stick it out slightly. Then inhale through your mouth while producing a hissing sound. When your lungs feel full, hold the breath as long as possible, then slowly exhale with both nostrils. Practice this breathing exercise for two weeks—five times in the morning, at noon, and at night.

- *Week 7, Expanding Breath.* The seventh and final breath exercise begins with exhaling all your breath by sucking in your stomach muscles. Next, use your right thumb to close your right nostril and slowly inhale through the left nostril. Take care to not overinflate your lungs. Once your lungs are filled to a comfortable capacity, close your left nostril with whatever finger feels most natural to you. Keep holding your breath for as long as possible. The length of time you can retain your breath will increase with practice. When you feel you've held your breath as long as you can, open the right nostril while keeping the left side closed, and slowly exhale. Repeat this cycle five times at each session during the first days of your practice. Gradually increase the number to twelve times. This can be practiced many times during the course of a day. However, once a day is sufficient.

---

If you have done this exercise correctly, you should begin to feel the electromagnetic pulses flowing through your body calming and grounding you. Now you begin to experience the benefits of the sun and moon breaths.

## BUDDHIST MEDITATION TRADITIONS

Buddhism alone has given birth to hundreds of offshoots. What follows is a brief tour of three: Zen Buddhism, Tibetan Buddhism, and the Insight tradition of Theravadan Buddhism. The discussion of these methods and techniques is meant as an overview, not in-depth coverage. Where possible, a meditation technique has been included for you to try.

While these three heritages are by no means the only offshoots of Hinduism and Buddhism, they are chosen because they have been brought to the United States by some of their foremost practitioners. All of these traditions offer reputable teachers, teaching facilities, programs, and organizations within the United States. One, TM, requires you to attend a course and initiation at an approved teaching center.

In the Zen, Tibetan, and Insight traditions, it is highly recommended that you locate a reputable teacher and participate in the activities of a teaching center. The Resource section in this book contains information that will help you access teachers and organizations.

### The core of Buddhism

*Philosophically, a school of Buddhism is characterized by its recognition of the Four Seals, the fundamental convictions that:*

- *The nature of all phenomena is impermanent.*
- *The nature of all experience is unsatisfactory.*
- *The nature of all phenomena is essentially empty.*
- *True peace is found in Nirvana.*

### The Buddha

Buddhism arose from Hinduism 2,500 years ago and Buddhists share some of the central beliefs of Hindus.

Siddhartha, the Buddha's given name, was born in 563 B.C., the son of a prince of the Gautamas (hence he was also known as Gautama Buddha). The Gautamas were Rajas (kings or princes) of the Shakyas, whose small kingdom was in the foothills of the Himalayas.

In his twenty-ninth year, the problem of suffering was suddenly and impressively set before him, when prince Siddhartha was visited by four signs during four excursions. These were an old man, a sick man, a corpse, and a monk.

Filled with the thought of the impermanence of happiness and the omnipresence of suffering, he felt a growing unrest and dissatisfaction with his luxurious life.

For a time Siddhartha undertook the severest ascetic practices and self-deprivations, thinking to gain enlightenment from self-denial. Discouraged, Siddhartha found himself no closer to his objective. In this time of loneliness and failure there came to him the Great Temptation (very similar to that of Jesus in the desert five centuries later). Mara, the evil one, visited him and entreated him to give up the quest as futile and return to his old life.

## The eightfold noblepath

*The Buddha taught that enlightenment comes from balancing searching with surrender—the middle way. The middle way leads to release from suffering. The eight parts of this path are:*

- *Right seeing, not seeing the mote in another's eye and missing the beam in our own.*

- *Right resolve, making a commitment to good will toward others, self-denial, and non-harming of sentient beings.*

- *Right speech, refraining from slander, lying, and gossip.*

- *Right conduct, taking no actions that harm others or yourself.*

- *Right livelihood, turning one's back on livelihoods that involve harm to sentient beings, from drug dealing to pollution to exploitation to armaments to slaughter houses.*

- *Right effort, effort in accordance with what is karmically wholesome and which refrains from what is karmically unwholesome.*

- *Right mindfulness, in short...*

- *Right meditation.*

Unvanquished, however, Siddhartha wandered along the banks of the river Nairanjara and took his seat beneath a bo tree, vowing to persist in meditation until he had solved the riddle of suffering. After forty-nine days of unbroken meditation, his mind seemed to grow clearer and clearer, his doubts vanished, a great peace came over him as the significance of all things made itself apparent and he attained complete enlightenment. Siddhartha had become the Buddha, the enlightened.

For the next forty-five years, until his death at the age of eighty, Buddha tirelessly trudged India preaching to all who would listen. He told of his realization of the Four Noble Truths by means of which humanity could enlighten and free itself, and of the Eightfold Noble Path that led there. People were moved to follow his way to spiritual emancipation as much by his serenity and compassion as by the wisdom of his words. Eventually his sermon and dialogues were recorded and these *sutras* (or scriptures) now comprise the basic doctrines of Buddhism.

Buddha ("awakened one") was a wise teacher who achieved enlightenment through mediation. Those who gain enlightenment are supposed to be liberated from the pain of the world, enslavement to the senses, and freed from the cycle of existence. Like Jesus, The Buddha was a reformer who saw that the established religion (Brahmanism) as too tainted by mundane concerns to provide spiritual solace or liberation from materialism.

## Far is near

A monk asked his teacher for permission to journey around the world to try the intensive meditation techniques of some other famous teachers. Permission was granted. A few years later, the monk returned. In Living Buddhist Masters, Jack Kornfield describes this exchange between the monk and his teacher:

"What did you learn?" the teacher asked.

"Nothing," replied the monk.

"Nothing. Really?"

"Nothing that is not already around, that was not right here before I left."

"And what did you experience?"

"Many teachers and many meditation systems," the monk answered. "Yet, the more deeply I penetrated the Dharma [truth], the more I realized there is no need to go anywhere else to practice."

"Ah, yes," replied his teacher. "I could have told you that before you left, but you could not have understood."

## Zen

Zen is a specific school of Buddhism. It originated in India, moved to China in the sixth century and then to

Japan in the twelfth. The word Zen is the Japanese form of the Sanskrit word for meditation, *dhyana*. The Chinese version is *Ch'an*.

Zen tradition holds a special fascination for Westerners; there seems to be something very Western about this Eastern way that resonates for us. Maybe it's Zen's sensibility, its surreal sense of humor, its inscrutable riddles—a fusion of Yogi Berra and the divine.

The Zen scholar D. T. Suzuki said that the hallmark of Zen is its "spirituality, directness of expression, disregard for form or conventionalism, and frequently, an almost wanton delight in going astray from respectability." From Jack Kerouac and the Beat generation to the aphorisms of Sam Goldwyn and Woody Allen, and even to computer software applications, the word Zen has come to be synonymous with simplicity, elegance, and the ephemeral, paradoxical nature of life.

"Briefly stated, Zen is a religious practice with a unique method of body-mind training whose aim is awakening, that is, self-realization." This more formal definition is given by Roshi Philip Kapleau in the preface to his classic *The Three Pillars of Zen*. The fact of the matter is, a true definition of Zen goes beyond words. As an old saying goes, "Zen is like looking for the spectacles that are sitting on your nose."

## Zen and the meaning of life

"To a West, which in its concern to refashion heaven and earth is in danger of letting the presentness of life—the only life we really have—slip through its fingers, Zen comes as a reminder that if we do not learn to perceive the mystery and beauty of our present life, our present hour, we shall not perceive the worth of any life, of any hour."

HUSTON SMITH
Foreword, *The Three Pillars of Zen*,
by Roshi Philip Kapleau

### Yogi Berra—Zen Master

One of the great Zen masters of all time was the Hall of Fame catcher from the New York Yankees, Yogi Berra.

Yogi was the guy who said, "It's so crowded nobody goes there anymore," "It's not over until it's over," and many other aphorisms that rank right up there with the great Zen masters like Hakuin, Ikkyu, Dogen, and the Sixth Patriarch. Here's an example from a Zen master Nagarjuna:

As by churning the milk, its essence—butter—appears immaculately.

By purifying mental afflictions, the "ultimate sphere" manifests immaculately.

Now, Yogi, saying the same thing:

You can observe a lot just by watching.

Don't be misled into thinking that Zen is a dry, intellectual practice, filled with insoluble riddles. It is a vibrant meditative, spiritual, and religious practice: The object of Zen is nothing less than *satori*, the total awakening of the self to one's own true nature.

### Zen in America

*The ruggedly independent, do-it-yourself history of Zen is another reason for its popularity in America; perhaps we see Zen as a spiritual John Wayne movie.*

The ruggedly independent, do-it-yourself history of Zen is another reason for its popularity in America; perhaps we see Zen as a spiritual John Wayne movie. Zen training, in the words of the author and expert Christmas Humphreys:

...is designed to break through to Non-duality. This is the sole purpose of all Zen effort, and the effort must come from within.... Zen masters will help to point the seeker in the right direction, but...the road of Zen is a road of "Do it yourself."

This attitude that is Zen is one reason it has spread from Asia to America with surprising alacrity. Some of the famous Zen masters who brought Zen to America include Shunryu Suzuki Roshi, Joshu Sasaki Roshi, and Taizen Maizeumi Roshi.

### Two Zen roads—Soto and Rinzai

The two major schools of Zen are Rinzai and Soto. Both follow what is called the middle way—the balance between strenuous searching for and total surrender to the truth. As Zen Master Unmon told his monks centuries ago, "If you walk, just walk; if you sit, just sit; but don't wobble!"

While both schools demand a dedicated, intensive, and extensive commitment to meditation, they differ in methodology. The core of Soto meditation practice is called *shikantaza,* which defies definition but in English is loosely translated as "just sitting." In contrast, the roots of Rinzai practice are its *koans,* the mind-numbing, insoluble riddles designed to literally drive you out of your mind and into enlightenment.

## The Koan

Koan is a teaching method based on posing unanswerable questions to students, who in order to respond to them must go beyond normal discursive thinking, or as some might say, think "out of the box." Koan answers don't arise from the left brain, our seat of intellect and thinking, but from the right brain, the seat of intuition and true wisdom. The *Mumonkan,* or the Gateless Gate, is the legendary collection of forty-eight koans, or riddles that was collected in the twelfth century by the Zen monk Mumon Ekai.

Although there are hundreds of koans, one need not master all of them to achieve satori. D.T. Suzuki, in his *Essays in Zen Buddhism,* wrote, "For all practical purposes, less than ten, or even less than five, or just one may be sufficient to open one's mind to the ultimate truth of Zen...."

In *The Way of Zen,* Alan Watts says that this...

*In an article entitled "Climbing Frozen Waterfalls" (Los Angeles Times, 30 August, 1997), David Ferrell, describes in Zen-like terms the mystical experience of climbers who "laugh at death and dodge jagged ice shards":*

*The fear, [one climber] said, "Is that the ice will break away and you'll fall and drown."*

*As yet, no one has suffered that misfortune, but the danger is integral to the experience, wrapping itself around its beauty in a yin-yang way that climbers find mesmerizing. They are moved to poetry. They speak of attaining extraordinary focus while suspended on 1,000-foot limestone cliffs, becoming locked in Zen-like states of consciousness.*

seemingly illogical reversal of common sense may perhaps be clarified by the favorite Zen image of 'the moon in the water.' The phenomenon moon-in-the-water is likened to human experience. The water is the subject, and the moon the object. When there is no water, there is no moon-in-the-water, and likewise when there is no moon. But when the moon rises the water does not wait to receive its image, and when even the tiniest drop of water is poured out, the moon does not wait to cast its reflection. For the moon does not intend to cast its reflection, and the water does not receive its image on purpose. The event is caused as much by the water as by the moon, and as the water manifests the brightness of the moon, the moon manifests the clarity of the water.

### Do cats meditate?

*"Dhyana [meditation] and schools of dhyana have existed in Asia for as long as anyone can remember.... From close observation, I suspect that it is also practiced by cats."*

ALAN WATTS
*Alan Watts Teaches Meditation*

The process of give and take between Zen master and student is arduous, long, and requires a total commitment of body and soul. During every waking (and supposedly sleeping) moment of life, the student is expected to be engaged in a constant meditation on the particular koan he or she is attempting to pass.

A student will usually meet privately with the teacher several times a day. These meetings, called *dokusan*, may only last a few seconds. The student is given an opportunity to demonstrate to the teacher, in a non-intellectual way, that he or she has understood the koan. Depending on the student's performance, he or she will be sent back for more study of the koan, or be assigned another one. In this way, the student, constantly monitored by the teacher, progresses to the point of passing many koans.

Because of the intensive time commitment and almost constant need of access to a teacher, koan practice is virtually impossible to do alone. If you are totally committed to the satori of a Rinzai Zen realization, you will probably have to retire from your daily life for a few years and go to a Zen monastery. And remember, there is no money-back guarantee that you will become enlightened.

*The great path has no gates.*
*Thousand of roads enter it.*
*When one passes through this gateless gate.*
*He walks freely between heaven and earth.*

THE MUMONKAN

## KOAN EXERCISE—"WHO AM I ?"

1. Make the mind as empty as space, totally unattached to the phenomena that appear out of nowhere, going nowhere.

2. Try to become the question, "Who am I?"

3. When sound appears, become the question, "Who hears these sounds?"

4. When thoughts appear, become the question, "Who thinks these thoughts?"

5. When body sensations appear, become the question, "Who feels these feelings?"

6. The great poet William Blake said, "If the doors of perception were cleansed, every thing would appear to man as it is, infinite." Cleanse the doors of perception. Penetrate beyond the questions. Become the questions.

7. At work, at home, at rest, never stop asking yourself the question, "Who am I?" Abandon the answer.

## The many faces of the koan

John Winokur, in Zen to Go, says, "Koans are spiritually instructive conundrums designed to force the student beyond logic to sudden illumination." There are some 1,700 koans, many of which are compiled in the Hekigoanroku and the Mumonkan.

Here are just a few:

Most famous: A monk asked Joshu in all earnestness: "Does a dog have the Buddha nature or not?" Joshu said, "Mu." [Literal interpretation: "nothing"]

Most dangerous: Master Sekiso said, "How will you step up from the top of a hundred-foot flagpole?"

Most whimsical: "On top of a flagpole, a cow gives birth to a calf."
Most inscrutable: "What is the face you had before you were born?"
Most famous in the West: "What is the sound of one hand clapping?"

### Soto Zen

In the Soto sect of Zen, the koan is usually not employed as a tool for attaining enlightenment. Soto Zen relies on various meditation techniques, such as being with the breath.

A major meditative part of Soto Zen is called shikantaza, a loose translation of which would be just sitting, probably the understatement of all time. *Shikantaza* does not rely on breath techniques, koans, or even an object of meditation. This practice is based on the belief that the practitioner, by assuming the posture of the enlightened Buddha, manifests, by definition, that state of enlightenment.

Associated with Soto Zen is the *tokusan*, a double-flap bamboo stick formerly applied to the back of a student who was nodding off during meditation. Named after the Tong Koan master Tokusan, the stick made a wake-up sound to encourage mindfulness. It is no longer used unless the student requests it, which some do.

Shikantaza is empty, devoid of everything. Not only is it impossible to describe, it's virtually impossible to do on a consistent basis. A talk explaining shikantaza, given by the Zen Master Yasatuni Roshi (1885-1973), is described by Philip Kapleau in *The Three Pillars of Zen*.

> So shikantaza is a practice in which the mind is intensely involved in just sitting. In this type of zazen (sitting meditation), it is all too easy for the mind, which is not supported by such aids as counting the breath, or by a koan, to become distracted. The correct temper of mind therefore becomes doubly important. In shikantaza the mind must be unhurried yet at the same time firmly planted or massively composed, like Mount Fuji, let us say. But it must also be alert, stretched, like a taut bowstring. So, shikantaza is a heightened state of concentrated awareness wherein one is neither tense or hurried, and certainly never slack.

### A Soto Zen Meditation

For more than a millennium, Zen techniques have been taught orally by Zen masters. A contemporary Zen master is Joshu Sasaki, the abbott of a Zen monastery outside Los

*Shikantaza... is based on the belief that the practitioner, by assuming the posture of the enlightened Buddha, manifests, by definition, that state of enlightenment.*

Angeles. Sasaki Roshi teaches expansion-contraction meditation. His theory is that at any moment of time, the world
and everything in it, including our own bodies and minds,
oscillates between the points of total infinity and total nul-
lity. As the I Ching, the ancient Chinese Book of Changes,
says: "What is empty becomes full. What is full becomes
empty. That is, everything changes, all the time."

## EXPANSION AND CONTRACTION OF THE BREATH

The following exercise is inspired by Shinzen Young, a Buddhist monk, and the nationally
known Insight meditation teacher and founder of the Vipassana Support Institute (VSI) in
Los Angeles.

1. Let the body settle. Bring your awareness to your body. Feel the overall sensation of
   being in the body. Note how various kinds of sensations arise from within the body.

2. Bring your awareness to your breath. Become aware of your breathing. No matter what
   you think of it, no matter what judgments you have about it, do not try to control it.
   Just let it be.

3. You will begin selectively to attend to the breath. During the in-breath, confine your
   attention to those aspects of the body that are contractive, such as the tightening of
   your diaphragm. Ignore the expansive aspects, even if they are prominent. Let these
   thoughts, feelings, and perception of space pull in and collapse on the in-breath. Let
   them contract down to an effortless nothingness. There is no pressure in the contraction, no feeling of discomfort. There is only the simple feeling that distance is collapsing.

4. Bring the attention to your out-breath or exhalation. During this part of the breath
   cycle, confine your attention to those qualities of feelings, sensation, and thought that
   are expansive. Let your experience expand with the out-breath and contract with the
   in-breath.

5. Slowly, gently, open your eyes. Take an inventory of how you are feeling, right at this
   moment. As you move on to your next activity, try to bring this quality of calm awareness to it.

*Revelations in Insight meditation go much deeper than particular situations and conditions-- they penetrate into the very nature of personality itself.*

## Insight meditation

Vipassana, also called Insight meditation (the term we will use), is grounded in the Southeast Asian Theravada Buddhism.

Vipassana, which means insight in the Pali language, is a process of achieving total awareness of the present moment, with clarity and wisdom. Insight meditation is perhaps the earliest and simplest of the Buddhist meditative traditions, descended directly, without alteration, from the Buddha himself

Insight meditation is the purely meditational aspect of Theravada Buddhism, and as such, the practice has no religious aspects; Insight meditators include priests and rabbis, as well as agnostics.

Hinayana Buddhism (called the Individual Vehicle) is one of the two major belief systems, or vehicles of Buddhism (not to be confused with Rinzai and Soto, which are the two major schools of Zen Buddhism). The other is called Mahayana (the Greater Vehicle.) The Mahayana, or Great Vehicle, includes Tibetan Buddhism, which is discussed later in this chapter.

The primary purpose of Insight practice is the development of awareness, or mindfulness (*samatha* in Pali), and insight. The words *mindfulness* and *insight* as used here have special meanings.

Mindfulness in meditation means being aware of, but not concerned with, what's happening. To achieve this, the meditator brings a high level of awareness to all aspects of ordinary experience, while remaining neutral to them.

Insight, which arises through continuity of mindfulness, has a different definition in the East than it does in the West. In the West, the word insight is used in psychotherapy to describe the patient's revelations about his personality and current major life issues. By contrast, revelations in Insight meditation go much deeper than particular situations and conditions—they penetrate into the very nature of personality itself.

Although many forms of Insight meditation have been developed over the centuries, they all share a common premise: Insight and purification come through continuity of awareness. Insight meditation is a popular and accessible meditation practice in the United States today.

- *In contrast to other forms of Buddhist meditation, Insight meditation has very little ritual. There are no dietary restrictions or dress codes, even at retreats.*
- *One need not have grounding in Buddhism or any other theology to practice it.*
- *Most American Insight teachers are Westerners with backgrounds similar to their students. Many have the talent to translate Eastern thought into understandable Western concepts.*
- *Unlike those in other traditions, Insight teachers are not placed on pedestals and treated like gurus but are instead called kalyana mittas, or spiritual friends.*
- *Insight meditation lends itself to self-study, supported by a wide variety of books, audiotapes and videotapes, and other materials (see Resource section).*

### Direct Experience

In Insight meditation, there is no fixed object of meditation, such as the breath. In what is called bare attention, the object of meditation is whatever happens to be the most prominent sensation at any given moment. This could be your breath, a thought, a sensation in the leg, or all three at once. The idea is not to dwell or elaborate on the phenomena, but merely to observe them with mindfulness as they appear and effortlessly to allow them to pass away, like clouds in the sky.

Insight meditation demands full attention on your immediate experience. One teacher compares the alertness, calmness, and restraint required to that of a cat watching a mouse hole. If you have been meditating with the breath technique, the following noting exercises will seem familiar.

### Noting

As you practice breath meditation you may experience involuntary thoughts, feelings and body sensations which appear almost out of nowhere.

The technique called noting supports your meditation. It allows you to note temporary objects of meditation that seem to draw focus away from the primary object of meditation. Noting allows you to view feelings, emotions and thoughts in the context of your meditation and to defuse them.

Being able to label something as just a thought, with uninvolved, calm awareness, deprives the distraction of the fuel it needs to exist. You're not adding fuel to the fire. And so it subsides of its own accord.

For example, let's say you are following your breath, the primary object of meditation. You feel a sudden surge of energy in your right leg, which, before you are even aware of it, pulls you away from your breath. You may feel discomfort. Instantly, a barrage of thoughts arises. "Is something wrong?" "Am I hurting myself?"

Using the noting technique, you merely note that surge of energy as *feeling*, without adding characterization, judgment, and criticism. You defuse the situation. And return to your primary object of meditation, the breath.

If you try non-verbal noting, remain attentive. Try not to space out. If you find yourself experiencing the sensation of sinking, or that your thoughts are taking you for a ride, simply return to your verbal noting. The sound of your own voice will remind you that you are continuously paying attention. Remember what the Buddha said: It is better to be awake for a moment than asleep for a lifetime.

In the old Dragnet TV series, deadpan Sergeant Joe Friday always told a witness: "Just the facts, Ma'am." Joe was only interested in what happened. Meditation is like Sergeant Friday; it wants just the facts. When you simply receive the news without writing the editorial, something amazing happens—the melodrama of your life disappears, leaving you a lot more room for peace and joy. This is another way that meditation can give you a new

*It is better to be awake for a moment than asleep for a lifetime.*

outlook on life. Noting is more than a way of meditating—
it's a way of life.

The two following exercises are very similar. The second allows you to pay more attention to the content of thoughts than the first.

## *NOTING BODY SENSATIONS #1*

This is inspired by an exercise by Shinzen Young.

1. Take a moment to let the body settle. Bring your awareness to your body. Feel the overall sensation of being in the body. Note how various sensations arise from within the body.

2. Treat all of these sensations equally. Some may be physical. A tightness somewhere, a looseness somewhere else, the tensing of muscles, the coolness at the tip of your nose. Other sensations come from internal functions—your heartbeat, your breath. Still others sensations are emotional. If you are bored, or frustrated, or angry this will cause sensations. Do not give one precedence over another. Simply note them.

3. Let each sensation do what it wants to do. Let it stay or go as it will. Don't interfere with its dance. Notice that if you do not try to control your sensations, you will naturally be drawn from one to another.

4. Do not fixate your awareness. Allow it to float freely where it will, like a balloon in an air current. Whenever a part of your body comes to prominence, note, out loud, in a gentle voice, the name of that part of the body.

5. Be the non-interfering camera. Your awareness may be drawn to very broad areas, such as the whole body. Or it may focus in, almost like a microscope, on one particular sensation. It's like a zoom lens. Just note where the predominant region is. And when you note the region—for example, foot, or neck, or lower back—pour your awareness into that particular region.

6. Keep your spoken notes soft and gentle, but impartial and matter-of-fact. This is the balance of the middle way in action. Don't let the notes overpower the sensations. You are beginning to permeate your entire body with attentiveness and allowingness. And in time, this will become a positive habit.

### Adding Thinking

This technique expands on the previous exercise.

It's like learning to juggle. You've already learned the basic toss in exercise one. It's the same movement, but with additional balls. It may complicate things at first, but you can master the hang of it.

Remember, noting is a gentle, neutral process. When thoughts appear during this meditation, categorize them all as thinking. So, for example, the mundane thought "I must remember to buy dental floss" is simply noted as thinking. By the same token, the profound thought "I now understand the mystery of life" is also noted as thinking. Here's an example of what you might be noting out loud during your meditation period:

> "Face, chest, thought, hands, hands and face, thought, whole body, whole body, thought, thought...."

Emotions such as boredom, anger, and the like are regarded as hybrid, a thought-body sensation mixture. Categorize an emotion the same way you would its singular components, as either feeling, thinking, or both, depending on which is most predominant at the moment.

## NOTING BODY SENSATIONS #2

1. Bring your awareness to your body. Feel the overall sensation of being in the body and note how various sensations arise.

2. Some sensations may be physical. Others come from internal functions. Still other sensations are emotional. If you have a sexual fantasy, there will be sensual feelings within the body. Do not give one precedence over another. Note and pour your awareness on the sensation that is most prominent at the moment.

3. Let each sensation do what it wants to do. If it wants to leave, let it leave. If it wants to stay, let it stay. Don't interfere with it. Remember, you are practicing the art of opening to each moment of life with calm awareness.

4. Do not fixate your awareness. Whenever a part of your body comes to prominence,

note, in a gentle and assured voice, the name of that part of the body. If a thought arises, merely note it as "thought."

5. Your awareness may be drawn to very broad areas, such as the whole body. Or on one particular sensation, thought, or emotion. Maintain your neutrality. Keep naming thoughts as "thought," sensations as to where they originate, and emotions as thought, sensation, or both.

6. Try not to get emotionally involved with thoughts, or take a ride with them. Keep the awareness on the breath. Just label the thought, "thought." It will pass, just as everything else does. It recedes, just as it arose, from nowhere on its way to no place.

7. Keep your notes soft and gentle, but impartial, soft and allowing. This is the balance of the middle way.

8. Flood your entire body with attentiveness and allowingness. In time, this can become a positive, permanent habit.

## Body Scan

Although you probably won't be encountering jumpsuit clad versions of Stephen Boyd or Raquel Welch wielding ray guns, the technique called body scanning or body sweeping might be called the meditational version of the '70s movie, *Fantastic Voyage*.

Body scanning is a particularly effective technique for pain reduction. Several teachers, including Shinzen Young and Dr. Jon Kabat-Zinn, the founder and director of the Stress Reduction Clinic at the University of Massachusetts Medical Center, have extensive experience in helping people reduce chronic pain using this particular technique. Kabat-Zinn and his clinic were featured on the PBS series *Healing and the Mind* with Bill Moyers.

In the Theravada tradition, S.N. Goenka, a Burmese Insight teacher, is generally credited with being one of the foremost exponents of body sweeping techniques. If you want to go deeper into body sweeping, his book *Vipassana Meditation* is an excellent resource. There is a more complete discussion on meditation and physical pain in chapter 11.

This is how Jon Kabat-Zinn describes the theory behind body scanning in his book *Full Catastrophe Living:*

> Any deep feelings…that you might have about your body can't change until the way you actually experience your body changes.
>
> When we put energy into actually experiencing our body and we refuse to get caught up in the overlay of judgmental thinking about it, our whole view of it and ourselves can change dramatically….

*As you let go mentally of sensations, thoughts, or inner images you found associated with it, the muscles in that region let go too.*

The idea in scanning your body is actually to feel each region you focus on and linger there with your mind right on it or in it. You breathe towards and away from each region a few times and then let go in your mind's eye as your attention moves on to the next region. As you let go mentally of sensations, thoughts, or inner images you found associated with it, the muscles in that region let go too, lengthening and releasing much of the tension they have accumulated.

### A Simple Body-Scan Technique

The idea of body scanning is to bring microscopic focus to the body. You can do the body scan either in your regular meditation posture or lying on your back. Although the description is short, you should take as much time as possible to do the exercise effectively. The patients at the Massachusetts Clinic do a daily forty-five minute body scan. Try to duplicate that as you do the following exercise.

## BODY SCAN

1. Let the body settle, and feel the entire body. Close your eyes. Take several deep breaths. Totally relax.
2. Bring the attention to the toes of the left foot. Focus on the feeling in each toe. Direct your breath into each toe, into the top, the middle, the bottom. Let your breath flow in and out of each toe, starting with your big toe and working towards the smallest.
3. Move on to the left foot. Notice the feeling there. Direct your breath into the foot. Observe the inhalation and exhalation of the breath in the foot. Notice whether there is  any tension, and if there is, visualize that tension flowing out of your body with your

out- breath. When you inhale, visualize each inhalation bringing to that place the energy of revitalization and rejuvenation.

4. When you have finished scanning the entire left foot, begin moving up the left leg. Feel the sensations in each portion of your leg: the calf, kneecap, thigh. Direct your breath into each part of the leg, the tissue, the cells.

5. Continue this process and slowly move up the left leg to the left part of your pelvis. Scan with awareness and focus as you flood the area with your breath.

6. Slowly bring your attention back down to the toes of the right foot. Repeat the scanning process, as you did before, until you reach the right part of your pelvis. Scan it with awareness. Flood the area. Make your breath a healing laser beam.

7. When you are finished scanning the right pelvis, slowly move your attention up and into your upper torso. Imagine your body in cross-section, divided up into bands three inches thick. As you move up, examine the entire core of each cross-section, taking in the abdomen, the back, the spinal cord. Focus your entire attention on the cross-section. Breathe in and out of the cross-section. Notice any blockages to your breath. Notice whether there is any tension, and if there is, visualize it flowing out of your body with each exhalation. Then when you inhale, visualize each inhalation as carrying vitality, energy, and rejuvenation back to that place.

8. Continue to move up the body, through the chest and upper back and shoulders. When you have finished scanning and breathing into these areas, bring your attention to the fingers of both hands.

9. Move your attention and breath slowly and simultaneously up the fingers of both hands, into both arms, and up into your shoulders. Focus your attention and breath into wrists, elbows, biceps on the way.

10. When you have reached the top of your shoulders, begin to scan your neck. Slowly breathe in and out where it connects with your shoulders. Begin to move, very slowly, up the neck and throat, into the base of the skull.

11. Direct your attention to your skull. Breathe into your face, the back of the head, the top of the head, your nose, your ears, and eyes.

12. Direct your attention to the crown of the head. Imagine that there is a hole, like the blowhole of a whale, on the crown of your head. Let your breath flow through the entire length of your body, from the hole, all the way through, and out through your toes.

13. Now, inhale through your toes, and bring the air all the way back up through the body and exhale it through your blowhole.

14. Relax for several minutes. Make a calm, aware, overall survey of the body. Slowly, open your eyes. And begin your transition back to activity.

## Tibetan Buddhism

Tibetan Buddhism is the tradition brought from India to Tibet by several teachers, including the legendary Indian master Padmasambhava, at the invitation of King Trisong Detsen (755-797). It is also called in Sanskrit the Mahayana, or the Great Vehicle, and has as its goal the liberation of all beings. To many Westerners today, His Holiness the Dalai Lama of Tibet personifies this rich and compassionate way of living.

Included in the Mahayana teachings is Vajrayana, also called the Tantric or Diamond Vehicle. This is considered to be the pinnacle of meditation practice. At this highly refined level, the practitioner is empowered, it is believed, to perform a kind of spiritual alchemy, transforming the hindrances of worldly thought and sorrow into blissful states of enlightenment and realization. These insights are achieved through a sophisticated combination of mental and physical techniques that seek to open the body's various energy centers (chakras).

In *The World of Tibetan Buddhism*, the Dalai Lama talks about the high criteria for a person studying the *tantra*, or higher esoteric teachings:

> The practice of tantra can be undertaken when a person has a firm foundation in the essential features of the path to enlightenment as explained in the teachings of the Buddhist sutras [original teachings of the Buddha]. This means that you should have an attitude that wishes to abandon completely the causes of suffering, a correct view of emptiness...and some realization of bodhicitta—the altruistic aspiration, based on love and compassion, to achieve enlightenment for the benefit of all beings. Your understanding of these, together with your practice of the six perfections,* enables you to lay a proper foundation of the path.... Only then can you properly undertake a successful practice of tantra. [The six perfections comprise the practice of the bodhisattva, or the practitioner on the path to enlightenment and altruism.]

*The six perfections are: generosity, ethical discipline, patience, perseverance, meditation, and wisdom.*

### Tibetan Visualization

Tibetan Buddhist meditation techniques are many and varied. In Tibetan visualization practice, the meditator brings his or her sincere intention and attention to visualizing positive images that he or she would like to realize for himself or herself, a particular person, or even the world. Intention and attention are key here.

Some Tibetan visualizations are very elaborate, where colors, divine beings, and the base elements of fire, air, and water come into play. Light and a "source of power" are also very important elements in this visualization practice.

*Light* as used here has a dual meaning—the phenomenon of light on both the sentient and spiritual planes. The spiritual light, "the Buddha light of oneness and openness," as it is described in *The Healing Power of Mind*, by Tolku Thondup, manifests and is perceived by us as blue, white, yellow, red, and green.

The innate power of this dual light is thought to be able to heal physical and mental wounds, transform negative into positive energy, or surpass fear.

The "source of power" in Tibetan visualizations is usually a spiritual divinity, such as the Buddha. You can, however, create in your mind your own source of power consistent with your religious and spiritual beliefs. Thus, sources of power can be anything from Mother Teresa to the surf at Monterey Bay.

## VISUALIZATION EXERCISE

The following exercise is inspired by "Illuminating the Darkness of Sadness," from *The Healing Power of Mind*, by Tolku Thondup.

1. Visualize your whole body and mind as being filled with total darkness. Feel the sadness, without being overwhelmed by it. Now, prepare to invoke healing light.

2. Imagine the light as coming from your source of power. The light could come from

within you, in front of you, or from above See the beams of light—bright, warm, and joyful as a hundred suns. The warm light fills your entire body, penetrating each and every cell, down to the atoms.

3. Imagine the light shining beyond your body, lighting the whole world. Feel the nature of the healing light, which is not solid. There is nothing to hold onto, to grasp. So there is no stress, no nothing, just light.

You, the universe, and the light are now united in a global, pervasive, ethereal light that bathes the universe. The darkness of sadness is no match for this light. It is gone. Vanished.

## CHAPTER RECAP

- At their core, the major meditative traditions share a common goal—to allow the meditator access to a new, higher level of conscious awareness. There is no one perfect meditation technique.

- The East might be spoken of as the cradle of meditation.

- Yoga was developed in India and has many branches, including karma yoga, hatha yoga, and tantric yoga.

- Tantric yoga aims at arousing and directing kundalini, a bio-spiritual energy we all have in us.

- Activating the chakra centers supercharges our bodies and minds.

- Buddha found enlightenment was through meditation, not extreme self-denial.

- Koan, used in Rinzai Zen, is a teaching method based on posing unanswerable questions to students, who, in order to respond to them, must go beyond normal discursive thinking.

- A major part of Soto Zen meditation is called shikantaza, or just sitting.

- Vipassana, also called Insight meditation, is a style of meditation grounded in Southeast Asian Theravada Buddhism.

- Body scanning allows you to feel each region of your body in a microscopic way.

> "...Zen is a religious practice with a unique method of body-mind training whose aim is awakening, that is, self-realization."
>
> ROSHI PHILIP KAPLEAU

# Western Meditation Traditions

## 6

Traditions inside Judaism, Christianity, and Islam are most likely to come to mind when Western meditation tradition is mentioned but the fact is that Druids, Gnostics, Greeks, and the first worshippers of Ishtar in Babylon all meditated. And meditation continues in Europe and America among members of Rosicrucian, Romany, Unitarian, and Theosophical groups.

This chapter offers a small sampling from this very rich stream of meditational philosophies and practices. You will discover insights and practical exercises drawn from the Gnostics, the early Christian practice known as Hesychasm, Gregorian chanting, Jewish mysticism, and Islam.

## MEDITATIVE PRAYER

The practice of mindful, meditational prayer begins with humankind's first desire to commune with, or receive the light of, Deity. It is known to have existed in Sumeria, and in fact existed throughout the pagan world. Clear mention is made of it in one late pagan text, *Allogenes*, based on practices of centuries standing: "There was a stillness of silence within me, and I heard the blessedness whereby I knew myself as I am." Direct mention of it is made many

- *Gnostic meditation*

- *Early Christian prayer*

- *Gregorian chant*

- *Jewish prayer and the Kabbalah*

- *Islamic prayer*

- *Sufi dance*

143

times in the Books of Ruth, Leviticus, and Exodus. Psalm 119 says, "O how I love thy law! It is my meditation all the day." Jesus was clearly describing meditational concentration when he said in Luke 11:34, "When thine eye is single thy whole body also is full of light." And of course, the prophet Muhammad endorses the practice, noting of the faithful, "Do they not meditate on the Koran?"

The goal of meditational prayer, as practiced in the Western traditions of Christianity and Judaism, is to awaken the participant to the immediate proximity of God.

The anonymous author of the Christian mystical treatise, *The Cloud of Unknowing,* defined meditative prayer as a means of reaching a state of constant consciousness of God's presence:

> And there are some that be so spiritually refined by grace and so intimate with God in this grace of contemplation, that they may have it when they want in the common state of man's soul: as in sitting, walking, standing, or kneeling.

In our time, the Trappist monk and scholar, Thomas Merton, reaffirmed meditation as a way for man to establish a vital connection between his soul and the living God. In *New Seeds of Contemplation,* Merton said that the real goal of meditative prayer is "to teach a man how to work himself free of created things and temporal concerns, in which he finds only confusion and sorrow, and enter into a conscious and loving contact with God . . . and to pay God the praise and honor and thanksgiving and love which it has now become his joy to give."

The capacity for meditational prayer is something we are all born with. We may use words from the Bible, or a phrase from the Mass, such as *Kyrie eleison.* We may choose to say them out loud or silently, or we may choose no words at all, simply surrendering to the ultimate stillness of that place in the heart where God dwells.

Meditative prayer has no expectations. As the author and scholar Thomas Moore says in *Medita-*

*The goal of meditational prayer, is to awaken the participant to the immediate proximity of God.*

. . . . Work [yourself] free of created things and temporal concerns . . . and enter into a conscious and loving contact with God.

THOMAS MERTON
*New Seeds of Contemplation*

*tions,* "Pray—period! Don't expect anything. Or better, expect nothing. Prayer cleanses us of expectations and allows holy will, providence, and life itself entry. What could be more worth the effort—or the noneffort."

Along these lines, the Christian mystic Meister Eckhardt (1260-1327) said, "...whenever the free spirit is to be found in true detachment, it forces God into being." He goes on to describe this state in detail:

> A man should receive God in all things and train his mind to keep God ever present in his mind, in his aims and in his love. Note how you regard God: keep the same attitude that you have in church or in your cell, and carry it with you in the crowd.... If you were equal-minded in this way, then no man could keep you from having God ever present.

Let's now look at some of the major meditative traditions, keeping in mind that they are at once unique unto themselves, yet alike in their commonality of purpose: to awaken us to the truth of who we are.

*"The way to receive light from God is through praying. The only difference is that some people pray unconsciously, some pray consciously, some pray superconsciously."*
RABBI SCHLOMO CARLBACH

## GNOSTIC MEDITATION

Gnostic meditations have existed from before the time of Christ. Gnosticism (from *gnosis,* Greek for knowledge, wisdom) was a spiritual/meditative movement-cum-religion that surfaced just before the time of Jesus and flourished in the early centuries of the Christian era. It fused past and present, old and new, Eastern and Western beliefs. Gnosticism took on the rational tradition of Plato and Homer and the mysticism of the oriental mystery cults popular throughout the Graeco-Roman world. Sources for Gnostic belief and mediation include Egyptian mythology, Greek philosophy, Zoroastrianism, Jewish apocalyptic beliefs, Chaldean astrology, the baptizing sects of Palestine—and toward the end, Christianity.

*"The gospel of truth is a joy for those who have received from the Father of truth the grace of knowing him. For he discovered them in himself, and they discovered him in themselves, the incomprehensible, inconceivable one, the Father, the perfect one, the one who made all things."*
THE GOSPEL OF TRUTH
*one of the Nag Hammadi scrolls*

*Gnostics believed in the presence of the divine within.*

In Gnostic practice, gnosis was intuitive, direct experience (i.e. knowledge) of God, reached not through reason but through contact with the divine through meditation. They believed this transcendent knowledge of God necessary for human salvation. It played a far more important role than faith in bridging the gulf between God and matter. Gnostics believed in the presence of the divine within and, like Quakers and Baptists, were certain that anyone who receives the spirit of God communes with the divine.

Christian persecution ultimately drove Gnostic belief underground, though it would influence Western thought for centuries. The legacy of Gnosticism shaped mystical schools, philosophical schools, and religious movements like the Manicheans. Swiss psychoanalyst Dr. Carl G. Jung wrote that, "All my life I have been working and studying to find these things, and these people knew already."

## THE POWER OF SILENCE

Gnostics believed in the power of silence. They derived this notion from their belief in a God who is both Father and Mother. Gnostic poet and teacher Valentinus suggests that the divine can be imagined as a dyad. One part of this dyad is the Ineffable, the Depth, the Primal Father; the other is Grace, Silence, the Womb and "Mother of the All." According to Valentinus, Silence is the appropriate complement of the Father. Here is a silence meditation inspired by a Gnostic text, *The Great Announcement*.

1. Extinguish or cover your light sources (light, candles, sun, etc.) and sit down. This can be a chair or a meditation rug—whatever is comfortable.

2. Close your eyes, breathe deeply, and take a minute to prepare to focus your inner vision.

3. For three to five minutes, conceive of the masculine Mind of the Universe. This is the Mind that manages all things.

4. In the next three-to-five minute period, conceive of the feminine Intelligence of the Universe. She produces all things.

5. Visualize the two joining in union within you. Discover that while Mind and Intelligence are distinct from each other, yet, they are One, found in the state of unity. Mother-Father is in every one of us. Let the images flow into each other like the water of two streams that converge to create a new, more powerful river.

6. Take this divine power, which now exists in a latent state, and let it fill your body. Open your eyes and adjust to the return to the world.

7. Break the silence and say aloud, "The Power is divided above and below. The One generates itself, makes itself grow, seeks itself, finds itself," "The One is mother of itself, father of itself, sister of itself, brother of itself, spouse of itself, daughter of itself, son of itself, source of the entire circle of existence."

8. You can continue the meditation after you are done with the silent, seated portion. Become observant of details in the universe. Look for this power in your daily life.

---

Gnostics saw God, and therefore, humans as divided against themselves inwardly. God, on the one hand, was a Creator, while on the other hand, God was also seen as an evil power (the Demiurge or the God of the Old Testament), who imprisons the divine spark of the spirit within flesh. The Gnostics, rather like the Kabbalists, believe that the return to the unified God (and/or self) is through a series of progressively less dense emanations of reality, ranging from the heavenly to the hellish, with many levels in between. Some Gnostics filled these levels with intermediary beings going upward (angels, demigods) and downward (demons, devils).

> "Some Gnostic groups believed in a God who was both Father and Mother, and that women and men were spiritual equals."
> ELAINE PAGELS, PH.D.
> *The Gnostic Gospels*
>
> • • •
>
> "Gnosticism involves no recoil from society, but a desire to concentrate on inner well-being." ARTHUR DARBY NOCK
> *Early Gentile Christianity and its Hellenistic Background*

## RECONCILING CREATIVE OPPOSITES

The following Gnostic meditation will help you move to a more harmonious integration of all these aspects in your own being.

1. Begin as in steps 1 and 2 in the previous exercise.

2. Now that you realize your bondage to the physical universe, you need to visualize yourself creating your own escape from bondage. Feel the earth's gravity keeping you down.

3. The Demiurge, as creator of the visible world, formed both material things and the spiritual realm. Reflect on how material possessions and spiritual obstacles get in your way of knowing God.

4. You must appeal to the Mother of the Demiurge: "Mother of the Lower Powers, the Divine Thought, appear above the Demiurge." Feel the negative pull of the Demiurge begin to weaken. Visualize your own Divine Mother.

5. Now visualize the Father entering the picture and standing next to the Mother. The Divine Mind fertilizes Mother Thought. See the Demiurge as the Son of the Divine Father; feel the positive power of the Demiurge.

6. Visualize the union of Mother and Father at the beginning of time, the creation of the universe. Watch the centuries roll back.

7. Now see yourself being created by the Demiurge. Follow and retrace the cycle back to the beginning.

## JEWISH MEDITATION

That Jewish prayer is meditation is affirmed by Rabbi Ted Falcon. As Rabbi Falcon tells the story, he had just finished praying, "Hear, O, Israel: The Eternal is our God, the Eternal is One" (the "Shema Yisrael", Judaism's most important profession of faith). "I was pondering the subsequent verses," he writes, "which instruct us to love the Eternal with all our heart, soul, and strength and to keep these words in mind when we lie down and when we rise up, when we are at home and when we walk on our way. Suddenly I realized that these verses were instructions for chanting a mantra!"

The *Shema*, Rabbi Falson elaborates, is a meditation that focuses us on the immanent and transcendent natures of God. It does this by juxtaposing one traditional name for God, Adonai ("the Eternal"), which refers to the transcendent aspect of God; with Eloheynu ("our God"), which signifies God manifesting within nature and ourselves. Rabbi Falcon compares "Shema Yisrael" with the Vedic mantra of India, which says, "The inside and the outside are one—as above, so below."

> *"What does it amount to—their expounding the Torah! A man should see to it that all his actions are a Torah and that he himself becomes so entirely a Torah that one can learn from his habits and his motions and his motionless clinging to God"*
> RABBI LEIB

## THE SHEMA MEDITATION

Contemplating the Shema awakens us to "the primordial space from which these sacred words emerge."

1. Find a quiet space where you won't be interrupted for fifteen or twenty minutes.

2. Sit comfortably. Gradually feel your body relax. Take a few deep and easy breaths and let your eyes close. Enter into your meditation with a "Shalom," with a feeling of calmness and peace.

3. Begin reciting the six words of the Shema in your mind: "Shema Yisrael: Adonai Eloheynu Adonai Ecbad." ("Hear, O Israel: The Eternal is our God, the Eternal is One.") Bring your attention back to these words when your mind wanders.

4. After a few minutes, begin to meditate on the heart of the Shema, the two central words, "Adonai Eloheynu." Continue meditating on two words until you are ready to conclude.

5. Begin meditating on the entire Shema again. After a few minutes, take a deep breath, relax and return to normal.

Prayer has been the traditional form of Jewish meditation. However two branches of Jewish mysticism—the Kabbalah and Hasidism—long discouraged by mainstream

Jewish leaders, appear to have developed a set of practices and techniques as extensive as any Eastern discipline. Fortunately, renewed worldwide interest in meditation and spirituality has brought renewed attention to both, and they are currently attracting new followers and credibility, both among Jews and non-Jews alike.

## The tree of life

It is said that the original teachings of the Jewish mystical tradition, or Kabbalah, were given to Moses by angels who were directed by God.

There are several different systems of Kabbalist teachings. One, called the tree of life, is based on the story of the Garden of Eden. Legend has it that there were two trees in the Garden, the tree of knowledge of good and evil and the tree of life. Kabbalists believe that before Adam and Eve were cast out of Eden for eating the fruit of the tree of knowledge, they were given a glimpse of the tree of life, and this insight became the basis for Kabbalah.

The tree of life is a roadmap that charts the stages meditators progress through as they move from our mundane world into higher states of consciousness. The tree consists of ten *sephiroth* (spheres), each symbolizing a major stage in the unfolding of the divine energy as it manifests from the highest plane to the earth plane of our physical reality—and in the individual human soul.

As the authors of *As Above, So Below* describe the process, "Via this spiritual roadmap, the meditator lifts his or her consciousness from the everyday world of Kingdom, ascends in stages to beauty (seen by some Kabbalists as the higher self), then continues onward through transpersonal realms to the transcendental crown (*kether*), a point of pure, formless being untouched by the pairs of opposites. Beyond this lofty height lies the *ein sof*, the boundless radiance of the infinite. After dwelling briefly in this endless light, the meditator visualizes the light descending through each of the spheres, healing and transforming his or her being, from the highest to the most earthbound levels."

*The tree of life is a roadmap that charts the stages meditators progress through as they move from our mundane world into higher states of consciousness.*

Typical tree of life meditations include using the entire tree as a mandala or a specific sephiroth as an object of contemplation.

As in the Christian mystical tradition, the focus of the Kabbalah is to transport the practitioner from the mundane state of everyday existence to a higher, clearer level of consciousness. Kabbalah is not manifested through the traditional rituals, services, and prayers that define mainstream Judaism. Instead, Kabbalists study with a *maggid*, a qualified spiritual teacher who directs the student in different techniques, among them *hitbodidut* meditation, a form of unstructured, wordless self-expression, much like that described by Christian mystics.

One such master, Rabbi Nachman of Breslov, an eighteenth-century Hassidic scholar, described the purpose of hitbodidut:

**The height of Hitbodidut meditation is when, because of your great longing to unite with God, you feel your soul bound to your body by no more than a single strand. Is there anything better to strive for in this life?**

Thus, through hitbodidut meditation and other mystical teachings, the Kabbalist works toward the moment when he or she will transcend the mundane trappings of the human ego and be afforded a glimpse into the true nature of the divine.

Until recently, the mystical teachings of the Kabbalah were secret. In recent years, however, some of these teachings have become publicly available. For example, in the Los Angeles area, formal teaching sessions are announced with advertising in various media. These techniques have surprising parallels to the philosophies and methods found not only in Christian Mysticism, but also in Zen Buddhism.

## Ten levels

Inner development, Kabbalists say, consists of balancing feminine forces with masculine forces creating a harmonization of forces. Some commentators compare the movement of energy on the tree to the movement of energy in the human body.

In the words of nineteenth-century hermeticist Eliphas Levi, the ten levels or sephiroth of the Tree of Life, from the top down, are:

1. *Kether*. The Crown, the equilibrating power that makes the manifest universe possible.

2. *Chokmah*. Wisdom, equilibrated in its unchangeable order by the initiative of intelligence.

3. *Binah*. Active intelligence, equilibrated by wisdom.

4. *Chesed*. Mercy, which is wisdom in its secondary conception, ever benevolent because it is strong.

5. *Geburah*. Severity, necessitated by wisdom itself, and by good will. To permit evil is to hinder good.

6. *Tepereth*. Beauty, the luminous conception of equilibrium in forms, intermediary between the crown and the kingdom, mediating principle between creator and creations, sublime conception of poetry and its sovereign priesthood!

7. *Netsah*. Victory, that is, eternal triumph of intelligence and justice.

8. *Hod*. Eternity of the conquests achieved by mind over matter, active over passive, life over death.

9. *Jesod*. The Foundation, that is, the basis of all belief and all truth-otherwise, the absolute in philosophy.

10. *Malkuth*. The Kingdom, meaning the universe, entire creation, the work and mirror of God.

## The names of God

Many Kabbalistic meditations center on the various names associated with God in the Torah. According to *The Book of Names,* an anonymously written Kabbalistic text, "The tree of life has to be lighted by one of the names of God. Without the name, the tree will be dead, lifeless."

There are as many divine names as there are appellations for God in the Torah, Bible or Koran. Any one will light the Tree, but Kabbalists advise meditators to use only the twenty-five names said to be "good and holy." Without these names to guide our spiritual way up the tree, the *Book of Names* states, our path will "only lead to the pit of Gehenna, from which, God forbid, a long time may be required to come out."

Kabbalists write that when the correct name is chosen for meditation and finally lights the tree for us, heaven and earth pass away for the meditator. This state may deepen slowly over a long time, or deepen swiftly in the space of minutes. We enter a fourth state of consciousness in which, the *Book of Names* tells us, "the Sephiroth of the Tree flash into our consciousness in a way which may be very profound and quite different from the way we imagined it." When the tree flashes into life—becomes living, pulsating—then the meditation, which has started in the heart, moves into the head, deepening until the tree completely disappears.

> **When the correct name is chosen for meditation and finally lights the tree for us, heaven and earth pass away for the meditator.**

## The Kabbalists' twenty-five names of God

*Abicha.* Our Father
*Abir.* Mighty One
*Adonoi.* Lord
*Ahavah.* Love
*Ehyeh.* I Am
*Elohi.* Great Living One
*Anochi.* I
*Eshda.* The Firey Law
*Gabor.* Mighty
*Gadol.* Great
*Ha Tzur.* The Rock
*Chaim.* Life
*Kabud.* Honor

*Masika.* Messiah
*Nora.* Full of Awe
*Olam.* Everlasting Worlds
*Tsaddik.* Saint
*Zion.* Place of God
*Kodosh.* Holy One
*Ra 'a Ya.* Shepherd
*Shalom.* Peace
*Torah.* Law
*Tehom.* Great Deep
*Tamim.* Perfect
*Yod He Vav He.*
    Brilliant Name of Fire

## Picking the right name

Many Kabbalists believe it's important for each person to select the right name for their individual meditation. They also caution that doing this may prove more difficult than it sounds, since the basic nature of our minds may not be what we think it is at any given moment. If we choose a wrong name, that is, a name unsuited to our minds, the *Book of Names* warns, "then the arrow has no force, as our minds cannot easily turn completely into this name, the results will be unsatisfactory, and may be accompanied by some initial disturbances until a name more suitable to our mental makeup is obtained, by happy choice or experimentation." One good method of choosing a name, the books says, "is to examine the list of divine names slowly, one by one, reflecting on the meaning of each." When a suitable name for your practice is reached, "a welling up of love in the heart will be experienced as deep calls unto deep."

The name most used is Yod He Vav He (Jehovah), a.k..a. the Brilliant Name of Fire. However, many Kabbalists recommend Ahavah (Love). *The Book of Names* says that Ahavah is best suited to meditation because "the Tree was made by Messiah with Ahavah alone, hence when this name is used as a meditation, there is Ahavah (Love) within and without."

When nothing seems to work, and you can't seem to hit on an appropriate name, Kabbalists advise letting a "Holy Person, who has realized the ultimate nature or the Tree of Life, choose for you." How to find such a holy person? "Make a beginning in this work, and such a Holy Person will appear."

## LIGHTING THE TREE

Here is a name of God meditation:

1. Find a quiet restful place.

2. Relax and clear your mind with meditational breathing.

3. Sit quietly and reverently for a moment.

4. Ask God to favor you with grace, love and wisdom.

5. Repeat the name you've chosen over and over many times while visualizing the harmony, beauty, and splendor of the name you've chosen glowing in your heart.

6. You should begin to detect a decided warmth in your heart area after only one meditation.

7. After a while, thank God for what you have received this time.

8. Begin each morning and end each day with a brief meditation on the name.

9. Repeat the name to yourself anytime something distresses or disturbs you. For many people this brings a powerful centering effect, creates greater love for others, and eventually lights the heart.

# CHRISTIAN MEDITATION

If you were raised Catholic, you may have noticed how similar the chanting of mantras is to the way you learned to pray as a child. Like mantras those prayers were often chanted over and over silently with the aid of rosary beads, or out loud, perhaps as assigned penance for some misdeed.

The connection between meditation and Christian prayer goes back at least to the fourth century A.D., and the first Christian monks. These monks later became known as "the desert fathers," because of their choice of location—the most remote regions of the Egyptian desert. There, far from distraction or temptation, they hoped to devote their lives to uninterrupted meditating on Jesus. Their teachings have been particularly influential in the Orthodox branch of Christianity (which split from the Roman Church in the fourth century A.D. and is the dominant form in Greece, Russia, and Slavic countries.)

> "When the attention of the mind is wholly turned away and withdrawn from bodily senses, it is called an ecstasy. Then whatever bodies may be present are not seen with open eyes, nor any voices heard at all. It is a state midway between sleep and death: The soul is rapt in such wise as to be withdrawn from the bodily senses more than in sleep, but less than in death."
>
> ST. AUGUSTINE
> *Confessions*

## Christian Hesychasm

The principle focus of the desert fathers was the "Prayer of Jesus." The practice of repeating this prayer became known as Hesychasm, from a Greek word meaning prayerful quietness.

*"[One who has attained a state of constant, effortless prayer] has reached the summit of all virtues, and has become the abode of the Holy Spirit.... When the Holy Spirit comes to live in a man, he never ceases to pray, for then the Holy Spirit constantly prays in him.... In eating or drinking, sleeping or doing something, even in deep sleep his heart sends forth without effort the incense and sighs of prayer."*

ST. ISAAC

The practice of constant prayer sounds very much like mantra meditation. Monks were told to "unceasingly" repeat the prayer, "Lord Jesus Christ, Son of God, have mercy on me", over and over. They were to devote themselves to the prayer "with perfect attention, resisting all other thoughts."

Such unceasing repetition of this prayer, these early aescetics believed, would block out all the diversions of the senses and the world, creating an inner peace that would bridge the gap that normally separates human beings from Jesus.

## The desert fathers

The desert fathers dedicated themselves to a search for selfless love through constant remembrance and cultivation of a feeling for the presence of God. They worked to achieve this through what they called the contemplative state. For the desert fathers, the ability to maintain the state of contemplation was of the highest importance. St. Abba Dorotheus, an early desert father, had this to say in his instruction for spiritual training:

> Over whatever you have to do, even if it be very urgent and demands great care, I would not have you argue or be agitated. For rest assured, everything you do, be it great or small, is but one-eighth of the problem. whereas to keep one's state undisturbed even thereby one should fail to accomplish the task, is the other seven-eighths. So if you are busy at some task and wish to do it perfectly, try to accomplish it—which, as I said would be one-eighth of the problem—and at the same time to

preserve your state unharmed which constitutes seven-eighths. If, however, in order to accomplish your task, you would inevitably be carried away and harm yourself or another by arguing with him, you should not lose seven-eights for the sake of preserving one-eighth.

The desert fathers threw themselves wholeheartedly into the attempt to free themselves from worldly distractions and enter the contemplative state. They lived in quiet, dimly lit cells, ate as little as possible, went months and years without speaking, fasted for long periods of time, and most importantly, devoted themselves to the endless repetition of, and concentration on their Savior. They believed that only through such a strict life could they cleanse their minds of preoccupation and temptation ("the soul, unless it can be cleansed of alien thoughts, cannot pray to God in contemplation") and truly be able to be "at one with God."

## The prayer of Jesus

The prayer of Jesus became the mainstay of the lives of many of the desert fathers. It was praised as the "art of arts (and) science of sciences." It was believed that meditation on this prayer, would eventually lead the meditator toward the highest form of human perfection. Prerequisites for success with the prayer were "genuine humility, sincerity, endurance, [and] purity."

St. Nilus, a teacher of the prayer, left us some specific instructions for attaining stillness necessary for the prayer to work. When he first wakes up, the monk must sit for an hour or more on a low stool in the solitude of his cell and "collect the mind from its customary circling and wandering outside, and quietly lead it into the heart by way of breathing, keeping this prayer: 'Lord Jesus Christ, Son of God, have mercy on me!' connected with the breath." When practiced correctly, the prayer of Jesus was said to become "as spontaneous and instinctive as breathing" and was to accompany—and bring purity to—one's every activity throughout the day.

By learning to "pray always," as St. Paul had instructed, even in the midst of activity, the desert fathers are said to have attained "the stature of Christ, and enjoy(ed) perfect purity of heart." This was known to the Fathers as *quies* (rest), the Christian version of Nirvana, described by the Christian scholar Thomas Merton as "nowhereness and no-mindness," the loss of all preoccupations. Quies allowed the "superficial self" to be purged away and permitted "the gradual emergence of the true, secret self in which the believer and Christ were one spirit." Or, as St. Nilus puts it, the practitioner would be able to "...abandon...the many and varied, (and) unite with the One, the single and unifying, directly in a union which transcends reason."

## Mantra in the West

Reliance on a mantra as object of meditation has continued to be a part of Christianity, East and West. For example, the anonymous fourteenth-century Christian work The Cloud of Unknowing gives this advice, "If you want to gather all your desire into one simple word representing God that your mind can easily retain, choose a short word rather than a long one.... But choose one that is meaningful to you. Then fix it in your mind so that it will remain there come what may.... Let this word represent to you God in all his fullness and nothing less than the fullness of God. Let nothing except God hold sway in your mind and heart."

Hugo Enomiya-Lassalle, a German Jesuit priest who is also a Zen master, argues in Living in the New Consciousness, that meditation can benefit Christians in several ways:

- The development of insight—a natural by-product of meditation practice—awakens our faith as we penetrate deeper into the mystery of God beyond conventional discursive thinking.

- We experience a new appreciation of the scriptures through an intuitive understanding. Doubts based on textual disharmonies dissolve as the soul penetrates its own depths to encounter all-embracing existence. Our increased capacity to concentrate makes it easier to keep attentive during prayer and liturgical ceremonies.

- Increased self-control and inner freedom make it easier to serve others. As we meditate away envy, hatred, and dissatisfaction, we find it easier to make ethical progress.

- As our dedication deepens and our practice intensifies, we experience loving union with God that is typical of Christian mysticism. This brings freedom from fear and doubt, along with deep peace and joy.

# THE PRAYER OF JESUS

This prayer should be approached with sincerity, reverence, and passion, with "with perfect attention, unceasingly, resisting all other thoughts." It's purpose is to bring you in to a sense of the presence of Jesus as a divine being—and it can.

1. Find a quiet place, preferably where you can be alone and undistracted. To emulate the ways of the desert fathers, you could even do this meditation first thing in the morning.

2. Relax yourself with deep breathing and eliminate distractions, as you learned to do in chapter 2.

3. When your being is relaxed and still, begin to repeat to yourself, either aloud or silently, as you exhale, "Lord Jesus Christ, Son of God, have mercy on me!" (If you are not Christian, you may want to substitute a different phrase of the same length, invoking your favorite figure of mercy, kindness, infinite love. It could be the spirit of your favorite animal, your grandfather, or the infinitely giving and loving Universe. Some people also feel better saying something celebratory, like, "…thank you for having mercy on me!" What's important is that you completely trust the spirit of this being to have an infinite reserve of compassion and mercy, and that you feel about her, him, or it the same intense love that the desert fathers felt for Jesus.)

4. As you repeat your phrase with your out-breath, begin to imagine this figure, Jesus or the mercy figure of your choice, in your mind's eye. What does he or she look like to you? Imagine the face of this figure to be radiant with mercy and love for you, and the hands to be turned upward, offering palpable rays of compassion. Now, as you continue to exhale your prayer for mercy, inhale slowly and deeply the soft rays of love you are being offered. Know as you breathe them in that they come from an infinite source.

5. After a while, be sure to express to Jesus or your mercy figure your thanks for being present with you, not only while you pray, but all the time. Imagine that, even as you begin to become aware of the room and your surroundings, this figure is with you at all times, surrounding you on the outside as well as residing in the center of your heart.

6. As you become aware of the world once again, continue breathing slowly and deeply, this time extending the love you feel outward, from an infinite source within yourself. Remember that at any time during the day you can draw upon this source, and breathe peace and mercy, the divine spirit of Jesus (or your mercy figure), into yourself, and then outward into your environment, wherever you are and whatever is going on. With practice, you will find the constant flow of mercy through you to be as natural as your own breath.

## A typical Christian meditation

Basil Pennington, a Trappist Monk, teaches a meditation he calls "centering prayer," which has similarities to other meditations in this chapter, such as the name of God meditations of the Kabbalists and the Prayer of Jesus of the Christian desert fathers. As Father Pennington teaches it, centering prayer involves focusing on a simple prayer word, such as "Jesus" or "love," then effortlessly sinking beneath discursive thought to the center where "the Spirit prays within us." Pennington's modern packaging of this ancient meditation inspired the exercise below.

## CENTERING PRAYER

1. Find a quiet place, relaxing and stilling your mind with a few deep breaths and a quiet period.

2. Put yourself in a reverent frame of mind with "Our Father" or some other prayer.

3. In faithful love, contemplate the concept of God dwelling in your depths with faithful love for you.

4. When you feel centered by your love for God and God's love for you, meditate on a single, simple word (like "Jesus" or "love" as noted above) that expresses this response and begin to let it repeat itself within you.

5. Take several minutes to come out, mentally praying the same prayer you began with.

## Walking meditation

Meditation can also involve movement. Walking meditation techniques that follow a defined pattern, or "sacred geometry," are found in many of the great Western and Eastern religious and meditational traditions.

Over the past several years, there has been a renewed interest in the ancient tradition of walking the labyrinth, which originated in the Catholic church. (One labyrinth widely copied elsewhere is from a design in the floor of Chartres cathedral.) In this form of contemplative prayer, worshippers engage in prayerful meditation and contemplation as they tread a tiled or painted labyrinth design on the floor of a church's nave. Labyrinth walking has become popular in America, where various groups have recreated this experience using both permanent and portable labyrinths

In her book *Walking A Sacred Path*, Dr. Lauren Artress (whose business card reads, "Have Labyrinth, Will Travel") describes this ancient practice as "a spiritual tool meant to awaken us to the deep rhythm that unites us to ourselves and to the Light that calls from within."

Labyrinths are usually circular patterns of different diameters, with a path wide enough for the average person to walk on comfortably. There is only one route in and out of the labyrinth, and thus this path serves as a metaphor for life: We choose our path, follow it, and accept what comes.

In the East, where it is called *kinhin* in Zen practice, walking meditation is seen as just as important as sitting practice.

At meditation retreats in Eastern traditions, walking meditation periods are alternated with sitting meditation periods. Walking is an especially good technique for meditating on those days when one experiences an unusual amount of restlessness.

The object of walking meditation is not to get to some particular place, but rather to be totally aware of the place where you are. Christopher Titmuss, an Insight meditation teacher, describes walking meditation as a metaphor for how we want to live our daily life—making each step count. Learning to walk without a purpose or compulsion, in an undriven and relaxed way, greatly enhances the happiness we can experience.

Walking meditation is usually done very slowly, and for this reason some meditators feel self-conscious in the beginning about doing it in public. If you feel uncomfortable, or if the weather is inclement, you can always walk indoors.

> *The object of walking meditation is not to get to some particular place, but rather to be totally aware of the place where you are.*

## *Sole to soul*

*The revival of labyrinth walking in America has basically come through Catholic church groups. Some labyrinths are permanent, such as the one at Grace Cathedral Church in San Francisco, which is patterned after the ancient labyrinth in the Chartres Cathedral in France.*

*In a Los Angeles Times article ("Sole to Soul," by Berkley Hudson), Dr. Lauren Artress estimates that more than 70,000 people have now walked the Grace Church labyrinth and says that the church has distributed fifty-one labyrinth kits around the country.*

*The article describes what might be the experience of a walker: "As you follow a winding path for twenty minutes or so, you might cry tears of grief or joy, solve the riddle of a messed-up family or work life, feel better about an illness, or gain spiritual insight."*

Walking meditation can be done alone or in a group. If in a group, the student may either find himself or herself walking in a circle or in a straight line, side by side with fellow meditators. If outdoors, he or she might follow a safe path or the perimeter of a flower garden.

## *Walking meditation practice*

Walking meditation has the same foundations in concentration, awareness, and mindfulness as sitting meditation. But now the object of meditation is designated as "the changing phenomena associated with walking."

To do walking meditation, clear a ten-to-thirteen foot lane either in your house or outside. Walking barefoot or in socks allows greater sensitivity. If you wear shoes, make them light and comfortable. As with sitting meditation, start with a ten-minute period and add to that as it feels comfortable.

## WALKING #1

1. Stand still for a moment. Feel the entire body. Your hands should be comfortable. They can hang along your sides. Or if you prefer, clasp them together, palms open, and rest them on your abdomen. You may also clasp your hands lightly behind your back if this affords better balance and awareness.

2. Flood your right foot with awareness. Be aware of the sole of the foot, the toes, the ankle, the knee. Slowly shift your weight onto the right foot. Feel the global change in the entire body. Come back to an evenly weighted position. Now, shift the weight to the left foot and feel the change.

3. Become aware of the contact area of your foot with the floor. Now begin to lift your

foot slowly, making a mental note of each increment of movement. For example, you might make the following notes of the movement of your right foot as you lift it:

> lift...lifting...lifting...swinging...swinging...
> descending...touching...shifting weight...or...
> Starting up...up...up...up...forward...forward...forward...
> down...down...down...or...Heel...heel...up...
> rolling...rolling...ball...toes...lifting...extending...
> down...down...toes...ball...arch...heel....

4. If thoughts arise, such as "I hope no one sees me," acknowledge the judgment and let it go, just as you would in sitting meditation.

5. Stay in the continuing flow of awareness of walking. Do not freeze or congeal your thoughts on a particular part of your leg or foot. Keep an unbroken stream of awareness.

6. As you walk, keep your eyes downcast, focusing on a point several feet ahead of you. When you reach the end of your walking lane, stop and turn. As you turn, remain in the state of mindfulness. Notice the complex series of sensations and feeling as your body performs this maneuver. You may discover for the first time how remarkable "just turning" is. Note it and return to your labeling technique.

7. Begin to walk back up your walking lane. Try to maintain a steady state of awareness in both feet. Notice the stillpoint, as in observing the breath, between strides. Experience the feel of each part of the walking movement. It is a continuously changing experience. As with other meditation techniques, you may label out loud or silently.

8. When you finish your walking meditation period, stand still and silent for several moments. Notice the peace and calm in the body. Take that feeling with you through the rest of your day.

Try to coordinate the amount of time you sit with the amount of time you walk. You can alternate periods of walking and sitting, or you can intersperse them at times that you feel particularly restless. At any rate, try to do a walking meditation at least once every two days.

The object of the following exercise is alertness, sensitivity, and fullness of experience of the phenomena associated with walking.

# WALKING EXERCISE #2

1. Become aware of the contact area of your foot with the floor. Note that the weight of your body causes a compressed or contracted sensation in the weight bearing leg.

2. Notice as you raise the weight-bearing leg, how the sensations in that leg change from contracted to expansive. And as you shift your weight to your other leg, observe that it now takes on those qualities of contraction.

3. Continue walking and meditating in this mode. You can label this constant flow of expansion and contraction. For example:

    > ...Compression...decrease...decrease...
    > none...expansion...expansion...compression...
    > contraction...increase... increase....

    You may feel the sensations of expansion and contraction simultaneously. This is fine. As you experience contraction in the right leg, you may simultaneously experience expansion in the left. Excellent. You are bringing mindfulness to the object of meditation: the expansion and contraction that comes from the shift of weight.

4. If thoughts come up, simply acknowledge them and release them. Stay in the continuing flow of awareness of walking. Do not freeze or fasten your thoughts on a particular part of your leg or foot. Keep an unbroken stream of awareness.

5. As you walk, keep your eyes downcast, focusing on a point several feet ahead of you. When you reach the end of your walking lane, stop and turn. As you turn, remain in the state of mindfulness. Notice the complex series of sensations and feeling as your body performs this maneuver. You may discover for the first time how remarkable just turning is. Fine. Note it and return to your labeling technique.

6. Now begin to walk back up your walking lane. Try to maintain a steady state of awareness in both feet. Notice the stillpoint, as in observing the breath, between strides.

7. When you finish your walking period, stand still and silent for several moments. Notice the peace and calm in the body. Decide to take that feeling with you through the rest of your day.

## Gregorian chant

Gregorian chant is a type of Christian religious music extending back more than fifteen hundred years. Chants are vocal psalms, hymns, or prayers. They are for voice alone unaccompanied by musical instruments and sung without harmony. The music follows the flow of the words in free rhythm. (Because of their simplicity, Gregorian chants are often referred to as plainsong.) Chants are often sung by choirs, but also by soloists, and even as call and response between cantor and choir.

Gregorian chants were the principal music used in religious observances during Christianity's first millennium. They are sung primarily in mass and the divine offices (hourly meditational devotions). Chants are used to pray, to celebrate God, to mark the hours of monastic life, and for a wide variety of other spiritual purposes.

Around 600 A.D., Pope Gregory I (after whom these chants are named) embarked on an effort to collect and preserve this sacred music. During the 1960s, chant fell out of favor, but there has been a resurgence of popularity, even outside of the church. Gregorian chants have caught on so widely that they've become bestsellers on the CD racks.

Chant is a wonderful way to escape stress and the concerns of the modern world, says Benedictine father David Steindl-Rast author of *A Listening Heart,* because chant exists in the eternal, eliminating the pressures of linear time. That's how it was composed, that's where it lives, because it was composed to glorify the eternal God. It exists for the sake of pure praise, thereby adding to one's life a dimension of rich meaning and beauty to balance out our society's enormous emphasis on efficiency and practicality.

*Chant...exists for the sake of pure praise, thereby adding to one's life a dimension of rich meaning and beauty*

### Joining In

As a method of meditation, one of the most important aspect of Gregorian chant is its emphasis on group participation. For monastics, chanting together, like meditating together has a healing and harmonizing effect on both individuals and the group. By blending dozens of voices in music of praise points singers beyond their individual lives toward their place in God's greater scheme of things. As in meditation, success not so much found in achievement, observes Steindl-Rast, as in untiring striving. "That ordinary people give themselves to the Chant" he writes, "is the remarkable beauty of it."

*"When night in its swift course had reached its halfway point, and deep silence embraced everything, when night was at its darkest and deepest, there the eternal word leaped from the heavenly throne. Silence burst into song."*

T.S. ELIOT
*Book of Wisdom*

Participation in this amazing form of musical meditation is not limited to monastics. Many monasteries and convents, churches, and other organizations of many denominations have formed groups for lay people who want to get involved in creating this special form of religious observance. Contact a local sponsoring organization—you will find them in the community and Sunday listings in your daily paper, through the internet, or by phoning your own church.

Should you wish to study chant more intensely, the best way, says Cantor Donald Casadonte, is to attend a school or summer seminar. "...Studying a manual, even the best one, is not enough.... Sing in a choir for several years. This is the way."

## The canonical hours

In monasteries and convents, the divine offices are sung at appointed times and places each day during the Canonical Hours. (In liturgy, "hour" is not a mathematical interval, but a soul interval.) A bell is rung at the start of the hour, calling everyone to drop what they are doing and assemble for chanting and prayer. "It's as if the day was broken up into seasons, each with a particular character and call to answer," writes Steindl-Rast.

The divine offices of the canonical hours are called in the following succession:

*Vigils* (a.k.a. *Matins*). The day begins with the call to Vigils in the wee hours. The darkness of night is celebrated as an immense mystery, which is of God and therefore to be trusted completely.

*Lauds.* As the sun begins to rise, lauds is called to celebrate the gift of life.

*Prime.* This is the hour of deliberate beginning, when the monastic community is called together to receive its work assignments. The focus is on work as a form of prayer, to be savored for its own sake.

*Terce.* Terce is called at midmorning as a break to refresh the spirit and remind us of the primal energy of life.

*Sext.* At noon, Sext is called, for a renewal of the resolution and commitment.

*None* (Pronounced "noan"). In the mid-afternoon, none is called, bringing the community together again to consider the day's descent, and likewise the impermanence of creation. This serves to remind all assembled to live in the present, as if every moment were the last, finding forgiveness for oneself and others.

*Vespers.* At the hour when the lamps are lit, vespers is called. This is the hour when the community is entreated to let go of the day, to reconcile contradiction, and to find inner peace.

*Compline.* Before retiring, many communities call compline to confess the day's misdeeds, seek forgiveness and resolve to do better tomorrow.

## *Peace of mind*

A young monk made a long journey to visit an old master in the Egyptian desert. When the young monk finally found the master, he put his question before the sage. He kept losing his peace of mind, the young monk confessed, and desperately wanted a recipe that would help him preserve it. The Old Master had been meditating all his life, surely he could supply the answer. The old master replied, "I have worn this habit for seventy years, and not in a single day have I found peace."

The young monk despaired. If even the master knew no peace of mind, where did that leave the rest of humanity? Later the Young Monk understood the true intent of the master's words. We can't hold peace of mind as a possession, and shouldn't fret over it. What matters is that we never cease to strive for it.

DAVID STEINDL-RAST
*The Music of Silence* (audio tape)

## OBSERVING THE DIVINE OFFICES
## IN YOUR OWN LIFE

You don't have to be a monk or a nun to observe the Canonical Hours. You can make them a part of your own day. Here are some suggestions:

- *Vigils.* Even if you definitely won't get up in the wee hours, you can still honor the dark, infinite pre-dawn potential of your own mind. Before leaving bed, write down your dreams and create something out of them—a poem, drawing, or even just a little bit of free writing. The important thing is that you are giving yourself time before the day begins to let go and be creative.

- *Lauds.* Before leaving for your work, reserve time to meditate on the day ahead, and life, as a gift. Steindl-Rast suggests thinking something like: "I'm being given a new day. The day is a gift. How can I best use and experience it as such?"

- *Prime.* Shortly after beginning work, take a minute to reflect on work as part of the spiritual dimension of God's universe. Meditate on these questions, Why am I here? How does this job fit into God's plan for me, now? What can I bring to and take from this work here that fits with my greater, overall life? How can I bless this work? How can I make work into prayer?

- *Terce.* At some point in the midmorning, take a moment to meditate on the blessings you have already received today. Consider ways you can take blessing into you and radiate it out to others again.

- *Sext.* Pause during the middle of your day to relax and review. Think about earlier this morning, when you remembered why your job is important in the larger scheme of your life. Now, at Sext, meditate on this question: Have you been living up to that realization so far today? Set your goals for the rest of the day accordingly.

- *None.* Meditate on this: What mundane concerns of the day can you drop to make room for more spiritual, timeless, and important values? Take the time to forgive wholeheartedly. Write your grievances on a piece of paper and then tear it into shreds and scatter them.

- *Vespers.* Do something peaceful, magical, and serene in the evening. Go for a walk before dinner, light candles and incense, take a long bath, even prepare dinner in a ritualized manner. Or just sit and meditate. Take the time to release the day's cares, tensions, and stresses. Concentrate on reconnecting with God's peace and blessing. Listen to an album of Gregorian chants.

- *Compline.* Before going to bed, take time to meditate on your place in the universe, that you are safe, that you are loved. Put children to bed with the same thoughts. Remember the dreams you recorded early that morning, and try to revisit them while you are still awake. Based on your day, think about what you want the night to teach you this time.

# ISLAMIC MEDITATION

Islam is a religion born of meditation. Like Jesus and Buddha, Muhammad was a reformer. When he was a young man, the Arab peoples traced their ancestry back to Adam and Abraham. They made pilgrimages to see legendary holy sites such as the *hajar al aswud,* the sacred black stone given to Adam by God. (The stone was in the Kaaba, a temple in the sacred city of Mecca said to have been built by Abraham.) But Arabs had also reverted to worship of idols, spirits, and a host of gods and goddesses by the time of Muhammad's birth. Surrounding the Kaaba, they had set up three hundred and sixty idols, one for each day in their year.

Because of the pilgrims, Mecca was a rich trading center, and its merchants did all they could to foster belief in the miraculous powers of all its idols. They had even seized control of the holy well, Zemzem, miraculously created by Abraham's son Ishmael. The local merchants sold its waters to believers. But people became disillusioned, doubting that water sold for money could be holy. In time, even their belief in idols and images—even the Kaaba and the legendary hajar al aswud—crumbled and the Arab peoples turned to gambling, fornication, magic, and an unbridled love of money.

## The life of Muhammad

Muhammad was born in Mecca. As an adult, he became a camel driver, leading caravans to Egypt, Persia, and Syria. Later, he became one of the city's wealthiest merchants. All this while, the thought of his people's idolatry, drunkenness, gambling and whoring, greatly depressed Muhammad, and he often walked into the desert at night to meditate on how to reform his countrymen.

One night, in his fortieth year, as he sat meditating in the desert, an angel appeared to Muhammad, telling him that God (Allah) had appointed him a divine messenger and prophet to deliver his people from iniquity. At first,

Muhammad resisted, but the angel reappeared, and Muhammad began to preach his message of the all-powerful God of Abraham who was sorely displeased with his people for their ways, demanding a return to strict obedience to his worship and his laws. Among his targets were the rich merchants who profaned the sacred Well of Ishmael and the Kaaba for profit. This earned him their enmity, and they threatened his life and passed a law banishing all who followed Muhammad from Mecca.

*In order to be a good Muslim, a true believer, there are only five important rules to follow:*

- *Believe in Allah, and Muhammad, His Prophet.*

- *Pray five times each day.*

- *Be kind to the poor and give alms.*

- *Keep the fasts during the Month of Fasts.*

- *And make a pilgrimage to Mecca, the holy city.*

But travelers from other cities were intrigued by what they heard, and soon the people of Medina begged Muhammad to come preach to them. Afraid lest his ideas spread among other cities, and pilgrims no longer seek out Mecca, the merchants sent assassins to kill him. But on that night, Muhammad, warned by an angel, fled safely to Medina. The date of his escape (622 A.D.) became known as the year of the *Hegira* (Flight of the Prophet) and marked the first year of the Islamic calendar.

Medina welcomed Muhammad as a leader with divine authority in spiritual and worldly affairs. Muhammad named his new religion Islam (submission), meaning submission to the commands of Allah. His followers he called Muslims (true believers). Because Mecca held the hajar al aswud, given directly by Allah to Adam, Muhammad said it remained the holy of holys; and all Muslims were to turn toward the holy city of Mecca that housed it when praying and make a pilgrimage to Mecca at least once during their lifetime.

Eight years after his flight from Mecca, Muhammad returned to worship at the Kabba with a following of ten thousand true believers, armed to ensure they would be allowed entry to the shrine. The people of Mecca fled into the hills in terror. But when they saw Muhammad came in peace, offering harm to none, they accepted him as God's true messenger at last, and became Muslims. Muhammad's first act was to have all the idols smashed and overturned, beginning with Habal with the golden hand. He announced, *"La ilaha ilia Allah, Muhammad rasul Allah!"* (There is no god but Allah, and Muhammad is the Prophet of Allah!)

# YOUR HOLY PILGRIMAGE

You don't have to be a Muslim or even believe in a supreme being to benefit spiritually from Muhammad's idea of a pilgrimage to a holy place. Even as a meditational exercise, it can have a surprising influence on your life. This should be someplace of real significance to you, preferably in another town or state. Making the journey should take enough effort and time that your spiritual commitment to making it is challenged. It could be a significant church, synagogue, cathedral or mosque. Or it could be a special place like Stonehenge, the Ohio Indian mounds, or the great pyramid. Or it could just be a scenic/spiritual spot outside, or even inside your own city.

1. Select a site and make arrangements for the pilgrimage. Ask God's or the Divine's or nature's blessing on it.

2. On the way there, meditate on the significance of the journey to you. What do you hope to get out of it? What feeling or insight do you hope to return with it?

3. Try to achieve a real sense of reverence and sincerity.

4. When you reach the spot, again ask a blessing.

5. Spend as much time there meditating as you can. Clear, center, and relax yourself. Open yourself to whatever feelings and sensations being there evoke. Ask yourself, What is its specific significance to me? Why do I consider it a holy place? Try to get in touch with that feeling.

6. Shift your meditation from yourself to the holy place itself. See it in your mind's eye as well as the physical one. Try to become one with it, to see with its eyes, feel with its heat, take on its form. What does the holy place feel like to itself?

7. When you leave ask for a blessing again.

8. At home, take time to meditate on your pilgrimage. What did you learn or feel? What did you come away with? Give thanks to God for allowing you a safe journey and for whatever you were allowed to experience because of it.

### Meditating Five Times Each Day

Like Christian monks who observe the canonical hours with prayer, Muslims believe you should take frequent breaks to pray and meditate on God. Muhammad mandated all Muslims pray five times each day. You don't have to be a Muslim to reap the rewards of meditating. Instead of meditating once each day for twenty minutes, schedule five five-minute meditation breaks. perhaps at dawn, noon, mid-afternoon, sunset, and bedtime.

## Sufi meditation

*"One who dies for the love of the material world, dies a hypocrite. One who dies for the love of the hereafter, dies an ascetic. But one who dies for the love of the Truth, dies a Sufi."*

SHEBLI
*Sufi teacher*

Sufism is a Persian offshoot of Islam. It has been described as "Islamic mysticism." Sufism concentrates more on meditation than traditional Islam. As P.D. Ouspensky says, "Persian Sufism is the most characteristic expression of Muslim mysticism. Sufism is both a religious group and a philosophical school which is very idealistic. It struggles against materialism, narrow fanaticism and the literal understanding of the Koran. The Sufis interpret the Koran mystically. "Sufism is the philosophical free-thinking school of Islam."

Sufism is a path towards the truth where the provisions are love. Its method is to look solely in one direction, and its objective is God. The Sufi is one who moves towards the truth by means of love and devotion. Since only one who is perfect is capable of realizing the truth, the Sufi strives his utmost for perfection. Sufis believe the only way to become perfect is to purify oneself under the training of a Sufi Master.

## Sufi stories

But all this makes Sufis seem stuffy. They are not. Sufism is a mysticism of laughter. Like Zen masters, Sufi's like to get people's minds working with teaching stories that pose paradoxical combinations of opposites. Unlike Zen teachers, Sufis tease the mind into engagement with humor, rather than austerity. Sufi stories might be considered something like the parables of Jesus as written by Woody Allen.

Most Sufi stories center around the misadventures of one Nasrudin, a mythical *hoja* (teacher). These stories are so delightful, anyone can enjoy them. There are several collections of Sufi and Nasrudin stories translated by Idries Shah available in book form. Two representative Nasrudin tales appear below.

A man came to Nasrudin and asked what the hoja would charge to teach his son to read. Three hundred piasters, " said Nasrudin. "That's too high," the man said. "For that I could buy six donkeys." "Buy them, then," the replied, "and your son will make the seventh."

One night, as he lay sleeping, Nasrudin dreamed that a man offered him nine piasters in a bar for his turban. "It's not enough," said the hoja, "give me ten." Just then, he woke up. Finding no money in his hand, Nasrudin closed his eyes in haste and said, "Give me the piasters quick. I'll take nine."

These stories may reflect the Sufi state of "being inwardly drunk and outwardly sober." This intoxication is spiritual, not alcoholic, and results from the inner ecstasy of a close communion with God.

*"Meditation for one hour is better than ritual worship for a whole year."*
I7TH CENTURY
SUFI MASTER

## SUFI STORIES AND THE SPIRITUAL PATH

Much Sufi literature, according to Dr. Javad Nurbakhsh, concerns itself with the spiritual path and deals with such issues as: How should one follow this path? What are the conditions of the path? What is the significance of the spiritual master? What is the role of the disciple?

1. Take this book, find a quiet place to meditate. Relax and clear your mind.

2. Reread the above stories.

3. Ask yourself: How does each comment on the spiritual path? What are its lessons? What message does it have for me?

## Zikr—the dance of remembrance

Sufis and their spiritual cousins, the dervishes, are famed for their ritual dancing in which participants chant mantras while dancing themselves into a state of spiritual (and physical) intoxication. As in Ti-Chi, Akido, and other martial arts, movement becomes a form of meditation.

*"There is a polish for everything that taketh away rust; and the polish of the Heart is the invocation of Allah.... Remembrance of God through repeating his name purifies the seeker's mind and opens his heart to Him."*

MUHAMMAD

Marathon dance sessions often last for hours as spiritual ecstasy fills the body giving it extraordinary powers of endurance. Dervishes chant their own form of mantra. The Sufi mantra is called *zikr* (remembrance). The zikr par excellence is said to "La ilaha ilia Allah!" (There is no god but Allah!) The Sufi aims for a purity that is total and permanent. The way to this purity is constant remembrance of God.

Zikrs are part and parcel of the Sufi dance. "The dance opens a door in the soul to divine influences," wrote Sultan Walad, the son of the Iranian spiritual poet, Rumi. "The dance is good when it arises from remembrance of the Beloved." Meditation on the zikr enhances the dance's spiritual effect by maintaining the remembrance of God throughout.

## CHAPTER RECAP

- At their core, the major meditative traditions share a common goal: to allow the meditator access to a new, higher level of conscious awareness. There is no one perfect meditation technique.
- Meditation is used in all known spiritual and religious traditions.
- The Gnostics meditated in search of a direct experience of God.
- At the center of Kabbalists' meditations is the use of one of the twenty-five names of God.
- Early Christian ascetics used Hesychasm, a form of meditation known as the Prayer of Jesus.
- Gregorian chants are a powerful form of meditation.
- Islam emphasizes continual contact with God and requires its members to meditate five times each day.

# *Meditation Among Traditional Peoples*

# 7

**M**editation is universal among traditional peoples. It is practiced by shamans and oracles to see the future. (In the ancient Mediterranean world, at the beginning of our own cultural tradition, oracles were often consulted. The priestess of Apollo at Delphi often figures in Greek dramas and was consulted before military campaigns and even to settle personal matters. Friends of Socrates consulted the priestess as he did himself. The priestess is described as speaking from a trance state which she arrived at, in part, through meditation. Shamans in Asia, the Americas, and Africa all meditate.)

Rites of passage in which young men and women are initiated into adulthood require sustained periods of meditation. Drumming and dance bring participants to a state of conscious like those arrived at through meditation.

Aboriginal peoples in Australia, described themselves as having access to a "dreamtime" in which the distinction between mythic past and present time was obscure and in which the gods and mankind were in contact. By Western standards, these people may have been in a perpetual state of meditation, in which the objects of meditation were features of the landscape which they associated with the deeds of gods, spirits, and ancestors.

*• Meditation in different cultures:*

*The African casting of bones*

*An African altar*

*Spirit and nature in early America*

*The dream vision*

The famous cave paintings of Cro Magnon man suggest a desire on the part of the hunter to understand and to identify with the hunted animal. Native American tradition suggests a similar union of pursuer and pursued. Anyone who has read Eugene Herrigal's *Zen in the Art of Archery* will see the similarity between contemporary Zen practice and these ancient and traditional modes of thought and feeling.

Dismissed by industrialized nations as primitive tribal superstitions, the manifold religious and meditative traditions of Africa, Australia, the Americas and elsewhere are only just being discovered in the West. Recently a few American and European writers have begun to base their own spiritual research on the teachings of tribal peoples. Carlos Castaneda's many books on the spirit world are based on conversations with a Mexican Native American *brujo* (male witch), Don Juan. But compared with the thousands of books available in English about Christian or Muslim or Buddhist meditation, only a handful have as yet been devoted to traditional beliefs and practices. Here we will look briefly at traditional practice in Africa and the Americas.

## AFRICAN MEDITATIVE TRADITIONS

Duchan Gersi, the explorer/author who lived with remote tribes in Africa, Java, and South America, cautions us that it is a mistake to see tribesmen as primitive, backward, ignorant, naive, acting from instinct, lacking intelligence, and believing in false realities.

Gersi prefers to call them "peoples of tradition." By peoples of tradition, he means all the remaining societies and tribal grouping who live "following age-old traditions instead of moving with the flow of the twentieth century, and which remain outside the modern world." Although every tribe could be said to have its own meditation traditions and religious beliefs, Gersi and others have identified certain common, core beliefs:

- There is a main God/dess who is the creator of all things.

- Religion enfolds the whole of life, there is no dichotomy between life and religion.

- Worship requires a fundamental attitude of strict discipline and reverence.

- There is high reverence for sacred places, persons and objects; sacred times are celebrated.

- An invisible, world of spirits and ancestors exists all around us and interacts for both good and ill in the natural, visible world; and care is taken to determine the will of spirits to whom sacrifices may be due or from whom protection may be sought.

- Magic is real.

- Their spiritual or religious leaders have special powers.

- They believe in three forms of healing:

    natural healing using plants,

    rebalancing of energies, and

    psychic healing.

## A Namibian bone meditation

In Namibia, in southwest Africa, Gersi met a group of tribesmen who meditate over objects of meditation that are like those of the earliest humans—chicken bones, bark, and pebbles. All early forms of divination, from the Chinese I Ching to the Teutonic runes, began with the casting not of dice but of bones, rocks, or even twigs. Before the development of writing, these were unadorned. Later, letters and words were inscribed on their surface.

You don't have to use bones, of course, you may use anything of different lengths, or colored stones. You may even want to make a bag to keep the elements of your oracle in. They are meditation devices, and deserve the same respect you bring to your meditations. The original Namibian Bone Oracle consisted of:

*"We in the United States or Great Britain should think twice before we dismiss the primitive beliefs of Africans as balderdash, or laugh at their occult customs."*

JOHN GUNTHER
*Inside Africa*

- six chicken bones (the two that join the knee to the foot, and four from parts of the feet),

- four colored stones (two red and two golden brown), and

- two small, flat pieces of tree bark.

These twelve objects are paired, symbolically, as male and female. The larger of each pair represents the male. The elements of the oracle represent human beings, good and bad forces, and character as follows:

- The two longest chicken bones (those that join the knee to the foot) represent the central characters—man and woman.

- The four smaller chicken bones (parts of the feet) represent the children—members of the family unit.

- The two pieces of tree bark represent the ancestral spirits— the positive forces symbolizing vigilance and protection.

- The two red stones represent crocodiles—the negative forces of the underworld.

- The two golden brown stones represent the seeing eyes of man and woman—wisdom and perception.

In the oracle, the state of health of each family member is determined by the position of the appropriate bone. If they are face up, it indicates good health. Those that fall face down denote illness and distress. Romance and fertility are indicated by the positive and negative forces between the bone representing man and the bone representing woman. Prosperity is foretold by drawing a line connecting the two golden brown stones (the positive forces), and a line connecting the two pieces of bark (the negative forces). If these lines cross any of the characters, they fall under the influence of either good fortune or bad. Those under negative influences can counteract the forces only if the golden stones (seeing eyes) lie closer to them than to the negative forces.

Generally, bone oracle meditations are held only at the full moon, for these Namibians "believe fortune is governed by the lunar cycle." In his book, *Finished*, Sir Henry Rider Haggard, who had served the government in Africa in the late 1800s, described the dramatic beginning of one full moon meditation, presided over by a Zulu *makoski* (master of many spirits), or medicine man, whose healing power is supposed to come not only from his potions, but because he has intimate contact with the tribal spirits.

> The edge of the moon's orb appeared above the hill and an arrow of white light fell into the little valley. It struck upon the jutting rock, revealing a...white-headed figure squatted between its base and the fire, the figure of Zikali. There he sat...staring at the sky, for the firelight shone on his deep and burning eyes. This went on, until the full round of the moon appeared above the hill. Then, at last, he spoke....

## MEDITATING ON THE ORACLE

Below, inspired by Gersi's *Faces in the Smoke*, is a basic bone oracle. It was intended to tell the future, of course. But as with the I Ching and the tarot, and other symbol-based systems of divination (oracles), the Bone Oracle also makes an excellent and highly illuminating object of meditation.

1. Blow on the bones.

2. Chant the following blessing to start the spirit flowing between you and the bones, "I breathe my soul and the soul of my guiding spirit upon you."

3. Cast the bones on the ground.

4. Meditate carefully on the way they have fallen. Ask yourself what their relationships suggest to you. Then simply keep your mind open to whatever thoughts and images arise.

## Altars—the faces of the gods

In Africa, altars form a very important part of Kongo meditative and religious traditions, as they do for Christians, Jews, Confucians, Hindus and others. They are frequently to be discovered at the bases of mountains, at the edges of forests, on river banks, at cemeteries, and other locations that designate the border between our world and the world of the spirits. These altars often contain magical pottery, ideograms and sacred medicine *fetishes* called *minkisi*, which are believed to promote physical and social harmony and healing.

And as with other traditions, the altars of the Kongo are symbolic links with deity or the supernatural. Each Namibian altar is dedicated to a specific orisha (god). As with the gods of the Norse, Hindus, and Greeks, each orisha represented and was responsible for a particular moral characteristic—justice, healing, and strength. And as with the traditions cited above, and many others, this pantheon was in turn ruled by a God of gods.

## The oldest form of meditation

Below are instructions for creating a simple Kongo altar and performing a sample orisha meditation on meditation on Shango, the Kongo thunder god. This is a variant of meditating on one's deity typified today by certain Christian churches and in Tibetan deity yoga.

## AN ALTAR MEDITATION

This meditation should be performed under a full moon, and ideally outdoors and under a tree (considered to be channels between this world and that of our ancestors and other spirits). If the idea of meditating on an African God (or any other god than your own) is disturbing, substitute meditating on one of your ancestors, a parent or grandparent, for instance.

1. Draw a circle on your altar cloth. Draw a cross within the circle. This is a basic symbol of the Kongo religion, a *dikenga*. It represents both the sun and what professor Robert Farris Thompson calls "a symbolic chart of the voyage of the soul. As a miniature of the sun, the soul is thought to have four moments—birth, efflorescence, fading and the return in the dawn of a coming day."

2. Draw (or paint) a diamond right above your brow. Like many yogic traditions, the Kongolese, who symbolize the soul as a diamond, believe the soul is located in the forehead.

3. Select an outdoors location where you won't be disturbed. Kongo altar meditations are best performed in nature, where the spirits and gods are at play.

4. Lay the cloth over a table or a special piece of furniture or even a large rock.

5. Sit, stand, or kneel as you feel most comfortable, relax with a few breaths.

6. Ask forgiveness and grace from your ancestral spirits.

7. Visualize a male figure dressed in fiery red robes, on his head, crowns of beads. He holds a double-headed ax in one hand, rattles in the others, gourds hang from thongs around his neck. (This is Shango, the thunder god, one of the orisha. The double-headed ax he holds is called the *oshe shango* and represents both judgment and balance. This symbolizes Shango's position as messenger of moral judgment.)

8. Meditate on Shango's significance as representing balance, fairness, and the thunder stroke of judgment when Shango finds we have perpetrated imbalance or unfairness.

9. Let any thoughts, feelings, and images this meditation stirs surface in your mind.

10. When they have subsided and your mind is empty of all but the image of Shango, silently thank the thunder god and your ancestral sprits for any insights this has brought. End your meditation.

## NATIVE AMERICANS—EVERYTHING HAS A SPIRIT

The native peoples of North and South America have a diverse range of spiritual and meditation traditions. The traditions have existed for centuries, and are beginning to get the attention of spiritual seekers of all backgrounds. It's not possible to explore any of them in detail, so what follows must be an all-too-brief summary of some elements common to most Native American meditation practices.

Living in close contact with nature, many Native Americans felt that everything that could be seen or touched—living or inanimate—has a spirit. The cornstalk, the tortoise-shell rattle, boulders and the mighty mountains are significant and alive. They symbolize the spirits that give them form and life. There is no separation between the sacred and secular aspects of life, as in

Christianity. Native American belief states that all things are woven together like a basket or fine rug. All are equal objects for meditation and veneration. Indeed, one of the objects of Native American meditation was to come to see the "spirit" in trees and rocks and rugs.

*"We live in a world of symbols where the spiritual and the commonplace are one. To you, symbols are just words, spoken or written in a book. To us, they are a part of nature, part of ourselves—the earth, the sun, the wind and the rain, stones, trees, animals, even little insects like ants and grasshoppers. We try to understand them not with the head but with the heart, and we need no more than a hint to give us the meaning."*

JOHN LAME DEER
*Miniconjou Sioux*

## Shamanism

For a long time, Native American shamans (of either gender), were disparaged by Western society as "medicine men" and "witch doctors." To Native Americans, their shamans were healers, judges, priests, weather forecasters, timekeepers, storytellers, even fools—but above all initiators into the mystic and instructors in powerful meditation practices. Shamans possess a host of ancient techniques—including ritual and meditation—using them to achieve and maintain well-being and healing for themselves and members of their communities.

## The Great Spirit

Many religions think of God as wholly masculine. Native Americans saw the universe as jointly ruled by a Male Spirit and a Female Spirit who were different yet complementary aspects of one divine being. Neither exists without the other. This divine being is called the Great Spirit.

Below is the text of a Sioux meditation on the Great Spirit. Stop and settle yourself before you read it. Take a deep breath and exhale slowly, letting any tension out. Now, read it as reverently as a Native American shaman might have two hundred years ago on the Great Plains. Return to it any time you find yourself in need of spiritual refreshment.

Grandfather, Great Spirit, you have been always, and before you no one has been. There is no other one to pray to but you. You yourself, everything that you see, everything has been made by you. The star nations all over the universe you have finished. The day, and in that day, everything you have finished. Grandfather, Great Spirit, lean close to the earth that you may hear the voice I send. You towards where the sun goes down, behold me; Thunder Beings, behold me! You where the White Giant lives in power, behold me! You where the sun shines continually, whence come the day-break star and the day, behold me! You where the summer lives, behold me! You in the depths of the heavens, an eagle of power, behold! And you, Mother Earth, the only Mother, you who have shown mercy to your children!

Hear me, four quarters of the world—a relative I am! Give me the strength to walk the soft earth, a relative to all that is! Give me the eyes to see and the strength to understand, that I may be like you. With your power only can I face the winds.

Great Spirit, Great Spirit, my Grandfather, all over the earth the faces of living things are all alike. With tenderness have these come up out of the ground. Look upon these faces of children without number and with children in their arms, that they may face the winds and walk the good road to the day of quiet.

This is my prayer; hear me! The voice I have sent is weak, yet with earnestness I have sent it. Hear me!

*Native Americans saw the universe as jointly ruled by a Male Spirit and a Female Spirit who were different yet complementary aspects of one divine being.*

## THE MEDICINE WHEEL

The Native American philosophy of the Medicine Wheel holds that all things and creatures on the earth are related and, therefore, must be in harmony for the earth to remain in balance. The same, they believe, is true of human beings. To achieve this balance, they meditate on the simple elegance of the circle, symbolized in the medicine wheel. (Its symbolism will grow naturally for you as you let its power, visualized as a light or fire, radiate to all areas of your life.) The following meditation, adapted from Native American sources, beseeches the Great Spirit through the wheel for whatever you most need. It will also center you powerfully, while revitalizing you spiritually.

1. Make your own personal medicine wheel. Find five stones. Mark the points of the wheel with them—north, south, east, west, and center—offering a prayer to each direction as you place its stone.

2. Determine exactly what it is you want. It can be a material, emotional, or spiritual desire.

3. Make this thought clear in your mind by thinking through what you want.

4. Use a Native American technique known as "smudging" to open and cleanse your aura, and to purify your environment of any negative or distracting influences. This is a technique known as smudging, which uses ashes from cedar, tobacco, sage, or other sacred herbs. Burn a little bit in a shell or similar vessel. Sprinkle the ash to the four directions. Offer the smudge to the Great Spirit with an upward motion. Sprinkle some around your feet for the Earth Mother. Now offer smudge to the North, East, South, and West. You may feel your aura gaining power.

5. Is there a light source around you somewhere, like the sun or moon, a lone streetlight, or a candle? Squint your eyes while staring at the light source until it looks like light beams are shooting out of it. Imagine that this is the inner light. Like a laser beam, you feel this light shooting through your body. You feel it first hit the energy center (chakra) at the top of your head and then course downward through your body.

6. Imagine that six energy centers are pumping out light beams.

7. Visualize a point of light at the end of the beam in front of you. Visualize this point moving clockwise in a circular route around your aura. You will find yourself at the center of a three-dimensional medicine wheel.

8. This is a master symbol that gives you access to the creative power of the universe. You may access it in your daily life in an instant. Ask it any question that you have, or beseech it for anything that you want.

9. Count ten in-out breaths before dissolving your astral medicine wheel, and close with a prayer to the Great Spirit. If the rocks are ones you have found within the area and you do not choose to keep them, let them stay with their Mother and bless her and the Great Spirit.

A Native American vision quest—particularly important to Native Americans of the Great Plains—often leads to a young man's adoption by a totem spirit, whose task it is to guide him through life. The totem will also let him partake of its powers and senses under the right circumstances. Typically, totems speak only in dreams or during intense meditation practices like vision quests or prolonged fasting and prayer.

The totem animal is ordinarily not a domesticated one. Some totem animals are buffalo, coyote, raven, skunk, and eagle.

# SEEKING THE TOTEMS

Your totem can both give you a point of focus for meditation and appear in your meditation. At the same time, keep yourself open to any other totems that may appear. One might choose to send you an important message.

1. Go to your place of meditation, preferably a natural place where your totem would feel at home. Find a position where you can be comfortable.

2. Let your mental, emotional and physical selves relax for a few moments.

3. Open your totem/medicine bag. Offer tobacco to the four directions plus up and down.

4. Close the totem bag and place it where your third eye would be (the top of a pyramid with your eyes at each base of the triangle). Close your eyes and breathe deeply and slowly. Allow your consciousness to permeate the third eye and medicine bag.

5. Invoke your totem. See it, become one with it. Feel yourself participating in the totem's existence. If it is an animal, look through its eyes at the world. If it is a plant, feel your roots reaching into the soil and your leaves turning toward the sun. If it is a mineral, enter the microscopic level to examine the patterns of its molecules and atoms.

6. Do whatever it is that the totem does. If it's an eagle, then flap your arms and fly! Put on the feathers and soar the skies. If it's a bear, growl and grunt like one. Don a bearskin cape and dance. If it's a stone, feel your very being change into new shapes with each movement of the Earth Mother.

7. Continue the imagery until you believe you have achieved oneness with the totem. It may take several sessions before you feel you have achieved it.

8. Look at any problems or interests you have through your totem. Let them teach you new perspectives. Move outside you totem and converse with it. Ask it to tell you whatever you most need to know.

9. End your meditation with a reawakening procedure. Gradually cease being the totem and return to your body. This should be a reverse process from the one you used to begin. Move your consciousness-center from your third eye to the top of your head. Feel your body transforming back to human. Put your hands and totem bag at your feet to ground yourself in the Mother.

## CHAPTER RECAP

- Traditional meditation has many connections with meditation associated with Eastern and Western meditation.

- Insights into our own beliefs and observance can be gained by studying meditation as it is practiced elsewhere.

- The African bones meditation is an excellent example of divination using simple meditative objects.

- The African altar meditation shows us how to create a holy gateway.

- There are many surviving Native American meditative traditions, and objects of contemplation include the totems and the Medicine Wheel.

- The Native American spirit search can be used as a basis for our own spiritual development.

# Contemporary Meditation Traditions

**8**

Centuries of monolithic left-brain rationalism came to an end in the West during the past three decades. Increasingly, people rediscovered the mental and physical benefits of tapping into right-brain qualities like holistic intuition, personal insight, inner calm, and empathy. The main vehicle to accessing the right hemisphere of our brain was, of course, meditation.

## MEDITATION AND THE NEW AGE

Meditation was new to the West in the early 1970s. "To be sure," Daniel Goleman notes in *The Meditative Mind,* Eastern teachers such as Yogananda and D. T. Suzuki had come to America much earlier and had gained followers here and there." But these were exceptions. Then, in the late 1970s and 1980s, "there was a blossoming interest in meditation like none the West had witnessed before."

Now the situation has changed. Meditation has been taken up big time in the West. Millions of Americans—business people, professionals, athletes, academics, movie stars, and the man (and woman) in the street—have given meditation a whirl, discovered its benefits, and made it part of their daily routine.

- *Adapting ancient techniques to modern lifestyles*

- *Benefits of contemporary meditation*

- *Don't go "meditation shopping"*

- *Sampling different meditative traditions*

187

*Unlike older meditative practices, New Age approaches don't require you to retire to a monastery or renounce the activities, pleasures and pains of the world.*

What turned the trick and brought meditation to the fore in the U.S. was the advent of the so-called "New Age." Beginning in the mid-1970s, the New Age was a period in the West of rediscovery of the very real potential for healing spiritual and physical which lies in ancient, and particularly Eastern, spiritual traditions. Led by individual seekers and visionary psychotherapists, the New Age encompassed interests in yoga, holistic healing, angels, crystals, the tarot, tantric sex, shamanism, meditation, and a host of other practices. Millions, for whom Western religion had become too narrowly focused and materialistic, sought what they were missing among the world's spiritual traditions. Others were drawn to New Age practices because science, which was now studying them seriously for the first time, was validating their ability to reduce stress, promote health and promote spiritual well-being.

Because meditation can produce all these benefits—and much, much more—it became extraordinarily popular. Tens of millions of Americans have discovered that its benefits justify making its practice, in one form or another, a regular part of their lives. Any large city has not dozens, but literally hundreds of meditation classes offered through various religious, educational, civic, and even for-profit organizations.

All this has given meditation a high profile in the media (which has in turn led to more people trying it). The last two decades have seen to a proliferation of newspaper articles, magazine features, and television reports focusing on the phenomenon. The number of resources available to veteran meditators and those newly interested in exploring its promise has also mushroomed in the form of books and web pages devoted to meditation. (See Resource section for lists of such materials.) As we enter the twenty-first century, it is virtually impossible to watch an entire evening of prime time television, or to open any issue of any magazine from *Marie Claire* to *Sports Illustrated* to *Time* and *not* find an article on some aspect of meditation, who meditates, and what they get out of it.

So many millions became involved in New Age interests that it spawned its own publications like *New Age Journal* and *Magical Blend,* its own bookstores nationwide, its own division at major publishing companies, its own conventions and expositions, its own music, its own organizations and movements, many of them meditation-oriented (see Resources section), even its own "superstars" like Ram Dass and Neale Donald Walsch.

Many contemporary meditators entered through the traditional meditative disciplines such as Yoga, Zen, Buddhism, Wicca, meditative prayer. But others found these unsuited to the patterns of their lives or were put off by esoteric terminology. This led people in the West to seek ways to adapt Eastern meditative practices to Western needs.

Western figures as diverse as Gurdjieff, Edgar Cayce, Herbert Benson, R. E. L. Masters, Ken Wilber, Jiddu Krishnamurti, Mary Baker Eddy, Carl Jung, Jean Shinoda Bolen, and Arthur Janov developed meditative practices free from esoteric terminology and easily fit into contemporary lifestyles. Among the thousands of contemporary traditions are found Infinite Thought, the Fourth Way, the Headless Way, transpersonal psychology, Primal Therapy, visualization, Transcendental Meditation, Gaiaism, transpersonal psychology, Jungian analysis, psychosynthesis, and the women's spirituality movement.

Unlike older meditative practices, New Age approaches don't require you to retire to a monastery or renounce the activities, pleasures and pains of the world. Nor do you have to learn complex, esoteric, mystical terminology. The core ideas of these meditative disciplines are expressed in terms of Western experiences and understandings, like psychology, biofeedback, brain studies, stress reduction.

In this chapter, you will be introduced to five of these traditions: Gurdjieff, Visualization, Transcendental Meditation, Edgar Cayce and his following, and Goddess/women's spirituality.

## GURDJIEFF AND OUSPENSKY

G. I. Gurdjieff (1877-1948) and his disciple P. D. Ouspensky are leading examples of those in modern times who have been inspired to leave behind significant meditative legacies for the twentieth century. In the next sections, you will find representative samples of both thinkers' contributions to contemporary meditation.

### A remarkable man

While Russian philosopher G. I. Gurdjieff (1877-1948), was traveling in Asia, having a series of what he would title in one book *Meetings with Remarkable Men*, he developed a unique spiritual system. One of his pupils described Gurdjieff's approach as "the religious teachings of the East disguised in a terminology which would not alienate the factual minds of Western thinkers."

Gurdjieff believed in "personal salvation," a kind of profound spiritual and mental rebirth achieved through a rigorous spiritual, physical, and meditative regime. In numerous cases, Gurdjieff's system transformed lives, including that of poet William Carlos Williams, who would write of the master later as "a flaming spirit that attacked and won many a fine victory for art and the good life."

Margaret Anderson was a student of Gurdjieff in a small group including Mrs. Enrico Caruso; A. R. Orage, former editor of the *English New Age;* singer, author and actress Georgette Leblanc; author Solita Solano; and Jane Heap, co-editor of the *Little Review.* In *The Unknowable Gurdjieff,* Anderson says that "Gurdjieff remains unknown, except to those followers who worked with him.... His science belongs to the knowledge of antiquity, and this knowledge is transmitted by word of mouth, never written about except in general terms."

"We are imprisoned within our own minds, and however far we extend them and however highly we decorate them we still remain within their walls. If we are ever to escape from our prisons, the first step must be that we should realize our true situation and at the same time see ourselves as we really are and not as we imagine ourselves to be. This can be done by holding ourselves in a state of passive awareness...."

KENNETH WALKER,
*Gurdjieff student*

## *The fourth way*

Gurdjieff called his approach to meditation and self-enhancement, the fourth way. He held that the ancient cultures had developed three major paths of meditative discipline and self-transformation, each appropriate to the peoples of long ago. As Gurdjieff saw it, these were:

- *The First Way.* The path of the *fakir*, who works on the physical body to conquer physical pain. This is the most difficult path. You must surrender everything and do as you are told.

- *Second Way.* The path of the monk. This way requires faith above all. You develop the emotional center on this path.

- *Third Way.* The path of the yogi. This is the path of knowledge and consciousness. You develop the intellectual center.

If these were the only three meditative paths available to people, there would be nothing for modern Westerners, says Ouspensky. Unlike the peoples of ancient China, Mesopotamia, Judea, and the Arab Peninsula, we are over-educated. Westerners need "a special way," Gurdjieff's fourth way, designed specifically to suit their lifestyle and needs.

Gurdjieff's fourth way synthesizes the work of classical Greek thinkers like Pythagoras, Plato and the neo-Platonists, with Slavic Orthodox Christianity, Tantric Buddhism, and Hinduism. Most importantly, it is adapted to Western needs. For example, to follow the fourth way:

- You don't have to give up everything you own. All the work goes on inside you.

- You continue to live the same life as before, in the same environment. These circumstances are the best for you anyway.

- If you start to work and study in these conditions, you can attain something valuable. Eventually you will be able to transform yourself and environment, but not before you sense the need to change. Nothing is harder than to change the inner you without changing the outer, external you.

*"Gurdjieff's Fourth Way tells how to do what popular religions teach has to be done, that is, transform one's consciousness."*
P. D. OUSPENSKY

This is the fourth way, the "Path of the Sly Man," one who carries out his meditation, not in solitary contemplation, but in relationships with the people, objects, social system and ideas around him (see chapters 9 and 10 for more on meditation in daily life).

Those who achieve self-development through the fourth way, Ouspensky writes, want to share their acquired knowledge and help other people advance even further. This has spawned numerous Gurdjieff groups, each with its own way of doing things. Today, Gurdjieff-Ouspensky centers can be found all around the world.

## Self-observation

Gurdjieff held that most people have been hypnotized by cultural brainwashing and become automatic, reflexive creatures who simply respond to stimuli. Like Buddha, he saw our normal state as suffering, and believed our only hope was to waken from the illusions of consentual reality through a deliberate program of self-transformation. Key to Gurdjieff's approach to personal liberation was recovery of the authentic self via a meditative technique called "self-observation."

Using self-observation, meditators detached from the distinction between themselves and the universe. Like the mindfulness techniques of Insight meditation or Christian centering prayer, when your mind wanders, the idea is to herd it back to job of watching yourself.

In the course of self-observation, the meditator realizes that his inner states are in constant flux and that there is no such thing as a permanent, single "I" or self within. We discover we are not a unified, whole personality, but instead, carry around within us an internal cast of characters or personality fragments. Depending on circumstances, different ones dominate the stage at different times, adding their idiosyncrasies to the shape of our personality.

*"We think we can study meditation or meditate ourselves. If you can remember yourself, you can meditate; if not, you cannot. Self-remembering means control of thoughts, a different state. Meditation is an action of a developed mind, and we ascribe it to ourselves. It would be very good if we could meditate, but we cannot; self-remembering is the way to it. You cannot begin from the end; you have to begin from the beginning like in everything else."*

P. D. OUSPENSKY
*Tertium Organum*

Through self-observation, these selves lose their hold as the meditator ceases to identify with them. As our observing "I" developes and becomes detached from all the little "I"s, the meditator will "wake up." In waking up, the little "I"s disappear, and there is what Kenneth Walker describes as "a sense of being present, of being there, of thinking, perceiving, feeling and moving with a certain degree of control and not just automatically." In this state, we see ourselves with full objectivity.

## SELF-OBSERVATION

You can do this meditation anywhere—walking around, sitting on a train, at home. All it requires is the ability to exercise the power of self-observation as if you were flexing the muscles of your arm or leg.

1. Begin by finding a quiet place and breathing slowly for a while to enter the still, calm meditative state.

2. Observe your body, as if you were a doctor or scientist. Notice one aspect about yourself—for example, a gesture that you make. (Throughout the rest of the day attempt to remain conscious of that aspect every time it comes into play.) There is a good reason to begin with the body. You cannot change your life with just your mind. You must use the body as a tool toward bringing your centers into line.

3. As you try to develop self-observation, you will find your inner selves are whirling around like a dust storm or blizzard. Observe these inner selves as they appear and disappear. When you observe them, these selves lose their power over you. You don't identify with them anymore. Instead, feel yourself waking up to complete objectivity.

4. You may be disturbed when you realize the rapidly changing nature of your mind. Self-observation requires constant effort toward perfection. Keep your attention on the physical. Note the action of observing rather than what you are observing.

5. Try to look at yourself and the entire universe through the eyes of objective consciousness. To do this, expand your perception to unite the subjects and the objects you are perceiving.

6. Continue until you feel you have gained all you can from this session.

Give self-observation time to produce its wonders. Don't expect to experience results in a day or a few sessions. Persist. It will prove worth your patience.

### Ouspensky and the tarot

Gurdjieff's leading disciple, P. D. Ouspensky, devoted much of his life to exploring his mentor's ideas. Ouspensky was forced to flee Russia during the Revolution, but found sanctuary in England and later the United States. In 1920 he published one of his major works, *Tertium Organum,* an attempt to understand humanity and its place in creation.

In keeping with Gurdjieff's incorporation of the best of all traditions in the fourth way, Ouspensky explored the meditative aspects of many esoteric magical and mystical systems. Like the great psychoanalyst, Carl Jung, Ouspensky became fascinated by the possibilities of what are ostensibly divinatory systems or oracles as meditative devices (see the previous chapter). He spent many years meditating on the tarot, and recommended his students do the same.

"There is more to the tarot than fortune-telling," writes European therapist Jan Woudhuysen. "We all have the gift of intuition, but most of us suppress it. The tarot has always been used for 'fortune-telling,' although, in fact, many traditional practitioners have used it for purposes which nowadays would be called psychotherapeutic. Via meditation the cards come to answer many types of questions, and suggest new ones. The ability to make use of the inherent powers of intuition is the reward given to those using the system; the ability to generate new questions the unique attribute. The tarot can be used to help you come to terms with yourself, or to understand other people. The subconscious knows and perceives all, and the conscious is bewildered by events. The tarot is a means of linking our conscious and our subconscious."

## TAROT MEDITATION

The meditation that follows is inspired by ideas in Ouspensky's books. Key influences on Ouspensky's concept of the tarot were Arthur Edward Waite and his Waite-Rider deck, the most popular of modern tarot decks.

1. Take out a deck of tarot cards. If you don't already have one, acquire one at a store. Pick a shop with a wide selection. There are literally dozens of different types of decks: Goddess-oriented, Gypsy, Golden Dawn, and many more. The quantity of the cards and their significance remains the same. But the cards' esoteric meanings are symbolized in different ways by different artists. Look them over until you find one that appeals to you visually or spiritually or both. If your vibes aren't working that day, many books recommend starting with the Waite-Rider deck, which is considered one of the most representative in the field.

2. Select an appropriate time and place for meditation. Use breathing to clear your mind of thoughts and your body of tension.

3. This meditation starts with the Magician, the first trump in the tarot deck. You can substitute any card that you want, of course.

4. Place the Magician (or your card) on the table or a flat surface. Make sure you have a cloth, preferably of black silk, to lay the card on for meditation. Meditators recommend the color black because it absorbs all the colors and is a good insulator and conduit of psychic energy.

5. Sit before it, centering yourself, relaxing and emptying your mind.

6. Let your meditation begin. Visualize the Magician in front of his table. What gesture is he making with his arms? While remaining silent and still, imagine that you are raising your arms in a similar motion.

7. Continue to meditate on the image on the card until it becomes a window into an ever-expanding landscape. Make the leap from "I see the man." to "I am the man." Become the Magician.

8. Gaze downward at the vines growing around you. Examine the magical weapons at your disposal—the staff, the chalice, the sword and the pentacle. Each channels a different form of ethereal/elemental energy: fire, water, air, and earth. Through your will you can use these tools for whatever you desire. But what would be your wisest use?

9. Now gaze straight ahead. Oroboros, the Serpent of the Universe, has coiled around your waist. The snake grips its tail in its mouth so that you can use it as a belt for your robe. Your two eyes are wide open, staring straight ahead. What do you see? Is something materializing that you have called down into existence?

10. Now, clear your mind with a series of breaths. Become a passive receptor of the symbolism that you have evoked. The meaning of the Magician is God, man, and the universe. What special message do they hold for you?

11. Bring your arms back to your side. Return slowly to everyday consciousness.

12. Say aloud whatever thoughts and words come into your head.

13. Bless the card and return it to its proper sequence in the deck.

# VISUALIZATION OF THE POSITIVE

Visualization was repopularized to the Western, scientific world in 1911 by Italian psychoanalyst Roberto Assagioli. His work led him to the conclusion that by allowing the mind's eye to see, a person will hear the tongue of the unconscious, and the strength of the unconscious is most directly aroused by the conscious exercise of visualization skills. He held that it is naturally within everyone's power and ability to imagine a wanted outcome and have that outcome materialize. Assagioli named his method of self guidance, psychosynthesis: The mental combination of elements, parts or substances into a whole. Assagioli's discovery is another example of twentieth-century psychologists rediscovering techniques that shamans may have used for more than twenty centuries.

> *"We cannot separate the special importance of the visual apparatus of man from his unique ability to imagine, to make plans, and to do all the other things which are generally included in the catchall phrase 'free will.' What we really mean by free will, of course, is the visualizing of alternatives and making a choice between them. In my view...the central problem of human consciousness depends on the ability to imagine."*
>
> JACOB BRONOWSKI
> *The Origins of Knowledge and Imagination*

## Visualization of the best

Visualization is summarized in the introduction to Part II. It is in wide use currently in psychotherapy as a way of helping people overcome phobias and fears, relieve pent-up traumas, and integrate disowned parts of the self. It's also in wide use among Olympic athletes and CEOs as a method of preparing for challenging encounters and peak performance in general. "Visualization works," writes Ronald Gross in *Peak Learning,* "because when you take the time to picture yourself doing something well and bring to mind each detail of the process, you are strengthening the pattern of behavior in much the same way you do by actually practicing it. Visualizing is like knowing how to play a piece of music and being able to go through the motions of playing it in your head without even touching the instrument." This approach is being used more widely in sports and in many other fields as well.

"Human beings have powerful imaginations. Why not use that power in positive, supportive ways rather than simply leaving your imagination focused on worrying about possible disasters?"

## Guided meditation

*In one form of visualization, guided meditation, the meditator is guided through visualizing a series of scenes deliberately designed to achieve a particular goal. Guided meditation has increasingly played a role in psychotherapy. It has been around since the dawn of history, but it has been rediscovered and applied by contemporary therapists. Someone suffering from tension, for instance. may be guided to visualizing a relaxing scene like a balmy tropical island. Someone afraid of heights may be guided through a series of images of increasingly grater height until they feel comfortable with heights. In this chapter, Answers from the Unconscious and Imagery Calisthenics (below) are exercises that demonstrate guided meditation.*

## IMAGERY CALISTHENICS

If you're just beginning to learn visualization techniques, or if you're someone who has a difficult time seeing images vividly in the mind's eye, "Imagery calisthenics" is one of two techniques you can strengthen your ability to visualize. Imagery calisthenics draws on ideas proposed in *Higher Creativity* by Willis Harman, Ph.D., past president of the Institute for the Noetic Sciences and virtual-reality maven Howard Rheingold.

Imagery calisthenics is a form of guided meditation. You are led through an intensely visual meditation that creates imagery so vivid it paints the images on your inner eye. This is another of those exercises that are more effective if someone reads them out loud (either a friend or yourself via a prerecorded taped). The more this is practiced, the clearer the images and their meaning become.

1. In a place where you won't be disturbed, use breathing to relax and clear your mind.

2. Listen to the following being read aloud and let any images it arouses come into your mind.

3. See yourself lying on a patch of thick, fragrant, green grass on a mild hillside slope under an old elm tree. The sky is spotted with full, bulging, white clouds that float slowly across the blue. The air's temperature is the same as your skin's temperature. You take many deep breaths, not concentrating on how many breaths you've taken, but rather on how relaxing those breaths are. See and feel yourself float into your surroundings, looking all around. Travel to different places, such as a forest or beach. Float to a lake, look into the dark water. Focus on what's in the water. Look into the trees. Smell a flower. When you're ready to end your journey, imagine yourself back on the hillside, under the elm tree. It is sunset now. Take one more deep breath. Open your eyes. Remember what you say and what you felt.

4. To reinforce the images, write down or sketch your impressions of the journey.

## Visualization on wisdom

Many contemporary schools of clinical psychology, including Jungian, Gestalt, Cognitive, and Humanistic use imagery or fantasy to access inner wisdom. A typical technique involves dialogue with the sage or inner teacher, in which therapist asks the client to imagine being in a safe, pleasant environment and meeting there a person of great wisdom. According to professor of psychiatry and philosophy, Roger Walsh, Ph.D., the client "is encouraged to allow a dialogue with this inner sage to emerge spontaneously and to ask whatever questions seem most helpful." These inner dialogues, Walsh contends, can produce "surprisingly insightful information" of which the client "was formerly unaware."

Martha Crampton, the Director of the Canadian Institute of Psychosynthesis concurs with Walsh, "Mental imagery techniques," she writes, "can play a valuable, integrative role by bridging the conscious and unconscious as well as the rational and effective dimensions of our personality. One technique with many varied applications is the method known as 'answers from the unconscious.' This method is generally

> "What our eyes behold may well be the text of life but one's meditations on the text and the disclosures of these meditations are no less a part of the structure of reality."
>
> WALLACE STEVENS
> *The Necessary Angel*

used to acquire information, obtain guidance and gain better understanding of our inner processes. The basic idea is to formulate a question, addressing it to one's unconscious, and allowing the answer to emerge in the form of a mental image. Such an answer will emerge spontaneously, in most cases with surprising facility. It is important not to reject images that may seem irrelevant. Usually, given sufficient attention, their significance will become clear. And if a sequence of unrelated images emerges, often the very first one turns out to be the most meaningful. The process is simple and straightforward.

## ANSWERS FROM THE UNCONSCIOUS

1. Find a quiet, relaxing spot.

2. Close your eyes and imagine you are in the presence of the wisest person in the world—picture him or her as vividly as you can.

3. Ask this wise person a question concerning a problem you have.

Many men and women are surprised at the accuracy of the answers this technique produces, according to a *Prevention* article. Questions aren't always answered directly. Sometimes your question may be answered "with another question." That's to help you see the problem in "a different light," the article says. Usually this will get you started "thinking in a whole new direction."

Tantra yoga has a number of visual kriyas (powerful meditative techniques) intended to help beginners develop their skills as visualizers. One is practice of *tratakam* or "clearing the vision." The purpose of tratakam is to strengthen the eyes by relaxing them, stemming from the belief that a focused vision will produce a focused mind.

## TWO KRIYA VISUALIZATIONS

1. With a lit candle in front of you, sit in a darkened, quiet room. Set the candle a few feet in front of you.

2. Look at the flame, concentrating on it. Do not blink.

3. When you feel your eyes get heavy or if they start to water, shut them. (Do not strain your eyes.) You should still be able to see the flame through your closed eyes. If it vanishes, try to refocus on it with your eyes still closed. If unsuccessful, open your eyes and look at the flame again. Repeat the process.

4. The flame may move around as you try to visualize it. Try to keep it still.

5. If practiced regularly, you should eventually be able to keep the image of the flame still.

A second kriya, uses color and the candle's flame to find your internal serenity while sharpening your visualization skills.

1. Begin this exercise as you did the previous one.

2. Once you have the image of the flame within your closed eyes, try to keep it still.

3. Once still, see the flame rising from the candle and floating toward your chest and into your heart. See how the flame's light grows, illuminating the color of spiritual love, magenta. Let the magenta light surround your body like an aura radiating peace and self-love.

4. When the moment is right for you, watch the flame return to normal.

5. Slowly open your eyes, still encompassing the warmth and strength of the inner love and solace the flame brought you.

## TRANSCENDENTAL MEDITATION

Transcendental Meditation is another of those developments of ancient yogic practices adapted to contemporary Western lifestyles. It was developed and introduced to the West by the Maharishi Mahesh Yogi. After graduating from Allahabad University with a degree in physics, the Maharishi studied for thirteen years with Swami Brahmananda

## Maharishi and the Beatles

*The Beatles became followers of the Maharishi Yogi in 1967. They visited his meditation retreat in Rishikesh, India. The original purpose of the trip was a two-month meditation course. However, the popularity of the British rock group turned the spiritual quest into a media circus. As a result, the Beatles became disillusioned with the Maharishi. John Lennon and Paul McCartney would write several songs about their experience with TM and the Maharishi. "Sexy Sadie" and "Dear Prudence" on their "white" album are thinly veiled commentaries about the Fab Four's much-publicized summit with the great guru.*

• • •

*"Transcendental Meditation opens the awareness to the infinite reservoir of energy, creativity, and intelligence that lies deep within everyone. "By enlivening this most basic level of life, Transcendental Meditation is that one simple procedure which can raise the life of every individual and every society to its full dignity, in which problems are absent and perfect health, happiness, and a rapid pace of progress are the natural features of life."*

MAHARISHI MAHESH YOGI

Saraswati, the world's foremost exponent of the ancient Vedic Science of consciousness. Then in 1955, after spending two years in silence in the Himalayas, the Maharishi began teaching his Transcendental Meditation approach to a small group of initiates, including several Westerners, in India. It worked so well for Westerners that by the mid-1960s the Maharishi had attracted an international following that included many celebrities. Then the Beatles, at the height of their fame, paid a visit to his enclave in India and made TM a household phrase. Since then, it has grown into a global movement, practiced by millions.

For many of the people who meditate the TM way, the technique reduces stress and fatigue; improves health; makes your mind more effective, orderly, dynamic, and creative;

enhances personal relationships; and increases job productivity and satisfaction. By practicing TM, they feel they have become more effective in daily life, in both personal and business affairs. Each person, of course, has a different experience with TM. It depends on the condition of your body, because mental clarity needs a stress-free system.

In essence, TM is mantra meditation stripped to its simplest, most effortless form practiced for fifteen to twenty minutes in the morning and afternoon while sitting comfortably with the eyes closed. "During this technique" TM literature states, "the individual's awareness settles down and experiences the simplest form of human awareness, transcendental consciousness—where consciousness is open to itself. The experience of transcendental consciousness develops the individual's latent creative potential while dissolving accumulated stress and fatigue through the deep rest gained during the practice. This experience enlivens creativity, dynamism, orderliness, and organizing power in one's awareness, which results in increasing effectiveness and success in daily life."

The Maharishi candidly admits that, of course, TM is similar to other kinds of meditation. But claims the "one advantage of Transcendental Meditation is its extreme simplicity. It is very simple for anyone to learn." He says the basic difference between TM and other meditative traditions, in addition to its simplicity, is that TM "concerns itself only with the mind. Other systems often involve some additional aspects with which the mind is associated, such as breathing or physical exercises. They can be a little complicated because they deal with so many things. But with Transcendental Meditation there is no possibility of any interference. So we say this is the all-simple program, enabling the conscious mind to fathom the whole range of its existence."

## TM in Action

TM may be the most thoroughly researched and widely written about of all contemporary meditative traditions. This is in part due to unprecedented canny marketing and promotional efforts on the part of the TM organization itself. For example, over five hundred studies have been completed at 210 different universities and research institutions in twenty-seven countries, on the physiological, psychological, and sociological effects of TM. All together, over four thousand pages of scientific papers have appeared in over one hundred different journals.

## TM in the work place

*R.W. (Buck) Montgomery owned a Detroit chemical manufacturing firm. He instituted TM at his company in 1983. Within three years, he said, fifty-two of the company's one hundred workers—ranging from upper management to production line employees—were meditating for twenty minutes before they came to work and twenty minutes in the afternoon, on company time. As Montgomery tells it, "At the end of three months, an independent firm reported that those who meditated said they had more energy, were able to handle stress better, had fewer physical complaints and had lower cholesterol levels. Over the next three years, absenteeism fell by 85%, productivity rose 120%, quality control rose 240%, injuries dropped 70%, sick days fell by 16%, and profit soared 520%."*

Kenneth Eppeley, a Stanford physicist, did an analysis of many forms of meditation and relaxation techniques and found TM to be the best stress buster. Gary Kaplan, M.D., Ph.D., Director of Clinical Neurophysiology, North Shore University Hospital, Manhasset, New York said, "This landmark study has enormous implication for our understanding of states of consciousness and the functioning of the human mind."

TM has also been touted as boon to business and the workplace, in articles in newspapers and magazines as diverse as the *Los Angeles Times*, *New Age Journal*, *Newsweek*, the *Kankakee Daily Journal*, *Time*, *The New York Times*, *Business Week*, and others. As the **Kankakee Daily Journal** put it, "Business people, locally and around the world, are jumping at the opportunity to offer Transcendental Meditation to their employees in order to increase job performance and decrease the number of work absences due to illness."

## TM for lawyers

*Meditation has become recognized as effective in reducing stress and anxiety, as well as increasing memory retention and productivity. The State Bar of California now gives credit towards their mandatory continuing legal education requirement to attorneys who learn TM.*

*The meditation program falls under the Substance Abuse/Stress Prevention and Law Practice Management category.*

One TM instructor told the Journal that, "There are companies in Japan and the United States that offer TM. Employers are noticing that an employee that has reduced stress and tension and feels more creative and energized, is more productive and less prone to illness." Research on TM is said to have shown that employees that do TM have "Seventy percent reduced hospitalization, reduced absenteeism, less alcoholism and less anxiety." In one study, workers who practiced TM for one year displayed a remarkable improvement at work compared to members of the control group. "Relationships with coworkers and supervisors improved, job performance and satisfaction increased, and the desire to change jobs decreased."

As a result, some businesses have recently begun to recommend that their employees meditate twice a day, in the belief that the benefits of meditation improve a company's bottom line. According the *Los Angeles Times,* "Businesses say the at-work sessions make for happier employees, increased productivity—even higher profits."

## Yogic flying

Perhaps the most amazing claim ever made for meditation is that it confers the ability to levitate, called "yogic flying." Yet, reports of advanced meditators levitating have an ancient and honorable history in both the East and West. As Michael Murphy writes in *The Future of the Body,* "Levitation of the human body has a long history in Christian lore and has been said to occur in adepts of other religions." Druids purportedly drifted down the lines that criss-crossed ancient Europe. Indian yogis were reputed to be past masters, Native American shamans were witnessed in the act, and Aboriginal Australian witch doctors called "clever men" and Hawaiian magicians possessed similar powers.

"There exist, it seems to me," Murphy says, "enough compelling anecdotes about the phenomenon to warrant our considering it a human possibility." Among those reported by eyewitnesses to have successfully mastered this technique are such worthies as Rabi'a of Basra, St. Terisa of Avila, and St. Joseph of Copertino. "Levitation, the name often given to the raising of the human body from the ground by no apparent physical force," says Butler's *Lives of the Saints,* "is recorded in some form or other of over two hundred saints and holy persons."

TM claims to have gotten the techniques involved in meditative levitation down to such an exact science that they can teach it to almost any one. TM literature reports that over 100,000 people have mastered the technique. In addition to bestowing the ability to levitate, yogic flying is supposed to greatly enhance coordination between mind and body. It is said to optimize coherence in brain functioning while producing the inner experience of "bubbling bliss." Moreover, many people claim to have achieved the goal of the course and levitated.

## St. Joseph of Copertino

Perhaps the most widely discussed historical account of levitation concerns Saint Joseph of Copertino, a seventeenth century Franciscan monk. Saint Joseph was said to have been observed levitating on more than a hundred occasions. Almost a century later the case was analyzed by the skeptical Prosper Lambertini, later Pope Benedict XIV. Lambertini's analysis of the evidence is said to have been "thorough and searching." His doubts appear to have been dispelled, for he published the decree of Joseph's beatification in 1753, when he was pope.

• • •

"Yogic flying brings waves of bubbling bliss creating happiness in the individual and peace in the world."

MAHARISHI MAHESH YOGI

## EDGAR CAYCE—THE SLEEPING PROPHET

The renowned Edgar Cayce (1877-1945), whose life has been detailed in several best-selling biographies, was a home-grown American psychic, mystic and healer. Born on a farm near Hopkinsville, Kentucky, Cayce showed mystifying powers from an early age. These include sleeping on his spelling book and memorizing every word

inside, telling his mother how to treat an injury, and talking to an invisible angelic being. Later in life, Casey would
discover many other amazing abilities—clairvoyance, the
ability to view people's auras, dowsing for water, and tapping people's unconscious minds.

## The Akashic record

*Asked where his trance-induced readings came from, the sleeping Cayce said his mind was tapping
both the mind of the subject and what he called "the Akashic records" (borrowing a term from
Hindu cosmology). In essence, these Akashic records seem to be what Carl Jung called the "collective unconscious." Other traditions speak of this phenomenon as the "Book of Life," the "Recording
Angel," and "anima mundi." All the thoughts and vibrations of everyone who has lived since the
beginning of time are recorded in this Akashic record. Cayce's sleeping mind was able to access
the storehouse of knowledge and draw from its bottomless well of wisdom. After a few introductory
phrases, Cayce's voice would say, "Yes—we have been given the records of the entity now known
as (person's name)," and the reading would begin.*

Cayce accidentally discovered his abilities at the age of
twenty-four. The year before, he had lost his voice from a
cold, but still hadn't regained it. A friend sent him to a
hypnotist for a cure. The hypnotist suggested Cayce fall
asleep, and Cayce went into a deep trance. To their aston-
ishment, he began speaking, telling the hypnotist how his
voice could be restored permanently.

When local people heard of this, they asked him if he
could go to sleep and dictate cures for ills they had that
doctors couldn't diagnose or relieve. At first Cayce resisted,
explaining that he did not have a medical education. In
fact, Cayce's formal education was nil. But friends and relatives pleaded for his help, and he finally gave in. In a
trance, Cayce's suggestions were on the money! Often the
cures were homeopathic, often they drew on obscure medical knowledge of medicines no longer on the market. But
even doctors had to admit that patients weren't just imagining their conditions had improved—they actually had
improved medically.

A visit from Arthur Lammers, who was interested in metaphysics, gave Cayce's subsequent readings a metaphysical bent. His early readings had stressed the physical aspect of an individual's illness. But now the sleeping Cayce produced "life readings" that analyzed a person's current distress based on character and pursuits in this life and past ones.

In 1925 Cayce's readings told him to move to Virginia Beach, which would survive a coming cataclysm. There he opened a hospital and formed the Association for Research and Enlightenment to research psychic matters (today it maintains his legacy, publishing compilations of the Cayce readings in book and audio tape form). Later in the 1940s, a national magazine article popularized Cayce, and he was besieged with twenty-five thousand requests for readings. The work load took a heavy toll on Cayce's body. He suffered a stroke at the age of 67 and died as his doctors ignored Cayce's last reading–on himself.

## Reading the future

During his lifetime, Edgar Cayce won fame not only as a healer but also as a prophet of the future. Many of his life readings give hints about is coming for the human race. The Cayce readings suggest the human race is in a transition period that will lead to a "New Dispensation," starting "in those periods in 1958 to 1998." In this new cycle, "the righteous" shall inherit the earth. Cayce called on people to prepare themselves to cooperate with one another. Only then, his readings said, could the "Brotherhood of Man" arise.

Preparing the way for the New Dispensation, Cayce said, would be the following series of events:

- Crises after crisis will weaken America's social, political, and economic systems.

- A period of severe public discord, strife, and turbulence.

- A major change in the geography of the North America due to rising tides on the East Coast, and an unprecedented earthquake on the West.

Following this, the New Era the Cayce readings foresee will bring:

- world peace,

- right, justice, mercy, patience,

- rewards to the most productive and able not the competitive and selfish,

- everyone working together for the good of all in a cooperative economic system, similar to the food coops of today, and

- an international currency or "stabilization of exchange values" urgently needed to prevent global inflation, depression and chaos.

## Meditation, prayer, and the universal laws

In his readings, Cayce referred to two universal laws of human nature:

*"The entity finds itself body, mind, and soul; which answers to the Godhead—Father, Son, and Holy Ghost—in the three-dimensional world."*

*"Not in the amount of moneys, lands, holdings, houses, cattle, or gold; but in the ability to serve thy brother lies strength, security, and the perfect knowledge of God."*

EDGAR CAYCE

1. There is a Oneness that pervades all Creation. According to Cayce, there is only one force or one energy in the universe. The one force expresses itself in millions of different forms. Through meditation, we give these energies new expression.

2. Human beings are three-leveled beings composed of body, mind, and spirit. They are so closely linked that poor health on one level (mind or spirit, say) can cause problems on the others (body or spirit). To maintain their mutually beneficial relationship, all three levels must be in alignment. Cayce's readings said the Lord's Prayer could do that.

According to one Cayce reading, Jesus taught this prayer as a meditation to the disciples because it awakens the spiritual energy centers (chakras). Cayce called these locations "the seven transducers." They are located at the top of the head, the forehead, throat, heart, solar plexus, abdomen and the genitals. Meditation on the Lord's Prayer, Cayce said, attuned all these center, bringing our spirits into harmony.

Cayce's oldest son, the late Hugh Lynn Cayce, has amplified on the reading's attitude toward this prayer:

> If I had to give a person one suggestion as to how to alter or raise his consciousness, it would be to practice prayer and meditation. I don't know of anything that would mean more. I am the custodian of a little part of the Creative Energy. And I have to manage this; I have to work with it every day. In meditation and prayer I am able to allow this energy to move back towards a union with the Creative Energies of the universe. I think this is the grace and love of God. It is constantly available to me; however, I move to touch it only as I move my own consciousness back to a level that can relate to it. This is what I mean by meditation, prayer and the quietness of attunement. There is nothing in the universe, that I've ever tried, that is more effective.

## MEDITATING ON YOUR IDEAL

Cayce, a devout Christian, believed that prayer and meditation went hand in hand. For Cayce, prayer is the active, outward appeal to God. Meditation is "Listening to the divine within." A Caycean meditation seeks to attune the mind, spirit and body to its spiritual source. The following is based on information from the Cayce readings:

1. Select an optimum time and place for meditation (Cayce recommended just after waking up and before bed. At both times, we are relaxed and near the *alpha state,* when the mind is naturally most receptive to meditation.)

2. Take a few moment to breath deeply and relax, clearing your mind of distractions (see chapter 2).

3. Say a short prayer such as the Lord's Prayer or a Native American invocation.

4. Say an affirmation that expresses your highest spiritual idea. It can be anything, Cayce emphasized, as long as it reflects your highest ideal. Here are two suggestions, culled from the Cayce readings: "God moved and said, Let there be light, and there was light. Not the light of the sun, but rather that light which—through which, in which—every soul had, and has and ever had, its being." and "All souls were created in the beginning, and are finding their way back to whence they came."

5. Repeat the affirmation several times until you begin to feel its meaning within your body, mind, and spirit. Feel intuitively; go beyond mere words until you have a sense of the spirit behind the words that represent your ideal.

6. Stop repeating the affirmation. Focus on that spirit. Hold it in silence. If your mind begins to wander, repeat the affirmation as many times as it takes to get back in contact with the spirit behind the words. As you become more skilled in this Caycean meditation, you will be able to keep your attention on the feeling for fifteen to twenty minutes.

7. Conclude with a prayer for peace and healing. Or meditate on sending love to people that you're concerned about.

## THE GODDESS TRADITION

Meditating on deity or the universe envisioned as a female being, Goddess (if you will), rather than God, is at once the newest and the oldest of all contemplative traditions. For over two thousand years, the Goddess tradition languished in obscurity while the world was given over to male-centered and male-created meditative systems. But with the

*"Feminist women encounter patriarchal religious systems that elevate the masculine without including much mention of the feminine. They feel resentful when told to worship God the Father, without including his feminine counterpart, God the Mother. Hence a new movement has developed that consciously elevates the feminine principle as something divine and nourishing."*

JEAN SHINODA BOLEN
*Goddesses in Every Woman*

• • •

*"Not until I said 'Goddess' did I realize that I had never felt fully included in the fullness of my being as Woman in masculinized or neuterized imagery for divinity."*

CAROL CHRIST

rise in feminism and a search for woman-centered spiritual and meditative traditions, many women (and men) have begun to return to the six-thousand-years-old practice of centering their meditations on the Goddess.

Common to many Goddess-related spiritual paths is the notion that the Universe is a maternal entity. Catholics might pray to Mary, Egyptians to Isis, and Native Americans to the Great Mother, but all envision her as a nurturing, endlessly creating force that loves and cares for Her creation. Long before the patriarchal tribes of Abraham and the Brahmans, women and men felt the Goddess's presence to be very much a part of their lives, guiding and protecting them, the way a mother protects her brood.

Today, people are beginning to rediscover her again. There has been an explosion of interest in the Goddess with the result that Goddess retreats, workshops, and worship services, are held in almost every city, year round. There are dozens of new books on the rediscovery of the Goddess. Video documentaries explore her roots and rediscovery.

*"I found God in myself and I love her fiercely."*
Ntosake Shange

## IN THE ARMS OF THE MATERNAL UNIVERSE

Many people feel most comfortable relating to the Goddess in her guise as the Great Mother. Or as theologians would have it, "God-the-Mother." The exercise below, inspired by *Life's Companion* by Christina Baldwin, will guide you through an initial contact with the nurturing, maternal aspect of the Goddess that may prove more moving and powerful than you expect.

1. Sit comfortably, close your eyes and relax your body.

2. Notice your breath. Let your breath slowly roll into you, deeply, slowly, like soft, heavy clouds that fill you with silence. Inhale slowly, exhale slowly, thoroughly. Feel your breath as a rhythm of calm. Exhale your thoughts, inhale silence.

3. You were once a child and the child you were still resides in you. Invite this child to sit on your lap, to sit with you. Place your hand palm up. Invite this child to place its hands on your hands. Feel the child's hands in your hands, the fingers warm and trusting, nestled in your grown-up hands.

4. Be your breath. Be still. You are grown, and yet you are still a child. You are a child of the universe. Inside you, the Universal Mother resides. Invite her, your guardian/companion, to sit with you. Feel yourself placed in Her palms, the backs of your hands resting in the larger palms of this universal support. Feel, also, the child's hands resting in your palms. You are sitting in the sacred lap, as surely as the child self sits in yours. Be still.

5. Be your breath. You are filled with the source of all knowing. You are attuned to your body, and your body is attuned to the universe. This is the light that you are traveling toward. This is the light that you came from. Here, in the light, everything is all right.

6. When you are ready, follow your breath back to this room. Emerge out of the silence of your body. There is no hurry. Stretch your body. Open your eyes.

## The many faces of the Goddess

There are hundreds of thousands of goddesses from spiritual traditions worldwide and each represents a different archetype of the female. These goddesses range far beyond the simple virgin/whore, mother/lover dichotomies that serve for female deities in most patriarchal societies. They can encompass achieving of one's goals, cool-headedness, intuitiveness, preservation of the family, and much much more.

Nor do these archetypes need to be seen as stereotypes. For, together, they comprise the full range of human possibilities. Indeed, each separate goddess, as feminist Gloria Steinem says, "...arose from the fragmentation of the one Goddess, Great Goddess, the whole female human being who once lived in pre-patriarchal times—at least in religion and imagination." Perhaps today, as then, she notes, imagining this ancient wholeness is, for women, "the first step to realizing it."

> "The image of the Goddess inspires women to see ourselves as divine...our bodies as sacred, the changing phases of our lives as holy, our aggression as healthy, our anger as purifying, and our power to nurture and create—but also to limit and destroy when necessary—as the very force that sustains life. Through the Goddess, we can discover our strength, enlighten our minds, own our bodies, and celebrate our emotions. We can move beyond narrow, constricting roles and become whole.
>
> STARHAWK
> *The Spiral Dance*

# SEVEN GODDESS MEDITATIONS

The meditations below are inspired by Jean Shinoda Bolen's *Goddesses in Every Woman*. They serve two functions. First, they are ways women (and men) can envision and thus call up needed strengths and qualities within themselves. Second, as Gloria Steinem writes, "If a glimpse in the media of a female role model can have such important impact on the lives of women, how much more profound might be the activating and calling forth of an archetype within her?"

*Athena.* (Meditation: "Help me to think clearly in this situation.") Her wisdom (she is often depicted with an owl) and role as a virgin goddess symbolize the part of woman that helps her keep a cool head in any situation. Undaunted by powerful emotion, Athena is a strong source of balance and fairness.

*Hera.* (Meditation: "Help me to make a commitment and be faithful.") Stately and queen-like, Hera (hero) is the goddess of marriage and its preserver. From her springs the primal urge to be pair-bonded, the aspect of relating to the world as part of a couple, and the spiritual fulfillment of the "sacred marriage."

*Demeter.* (Meditation: "Help me to be patient and generous.") Mother, protector, nurturer, and goddess of grain, Demeter is pictured as matronly and radiantly golden. Her untiring search for her daughter, Persephone, after she was abducted by Hades, symbolizes passionate maternal love. As the personification of "mother nature," Demeter is said to have inspired early peoples to cultivate grain.

*Persephone.* (Meditation: "Help me to stay open and receptive.") Spirited away by Hades to the underworld, Persephone, Queen of the Dead, represents a woman's unconscious. The ancient world conceived the unconscious, which mediates between the spirit world/transpersonal realm and that of everyday life, as "feminine" (and more easily accessed by women). Hence, woman's traditional role as witches, oracles, seers, and fortunetellers.

*Artemis.* (Meditation: "Keep me focused on that goal in the distance.") This virgin goddess of the hunt always hits any target she aims at. She symbolizes that part of woman that clear-headedly sets goals and reaches them.

*Aphrodite.* (Meditation: "Help me to love and enjoy my body.") Goddess of passion, beauty, and creativity, Aphrodite is the fount of the passion you feel when you are in love, and the pain you feel when that love is not requited. She also represents the deep fount of passion for living that is the source of woman's creativity.

*Hestia.* (Meditation: "Help me to find peace and serenity.") Goddess of the hearth, embodiment of what makes a house a haven, Hestia is another of the virgin goddesses. She represents woman's introspective quality—observing the world dispassionately from a centered, inner hearth, that keeps her from getting swept up into life's ongoing dramas.

## Gaia

Throughout human history almost all nations and societies have viewed the Earth as a living, conscious being, a woman, and possessed of the divine powers of a goddess. They hailed her as Gaia, Great Mother, Kujum-Chantu, Mother Earth, Ishtar, Lady Bird, Magna Dea, Mary mother of God, Danu, and by thousands of other names. From before the beginning of recorded history through the dawn of the Christian era, the Earth goddess was the most frequent object of meditation all over the globe.

*"Though I do not expect that I shall ever be reborn directly as a crocus, I know that one day my atoms will inhabit a bacterium here, a diatom there, a nematode or a flagellate—even a crayfish or a sea cucumber. I will be here, in myriad forms, for as long as there are forms of life here on Earth. I have always been here, and with a certain effort of will, I can sometimes remember."*

JOHN A. LIVINGSTON
*One Cosmic Instant*

Now a scientist has proposed that our ancestors may have had things right. James E. Lovelock in his book, The Gaia Hypothesis, suggests there is reason to believe that our Earth is not the huge non-living mass of rock Westerners have thought it. Instead, he has written that "the entire range of living matter on Earth, from whales to bacteria and from oaks to algae, could be regarded as constituting a single living entity...endowed with faculties and powers far beyond those of its constituent parts."

The Gaia Hypothesis (after the Greek Earth Goddess Gaia) has been hailed as "a wedding of the traditional intuitive wisdom to contemporary scientific insight." Lovelock says that, just as a human being is a higher organism than the individual organs and cells of which its body is composed, so the Earth as a whole is a higher organism than the rocks and soil and water of which it is composed. Humans, it follows to Lovelock, must be the planet's newly developing nervous system and mind, the beginning of the Earth's self-awareness. The planet, in short, is "awakening," say the authors of *Chop Wood, Carry Water*, "to some kind of incredible consciousness, greater than anything any individual human could ever hope to know."

If so, then it is fit subject, indeed, for meditation.

Conscious or not, the Earth nourished us and nurtures us like a mother, providing the food we eat, the elements of the homes we live in, the clothes we wear, and all the comforts of civilization. That, too, is fit subject for meditation.

> "Gaia was the primal Earth mother from whom all life came, including the Sky God, Uranus, who became her husband."
> JEAN SHINODA BOLEN
> *The Goddess in Every Woman*

## GAIA MEDITATION

Below is a very special meditation on Gaia. Inspired by ideas in *As Above, So Below* by the editors of *New Age Journal*. It will give you a sense of both your own place as part of the ecosphere and of communion with Gaia, the spirit of the Earth herself. Be warned, it is a rather long meditation, and you should schedule at least half an hour for it.

1. Find a good place to meditate, preferably a spot by a window letting in sunlight and, presuming it is warm outside, air. Better yet, if weather permits, go outside and sit on the lawn with a mat or blanket. The closer you are to nature, the better. Once you have found that spot, get comfortable. Make sure you are in a position where you will be comfortable for a while.

2. Begin to breathe. Slowly, deeply, in and out, making sure that you fill your lungs completely when you inhale and squeeze all the air out when you exhale.

3. Begin by tuning in on your body. What's going on with it? What parts do you feel? What sensations? Let any stray thoughts drift away with your exhaled breath. Sense the air you inhale nourish you, the oxygen soaking into your lungs, feeding your blood.

4. Begin to contemplate the many, many subsystems within your body that, working together, comprising "you." Every system is a part of another, larger one. Every system is made up of sequentially smaller ones. Each has its own identity, yet is part of a larger whole.

5. The smallest system we know of is the kingdom of atoms. Everything is composed of them. Visualize the atoms dancing in your cells. They were once dispersed in plants, animals, rocks. Now they are part of you, dancing together to make your life.

6. Expand your awareness outward to visualize the atoms coalescing to create your cells.

7. Visualize those cells. Feel the cells as individual entities, seething with life.

8. Expand your awareness outward to visualize your cells coalescing to form organs, bone, muscle, veins, and blood.

9. Focus on your heart beating. Consider, from the atomic level on out, how many different collective endeavors go into making it work. Do the same with your lungs, your blood, your skin, your stomach, intestines, muscles, reproductive organs, even your brain inside your skull.

10. Expand your awareness outward to visualize this collective of organs coalescing to create what you know as you.

11. Expand your awareness outward to tune in on all the larger systems that surround you of which you are a part: your society, culture, lover, family, workplace, friendships, town, nation, world. Feel the cultures you are closest to as living entities, with you a part of them.

12. Expand your awareness outward to tune in on the human race, of which you are a part, blanketing the globe, swarming in its millions, giving you context.

13. Expand your awareness outward to tune in on the entire planetary ecosystem of which you are a part, animals, plants, oceans, air.

14. Expand your awareness to feel Gaia, the Earth. She is immensely large, immensely slow, immensely old. Yet, by Her own calendar, She is still quite young. Each ecosystem is an organ in Her body, each species a tissue, each individual animal or person a cell.

15. Visualize her consciousness turning to you, looking at you, wise, benign, loving, maternal.

16. Visualize Gaia surrounding you with her arms, drawing you to her body, holding you close.

17. Realize that this is the situation every day and minute of your life, and give thanks to Gaia.

18. Take a few minutes to clear your mind and breath deeply before ending the meditation.

## TRYING DIFFERENT TECHNIQUES

When done for the right reasons, it is good to experiment with different meditation techniques. On the other hand, it is not recommended that you go "meditation shopping" whenever you find a hindrance or difficulty with the technique you have chosen at this particular time.

*The breath is a good port of embarkation.*

While it is fine to try any of the techniques you find either in this book or elsewhere, jumping from technique to technique is not what meditation is about. It is recommended that you stay with the basic breath meditation technique for at least two weeks before you try another. There is no one meditation technique that's right for you.

In the beginning, meditate by observing the breath. It's a centuries-old, time-tested technique that is taught in most of the Western and Eastern traditions. The breath is a good port of embarkation. Once you are comfortable with breath observation and counting, you can try other techniques.

Most meditators discover during the course of their practice that a certain technique or collection of techniques works best for them. You may find that you have a proclivity for mantra, or Tibetan visualizations, or Insight noting. Why one of these techniques resonates more strongly for you is not as important as the fact that it does. Stay with it. It intuitively is right for you at this time.

As we said in the beginning, the objective of all meditation techniques is the same: the development of that state of awareness that allows you to live every moment of your life with the fullest possible joy. In the words of T.S. Eliot, "And the end of all our exploring will be to arrive where we started and to know the place for the first time." Don't worry what route you're on. Just keep your eyes on the road.

Again, there is nothing wrong with changing your meditation technique. Just exercise restraint. In so doing, you'll get such added benefits of consistency as those described below.

## CHAPTER RECAP

- An explosion of meditative approaches tailored to Western needs has created thousands of individual modern approaches.

- A self-observation meditation method by G. I. Gurdjieff helps us see ourselves objectively.

- Gurdjieff's student P. D. Ouspensky, like the psychiatrist Carl Jung, found meditating on the tarot cards an aid to insight.

- Visualization is meditation on a mental image.

- Visualization can provide answers to inner dilemmas and help prepare us for challenges.

- Transcendental Meditation is one of the most popular contemporary systems in the West.

- TM is mantra centered.

- Edgar Cayce used meditative sleep to tap his unconscious.

- A Cayce meditation seeks to attune the mind, spirit and body to its spiritual source.

- The emerging Goddess tradition has produced woman-centered meditations.

- Goddesses represent female archetypes that both men and women can access by meditation.

Buddha          Dharma          Sangria

# PART 3
# *The Meditative Life*

An advertising slogan for DuPont once promised "Better Living Through Chemistry." This section is about better living through meditation in action. What we are talking about is nothing short of miraculous: an improved quality of life without having to do anything special.

There are several expressions that describe the act of being present in each moment of daily activity: meditation in action, karma yoga (*karma* means action), and work-practice. We're going to use the term meditation in action, because that's exactly what it is.

Meditation in action is the cultivation of the same process you've already been developing in your sitting meditation practice: the art of opening to each moment of life with calm awareness. In meditation in action, you bring precisely the same mindful awareness to your daily activities that you bring to your sitting, koan, or walking meditation. The only difference is that you're doing something purposeful at the same time.

Meditation in action is applicable to everything you do, from getting the kids to school to asking the boss for a raise. The goal is to be totally present in the moment whether that be cooking dinner, making love, or watching your favorite television show.

Bringing mindfulness to relationships with your spouse,

significant other, loved ones, children, friends, even your pets, allows you to experience these connections in an entirely new, richer way.

You may be skeptical that his ancient practice can change our lives for the better today. After all, how can this process, which looks like doing nothing, be of any benefit in the real world? Here and now, one issue of the Sunday *New York Times* contains more information than a sixteenth-century Zen monk would have encountered in an entire lifetime.

The fact that meditation has survived for more than 2,500 years is probably the best recommendation for the fact that—whatever meditation is—it works. Even Volkswagen Beetles don't last that long.

Prior sections of this book have concentrated on one wing—insight and wisdom, which you have begun to develop through your daily meditation practice. Now it is time to direct your focus outward, to begin to devote attention to the other wing of the meditative life, lovingkindness and compassion.

# Mindfulness— Meditation in Action

# 9

The ideal of meditation practice is to be awake in every moment of your life. There is no more joyful place in the world than exactly where you are, right now. Your meditation practice should not end when you rise up from your cushion or out of your chair. Every moment of your life is a golden opportunity to be awake and practice mindfulness. It is out in the world, where we really get to apply our practice of mindfulness, lovingkindness, and compassion.

## BEING PRESENT

You may already have experienced moments of total presence, in sports, perhaps, or even in your meditation practice, when the boundary between yourself and the feeling or thinking process has dissolved or disappeared—that is, where you are not a runner, but are running. Or where you are not the thinker, but are thinking. This state has been described at various times as:

- peak experience,
- being in the zone,
- going with the flow, or
- enlightenment.

• *Meditation in daily life:*

*working*

*recreation*

*driving*

*athletics*

*sleep*

221

There is no new or special technique you need to learn to be mindful in your daily life. In fact, you already began working on being mindful in daily life when you started meditating. This does not mean that you should shut your eyes and count your breath while driving, or sit in half-lotus in the middle of the annual sales meeting. It does mean that the awareness you're developing in your daily meditation practice naturally expands to encompass your day.

When you learned walking meditation, the objects of meditation were the phenomena associated with walking— the lifting, extending, and setting down of your feet.

### Remember

Insight meditation teacher Joseph Goldstein tells his retreat students that the problem of being mindful in the swirl of daily activity is not actually paying attention, but remembering to pay attention.

In meditation in action, the object of meditation will be the different phenomena that arise in the course of daily life. You'll attempt to be as present as possible in each moment of constantly shifting panorama of thought, feeling, and emotion.

There is no better or happier way to go through a day than to be totally present with exactly what is happening in it.

Consider your meditation practice as a great gift. The tools that enable you to live a mindful life also empower you to live it fully and gracefully. There are many benefits that are the natural outgrowth of mindfulness:

- clearer thinking in normal and stress situations,

- deeper enjoyment of sex, work, and play,

- increased patience with loved ones, children, colleagues,

- less aversion to and more acceptance of a boring or distasteful activity,

- better concentration in driving, sports, or work,

- healthier eating habits, and

- weight reduction.

Even more than in daily routine, meditation in action is of immeasurable help in crisis and catastrophe. But don't wait for a disaster to occur before you begin to practice.

Just as a novice sailor would meet certain doom venturing into a typhoon, a novice meditator can be wiped out by a major life challenge. For this reason, it is important that you begin right now:

- Establish and keep your daily meditation practice.
- Apply the mindfulness aspect of meditation to simple daily situations.
- Gradually work up to the point where you can deal with difficult situations in a skillful and mindful manner.

## Mindful living

Meditation in action means staying in touch with everything that is going on with us on a physical, emotional, and mental level.

Our bodies are perhaps the best touchstone we have for developing mindfulness in daily life. However, we are woefully out of touch with them.

Try this:

Right at this moment, as you are reading this book, become very aware of your body. Take an inventory. You may notice that you're hunched over a little. Maybe you're squinting because of sunlight. Get in touch with your body right now, exactly as it is. Notice what happens when you shift position. It's simple; you just need to remember.

During all your daily activities, try to be mindful of your body as you move from one task to another, one position to another, one place to another. This is ground zero for mindfulness in action—being aware of exactly what is going on right now. It's simply a matter of practice. You're going to move your left arm. Be aware of it.

*"I cannot say it strongly enough: to integrate meditation in action is the whole ground and point and purpose of meditation. The violence and stress, the challenges and distractions of modern life make this integration even more urgently necessary.... So what really matters is not just the practice of sitting but far more the state of mind you find yourself in after meditation. It is this calm and centered state of mind you should prolong through everything you do."*

SOGYAL RINPOCHE
*The Tibetan Book Of Living And Dying*

The other major area where you want to bring mindfulness to daily life is at work—in the awareness of your thoughts and feelings, especially in stressful situations.

> *"This basic effort, which paradoxically is a relaxing back into the moment, gives us the key to expanding our awareness from times of formal meditation to living mindfully in the world. Do not underestimate the power that comes to you from feeling the simple movements of your body throughout the day."*
>
> JOSEPH GOLDSTEIN
> *Insight Meditation*

For example, being undeservedly berated by your boss can induce angry thoughts, guilty feelings, and body tension. While these thoughts, emotions, and sensations may not be pleasant, if you can look at them mindfully, simply regarding them as thoughts or feelings, you will have an entirely different experience of this event, one less likely to upset you or result in your doing or saying something you'll regret.

Instead of looking at the content of those thoughts and emotions, you're observing their contour. This process defuses the emotional charge that ordinarily arises in this situation. More awareness results in less upset, less regret.

In the following pages we'll take a look at some strategies for opening to each moment of life—work, home, and play. They are by no means exclusive of one another. Consider this as the start of an entirely different, infinitely more pleasant style of life for you and your loved ones

## Mindful work

> *"Caring about our work, liking it, even loving it, seems strange when we see work only as a way to make a living. But when we see work as the way to deepen and enrich all our experience, each one of us can find this caring within our hearts, and awaken it in those around us, using every aspect of work to learn and grow."*
>
> TARTHANG TULKU
> *Skillful Means*

Though meditation and work may seem antithetical, most meditative traditions see them as complementing each other. Putting meditation into action at work can make your occupation as deeply enriching—and spiritual—as any other aspect of your life. Performed mindfully, as a meditation, even the most ordinary and routine work is transformed into a challenging opportunity to grow and ponder.

Approaching your occupation meditatively is critical, because, of all your environments, the workplace is where you probably spend the most time. Mindfulness at work can:

- lower your stress level,
- make you more productive,
- help you anticipate events before they happen,
- make a bad day better,
- make a good day even better, and
- help you connect with your colleagues.

## KARMA YOGA

In the Indian meditative tradition known as karma yoga, performing your work mindfully is considered integral to spiritual development. This is the approach taught by Maharajji, the guru of Ram Dass. "Maharajji did not generally encourage severe austerities, nor extensive meditation practice, nor complex rituals," Ram Dass explains. "Rather, he guided us to karma yoga, a way of coming to God through living life as an act of devoted service.... But Maharajji made it clear that hard work alone was not the essence of the matter. Rather, it was work carried on with remembrance of God; that is, work done with love in the presence of God's grace."

*The idea of work done, not for one's own sake, but as an act of devotion to God is...basic to many traditions.*

The idea of work done, not for one's own sake, but as an act of devotion to God is central not only to karma yoga, but is basic to many traditions. One thinks of the Puritans, Benedictines, and Quakers among Christians. Hindu, Christian, Muslim, and Native American teachers all emphasize that work should be dedicated to God and to serving others.

*"You know the story of the three brick masons. When the first man was asked what he was building, he answered gruffly, without even raising his eyes from his work, 'I'm laying bricks.' The second man replied, 'I'm building a wall.' But the third man said enthusiastically and with obvious pride, 'I'm building a cathedral.'"*

MARGARET M. STEVENS

Work without attachment to the fruits of one's labors is key to Karma yoga. As Henry David Thoreau explains in his contemplative classic, *Walden,* "The true husbandman

*"A vision without a task is but a dream,
a task without a vision is drudgery,
a vision and a task is the hope of the world."*
CHURCH INSCRIPTION
*Sussex, England*

will cease from anxiety, as the squirrels manifest no concern whether the woods will bear chestnuts this year or not, and finish his labor with every day, relinquishing all claim to the produce of his fields, and sacrificing in his mind not only his first but last fruits also."

## TAKING ON THE DAY

The following only takes a moment. Make it a part of your daily routine at work, no matter how worried, late, or harassed you feel. It will leave you refreshed, relaxed, centered. You'll find it a powerful benefit to your day.

1. Every morning, soon after arriving at work, pause for a moment.

2. Make a quick inventory of your body, using the body scan method (chapter 5).

3. Are there particular areas of tension in your neck or your arms?

4. Take a deep breath and let go of the tension.

5. Make a quick inventory of your immediate workplace concerns and priorities.

6. Take a deep breath and let go of them.

7. Take one last breath for yourself, to center yourself.

8. Let it out.

9. Now, take on the day.

## THE WORK DAY

Throughout the work day, have your awareness focused on of meetings, phone calls, and other interactions before they begin. The trick is to focus on each happening as if it is all that is important.

For instance, as you walk down the hall or get out the elevator, be aware of how you are at that present moment. Try to bring your awareness to walking, making it an object of meditation for the fifteen feet between the elevator and the reception desk. Just walk naturally. You don't have to walk in slow motion.

## The secret ingredient

*Bernard Tetesugen Glassman is abbot of the Zen Community of New York. In a book written with Rick Fields,* Instructions to the Cook, *Glassman makes cooking a metaphor for living. The Zen Community also owns and operates one of the finest bakeries in America, the Greystone Bakery, from which it derives a major portion of its funding.*

*Right livelihood is really at the heart of Zen, because of a secret ingredient that Zen Buddhists call "work-practice."*

*Zen sitting meditation or zazen is one way to practice, but not the only way. We can also meditate while we work.*

*In sitting meditation practice, we concentrate on our breath or a koan. In samu or work-practice, we concentrate on our work. If we are cutting grass, we just cut grass. If we are washing the dishes, we just wash the dishes, if we are entering data into a computer, we just enter data into a computer....*

*We use our work as a meditation practice that helps us stay in the present and aids our concentration. When we work in this way, our work actually gives us energy and peace of mind.*

Notice your body sensations. Are you tensing up, perhaps sweating a bit? Bring your awareness to your thoughts. The act of noticing what's what for you right now is restful in itself.

As you greet the receptionist, your colleagues, or your client, notice the sound of their voice. As you shake hands, be aware of the sensation of touch. Be aware that you are, for that moment, connected with another human being.

## Beauty in the ordinary

*"I also cherish the opportunity to hang clothes on a line out-doors. The fresh smell, the wet fabrics, the blowing wind, and the drying sun go together to make an experience of nature and culture that is unique and particularly pleasurable for its simplicity. Deborah Hunter, a photographer, made a study several years ago of clothes on a line tossed by the wind. There was an element in these photographs, difficult to name, that touched upon vitality, the deep pleasure of ordinary life, and unseen forces of nature, all of which can be found around the house."*

Thomas Moore
*Care of the Soul*

Do the same with phone calls, conferences, social encounters with workplace colleagues, anyone and everything.

Over a period of time you will discover you are anticipating each encounter and task with unusual accuracy, and finding the best way to flow through them all.

As your confidence grows, so will your calmness, performance, and level of satisfaction.

## MEDITATING AT MEETINGS

1. Sit comfortably, yet remain alert, with your spine erect, but not rigid.

2. Meditate on the meeting. It is your object of awareness. Open yourself fully to the experience. Focus fully on the speaker, but be equally aware of the overall significance of what is going on, and of the emotional currents in the room.

3. If you find yourself drifting off, inattentive, or bored, simply notice those feelings and bring your attention back to your object of awareness—what is going on, right now, in this meeting. If you become drowsy, sit up straighter. Open your eyes a bit wider. Notice how this action refreshes your attention.

4. If you are called upon to speak or asked a question, don't respond immediately. Pause for the length of a long breath, four seconds.

5. During that time use what you have learned from meditation be totally aware of your thoughts and body sensations. Are you nervous? Is your pulse more rapid? What is it you want to say?

6. Take a deep breath and let it all go. Then begin speaking.

7. If you find yourself in an acrimonious meeting, or you are put on the spot, pause longer. Take a deep breath, and for an instant make the breath your object of total attention. Try not to be overpowered by the words being thrown at you. Observe them simply as sounds.

Take inventory. Ask yourself if you are about to say something you may regret. This action alone will bring you back into your body and mind. Bring your attention to your breathing.

8. Now, do what you have to do. Respond, deflect, challenge, even apologize.

Whatever you do, you and the situation are now less highly charged, which means you'll be able to handle things much more effectively.

## Departure—taking back the day

Before you grab your briefcase and dash out for your commute, take a moment to sit or stand somewhere quiet in your workspace. This is, in a way, the opposite of transitioning after your daily sitting meditation; instead of taking things with you, you're going to leave them behind.

1. Sit in a comfortable posture.
2. Begin to reconnect with your breath. Notice the calming effect.
3. Get in touch with what is going on with you right at this moment in relation to work.
4. Take a deep breath and let it all go.
5. Now, continue on out the door, being mindful each moment of the journey home and each moment of the evening that follows.

## Mindful driving

Most drivers spend an inordinate amount of time thinking. Unfortunately, the thinking is about everything else but driving—thoughts about that great Chinese restaurant you're on the way to, that cute new FedEx guy, the fight you had with your son this morning.

This is mindfulness all right, but not the kind you want to have behind the wheel.

Here's a sample scenario of a typical driving situation, and how you, as a mindful driver, might handle it.

- You're driving.

- Your hands rest comfortably on the steering wheel. And you feel them there.

- You feel your foot on the accelerator.

- As the highway unfolds in front of you, moment by moment, you are alert, yet relaxed. You catch yourself thinking about a great Chinese restaurant and realize that you are not totally driving. You return to the object of attention: driving your car.

- You alertly double-check your speedometer to make sure that you didn't accelerate while thinking about that incredible Mongolian chicken dish. The needle shows fifty-five m.p.h.

## Please ring for mindfulness

*A film director in Los Angeles has placed a small bell on his dashboard. When he realizes he has lost awareness, he rings the bell to bring himself back to mindfulness—while, of course, keeping his other hand on the wheel and both eyes on the road.*

- With attention and calm, you look in your rearview mirror and see a highway patrol cruiser a quarter of a mile behind you, approaching rapidly. With total attention and awareness, you realize that you must get out of this lane quickly yet safely. You activate your right turn signal, feeling your hand on it.

- You put your hand back on the wheel. You focus attention on your rearview mirror. The motorist in the next lane is leaving room for you. You look to your right. A woman in a BMW is oblivious to what is happening, neither accelerating or decelerating to let you into the lane.

- The cruiser is almost behind you now, with siren wailing and lights flashing. It's very loud, almost disconcerting. You don't fight the siren. You allow the sound to pass through you as you maintain your attention on the car in the next lane.

- The siren rouses the daydreaming woman out of her trance. She accelerates. Now you can pull into the next lane, which you do with complete mindfulness.

- The cruiser speeds by at ninety m.p.h. You calmly check your rearview mirror, your speedometer. You continue driving. Mindfully.

The mindful driver responds to stimuli with relaxed awareness. Note that the mindful driver wasn't totally perfect. But immediately upon realizing that he or she had drifted off into thoughts of Chinese food, he or she returned to the object of meditation—driving.

### Awareness in Driving

- Keep the radio off.

- Each time you stop at a stoplight, at a stop sign, or in traffic, check your awareness level.

- Whenever you insert or remove the ignition key, stop for a moment. Feel your hand on the key. How does the metal feel? Cold? Warm? Take one or two breaths and follow your inhalation and exhalation. Now, slowly and mindfully, either start the car or remove the key.

- *Never, ever, listen to a guided meditation tape in your car while driving.*

## Mindful play

Physical activity is a great opportunity to practice mindfulness. Whether it's a ten-minute walk or a twenty-six mile marathon, whether you're a beginner or a professional basketball player, the object of awareness is, as it always is, whatever you are doing, right now.

Aerobic exercise is good for us. It is also inherently boring. Aerobic instructors and entrepreneurs incessantly labor to come up with ways to keep us from being bored to death while we get the heart-pumping exercise we need to live.

With meditation-in-action strategies you can turn your aerobic exercise session into a truly fascinating experience. And you don't need music, flashing lights, steps, or the latest gizmo. All you need to do is approach your workout with the same intention you would if you were going to sit down and meditate—calm awareness.

Remember your walking meditation technique, where the object of meditation was the phenomenon of walking? You broke it down into its components and were mindful of them, on a moment-by-moment basis. Now you're going to do the same thing with the particular aerobic exercise you are engaged in.

*The ability to exercise in a condition of heightened alertness leads to the experience of being in the zone.*

The ability to exercise in a condition of heightened alertness leads to the experience of being in the zone. This is the peak state of physical and mental balance and integration where the mind, body, and movement blend together seamlessly. Bringing the mindfulness techniques you are already working with to physical exercise can put you in the zone faster and keep you there longer.

**Mindful Sports**

Almost everyone has heard of *Zen in the Art of Archery*, by Eugene Herrigel. But peak athletic performance isn't only reserved for the world of Zen and archery. Performance in both competitive and non-competitive sports can be enhanced by applying the principles of meditation in action.

Mindfulness in sports is another place for present-moment awareness. The degree and depth of awareness are major factors in levels of performance, prowess, and personal satisfaction.

In *The Inner Game of Tennis*, W. Timothy Gallwey delves into the connection between mindfulness and tennis.

Gallwey says that mindfulness, when brought to sports, strengthens the inner game and makes better tennis players. It slows the thinking mind and brings a state of equilibrium to the mind-body connection. "In short," says Gallwey, "'getting it together' requires slowing the mind. Quieting the mind means less thinking, calculating, judging, worrying, fearing, hoping, trying, regretting, controlling, jittering, or distracting. The mind is still when it is totally here and now in perfect oneness with the action and the actor."

It also allows faster, effortless, skill development. Again, Gallwey: "No matter what a person's complaint when he has a lesson with me, I have found that the most beneficial first step is to encourage him to see and feel what he is doing—that is to increase his

## Mindfulness in golf

*You're involved in the action and vaguely aware of it…. I'd liken it to a sense of reverie—not a dreamlike state but the somehow insulated state that a great musician achieves in a great performance. He's aware of where he is and what he's doing, but his mind is on the playing of his instrument with an internal sense of rightness—it is not merely mechanical, it is not only spiritual; it is something of both, on a different plane and a more remote one.*

ARNOLD PALMER
quoted in John Winokur *Zen to Go*

awareness of what actually is.... This action unlocks a process of natural development which is as surprising as it is beautiful."

It encourages the swing to develop naturally. "As the player finally lets himself observe his racket with detachment and interest, he can feel what it is actually doing, and his swing has begun to develop a natural rhythm.... Then, when he goes out to play, he...can concentrate without thinking."

What Tim Gallwey has to teach us about tennis is applicable to any sport, whether competitive or non-competitive. Some activities such as yoga and *tai chi* are grounded in centuries of mindfulness tradition and are considered, in their own right, as much meditation as exercise. Western sports such as tennis and golf also provide the ideal environment for the practice of mindfulness in action.

## Mindful sleeping

For some people, the meditative day isn't over, even when we sleep. Tibetan Buddhism has a tradition known as dream yoga or lucid dreaming. This practice, when mastered, allows the meditator to be awake in their dreams. It also gives dreamers the power to change dreams as they unfold. Masters taught it as a cure for nightmares, a reliever of daytime fears, a vehicle for emotional and physical healing, and a method of seeking advice from the gods and other realms.

You don't have to be a yogi to take advantage of lucid dreaming. Oneironauts (who are to sleep as astronauts are to space) at California's Stanford University Sleep Research Center turned lucid dreaming into something of a science. There, dream researcher Steven LaBerge Ph.D. taught his oneironauts to wake up to the fact that they were dreaming while still remaining asleep and within the dream! Then, in a feat that rivals the first manned landing on the moon, LaBerge's oneironauts (of which he himself was one) sent signals, via a complex series of eye and body movements, from within their dream worlds to observers in the Stanford sleep lab.

*For some people, the meditative day isn't over, even when we sleep.*

Additional research by University of Northern Iowa psychologist Jayne Gackenbach seems to support some of the ancients' claims. Gackenbach found lucid dreamers are less neurotic, less depressed, and have higher self-esteem and better emotional balance than other dreamers.

Anyone can reap these rewards, says LaBerge. We've all had lucid dreams at some time. Suddenly, in the midst of a dream, some element strikes us as incongruous, and we suddenly become aware we are dreaming.

## MINDFUL DREAMING

Through his researches, LaBerge developed a simple process that helped tens of thousands of people master lucid dreaming. LaBerge believes there are only two essential requirements for learning lucid dreaming—motivation and good dream recall.

LaBerge's four-step method for inducing lucid dreams:

1. When you wake spontaneously from a dream, go over all the details until you have them fully fixed in mind.

2. Before you go back to sleep, tell yourself firmly several times: "Next time I'm dreaming I'll recognize I'm dreaming."

3. Visualize yourself inside the dream you just recalled—aware that you are dreaming.

4. Repeat steps two and three until the desire to remember your dream is firmly planted in your mind—or you fall asleep.

With a little practice, you should find yourself awake and lucid in your dreams. With patience and practice you will be able to converse with those you meet there, control the course of dreams, even change to a different dream.

The yogis even seem to be right abut lucid dreaming's effectiveness as a nostrum for nightmares. If you find yourself faced with a frightening situation in a lucid dream, LaBerge reports, simply face down the image that's threatening you. When that happens, the frightening image will vanish quickly and rarely return.

## CHAPTER RECAP

- Meditation in action is the practice of being totally mindful and in the moment during each activity throughout the day.

- Bringing your practice to work can lower stress, make you more productive, help you connect better with your colleagues, and even make a bad day better.

- Pausing to mediate for a moment at the beginning and end of each work day can clear and center your mind for the next part of your day.

- Mindful driving results in being able to respond with relaxed awareness to situations developing around you.

- In sports, a meditative attitude clears the mind and brings a state of equilibrium to the mind-body connection, allows seeing and feeling, increases awareness of what is, and allows the skills to develop naturally and intuitively.

- Even in sleep, it is possible to remain mindful via the technique of dream yoga, known scientifically as lucid dreaming.

# Meditative Home 10

monastery is designed to serve as a giant input mechanism, providing a monk or novice with instant feedback to every action and intention. Although it may seem just the opposite, your home—even with the TV blaring, phone ringing, and doorbell buzzing—is your monastery, the place where your intentions and actions can also elicit instant feedback. Bringing mindfulness home can be an illuminating experience, like replacing a twenty-five watt bulb with a floodlamp.

This section covers strategies for converting ordinary household situations into opportunities for meditation in action which then teachers call mindfulness.

## MINDFUL CHORES

Household duties take on a wonderful new perspective when approached through mindfulness. The ordinary chores of washing dishes, peeling vegetables, even taking out the trash can do double duty as an effective meditation experience. When done mindfully, the act of scrubbing a sink takes on the same beauty as watching the sunset.

Here are some meditation in action strategies to help you transform mundane chores into something more:

*• Mindfulness in:*

*chores*

*eating*

*relating to family*

*lovemaking*

237

- Do one thing at a time.

- Make each move count. If you find yourself doing something twice, you were not mindful the first time.

- Be aware when your mind begins to wander from what you are doing. Gently bring it back.

- Whatever you are doing, just do it. If you wash dishes, just wash dishes. Feel the water as it hits your hands. Notice how your arm moves as you wipe a sponge across a dish. Notice how the dish looks before and after you have cleaned it. Watch the thought, "Sometimes I wish I had a dishwasher" arise and pass.

- Convert taking out the trash into walking meditation.

- When cleaning, remember what Bernard Glassman says: "The cleaning process itself changes the cook as well as the surroundings and the people who come into those surroundings—whether we're in a Zen meditation hall, a living room, a kitchen, or an office."

- Arrange your grocery cart as if it were a Zen rock garden. At the checkout stand, mindfully take each item out of your cart and place it on the conveyor. Help bag your own groceries, mindfully separating cans, bottles, and chemical items from food.

## *Meditating seven days a week*

- *Monday. Meditate on work.*
- *Tuesday. Meditate on your home.*
- *Wednesday. Meditate on your partner or spouse.*
- *Thursday. Meditate on your children or parents.*
- *Friday. Meditate on your speech.*
- *Saturday. Meditate on play.*
- *Sunday. Meditate on spiritual matters.*

*(Change places with your own Sabbath if it falls on a different day.)*

## *Samu*

Manual labor is referred to as samu in Japanese Zen traditions. Samu is a very important aspect of the meditational life of Zen monks. Each day in a monastery, hours are devoted to chores like sweeping, dusting, polishing the floor, scrubbing the toilets, weeding and gardening--and to meditating on each chore as it is done.

Samu gives meditators a unique opportunity to quiet, deepen, and bring the mind to one-pointedness through activity, thereby invigorating the body and energizing one's mind. Meditating while working makes clear the most fundamental of Zen principles, that meditation is not merely a matter of learning to focus and concentrate your mind during sitting meditation (zazen), but instead to bring that state into even the smallest acts of our daily life.

> "Since the time when Hyaku'o first instituted it, more than a thousand years ago, manual labor has been an essential ingredient of Zen discipline. It is recorded of Hyaku'o that one day his monks, feeling he had grown too feeble to work, hid his gardening tools. When they refused to heed his entreaties to return them, he stopped eating, saying, 'No work, no eating.'"
>
> ROSHI PHILIP KAPLEAU
> *The Three Pillars of Zen*

*Meditating while working makes clear the most fundamental of Zen principles.*

"By undertaking each task in this spirit," Roshi Philip Kapleau says, "eventually we are enabled to grasp the truth that every act is an expression of the Buddha-mind. Once this is directly and unmistakably experienced, no labor can be beneath one's dignity. On the contrary, all work, no matter how menial, is ennobling because it is seen as the expression of the immaculate Buddha-nature. This is true enlightenment, and enlightenment in Zen is never for oneself alone but for the sake of all."

## MINDFUL EATING

In this day and age, food seems to be consumed more while standing or running, rather than in the traditional sitting position. Although we must respond to the exigencies of daily life, the process of nourishing our body is one that should be given proper attention. Mindful eating can have a positive effect on all aspects of life, resulting in increased energy, more stable blood sugar level, and less physiological wear and tear on the digestive organs.

Jon Kabat-Zinn, in *Full Catastrophe Living*, devotes an

entire chapter to what he calls "food stress." He says that bringing mindfulness to eating can help people make and maintain positive dietary changes: "Perhaps the best place to begin [a diet] is not by trying to make any changes at all but simply by paying close attention to exactly what you are eating and how it affects you."

When people begin to eat mindfully, they are amazed and shocked, not by their food selection, but the speed at which they eat and the impact it has on their digestive and nervous systems.

Bernard Glassman, of the Zen Community of New York, in *Instructions to the Cook*, says that we should eat,

*"Whenever possible, avoid eating in a hurry. Even at home, don't gobble up your food. Eating is an act of of holiness. It requires full presence of mind."*
RABBI NACHMAN OF BRESLOV
*The Empty Chair*

...in a way that expresses our appreciation of our food and all the effort that went into making it.... And we need to pay attention to what we are eating, as well as to the people sharing our meal.... Some people recommend chewing rice fifty times before swallowing it. That might be going a little too far, but at least we should chew our food well so that we can savor the six flavors: the bitter, sour, sweet, salty, mild, and hot.

*Mindfulness in action makes your meals an opportunity to reconnect with yourself and the people you are sharing your meal with.*

Mindfulness in action makes your meals an opportunity to reconnect with yourself and the people you are sharing your meal with.

The following eating meditation is inspired by the one Shinzen Young gives to students during meals at meditation retreats. It is adapted for you to use at home. Try it alone, or try it with your family.

During all phases of your meal, remain mindful, in the present moment. The object of meditation here is the taste, smell, and body sensations of food.

David Letterman once said that the most important meal of the day is the midnight snack. The world of snacking, noshing, or grazing is also an ideal opportunity to deepen your mindfulness practice, since the popping of a beer can may unconsciously trigger a Pavlovian response compelling you to reach for a Dorito.

## MINDFUL EATING

1. Sit quietly, with spine upright. Notice the way the body feels, the sensation of the body as it sits in its seat. Note the anticipation in your mind of the good meal to come.

2. Slowly begin to put food on your plate. Pay close attention to the color of the food and the size of the portion you are taking.

3. Set your plate in front of you, and for the next minute, observe as minutely as possible the food you have mindfully chosen. Notice the colors and the smells— perhaps there is smoke rising from a hot baked potato. Take a good look at your food.

4. Slowly begin to eat. As you place your fork into a particular food, notice the amount you are taking. Does food fall off the fork? Is this perhaps too much for a mindful mouthful? Pay attention. As you begin to eat, notice the texture and taste of your food. Each time you take a bite, note the taste sensations. If the taste is pleasant, there will be a kind of ripple effect in the body, like a pebble tossed into a pond. See if you can detect a spreading effect as this ripple spreads through your body.

5. Eat slowly and mindfully. If the food you are eating is tasty, there may be a tendency to gobble, to be impatient to consume as much as possible. Notice this. Notice your thoughts. They may be something like, "Wow! I love this." You may in fact be so carried away with thoughts of delight that you are not actually tasting your food at the moment. You also may be impatient to eat, annoyed at this slow process. Notice this "drivenness" to consume in your mind and body.

6. Eat slowly, mindfully. As you eat, try to keep your spine straight while simultaneously relaxing, much as you do in formal meditation practice. Rather than looking at this process as merely an "eating meditation," regard it as an extension of your overall meditation practice. If you become distracted by noises, sensations, inner thoughts, outward sights and sounds, gently return your attention to the process of eating.

7. Occasionally pause, put down your utensil, fold your hands comfortably, and close your eyes gently.

8. You may find that a rhythm develops as you eat. You are aware of your arm moving as you reach and bring food to your mouth, then the explosion of flavor and texture on your tongue or other parts of your mouth, followed by the "ripple effect" of pleasure throughout your body.

9. When you have finished eating, sit for several minutes and allow the pleasant feelings of physical satisfaction to permeate your awareness. If for some reason you have unpleasant sensations, mindfully note where they are coming from. Do you feel guilty that you did not eat food that was healthy? Or are there physical sensations of bloating or gas that indicate you have eaten too much or too quickly, swallowing excessive air? Perhaps there are both.

10. Keep your attitude of mindfulness as you rise from the table.

Here's one strategy for developing increased awareness and mindfulness about what you are munching and why:

- For one day, in between meals, try to notice the moment just before you reach for that snack. That is the moment, just before you reach for that food, when your mind has already formed the intention to eat a Pringles™ chip or Hershey™ bar. Don't look for any loud bells and whistles signalling the command, "Give me that Pepperidge Farm™ bag."

- The "just before" moment is very subtle. Don't be upset if you can't find it the first time. When you do spot it, flood it with your entire awareness. What is it? Where does it come from? Where is it going?

- Even noticing that moment once will enable you to be much more aware. If you still want that snack, fine. Have it. Enjoy it mindfully. And if you realize you don't want it, put it down mindfully.

## WATCHING YOUR WORDS

Unskillful communication is a leading cause of family tension and problems. Meditation in action means being as highly aware of your words and intentions as you can. Here's a common example: Your child or spouse does something you think is very inconsiderate. Before you know what you're doing, you've laced into him, or spoken sharply to her. Then you find out that the motive for the inconsiderate action was to comply with something you said! Nobody's to blame. It's just bad communication on your part.

If there's anyplace you should make a total commitment to meditation in action, it is in your communication to loved ones. Your every utterance, every statement, is heard more closely, interpreted more quickly, and acted on more directly than in any other area of your life. It is crucial that your words clearly and unequivocally express what you mean.

## Letting the water clear

*"So long as our words have the slightest ego attachment, they are dishonest. True words come when we understand what it is to know we're angry, to know we're fearful. And to wait. The ancient words say, 'Do you have the patience to wait until the mind settles and the water is clear?...' Can we be quiet for a moment, until the right words arise by themselves—honest words that don't hurt others?"*

CHARLOTTE JOKO BECK
*Nothing Special*

Mindful communication means not only being as clear as possible, but as compassionate as possible. Both of these qualities contain within them the tenet of non-harming, which means that we will not engage in any act that causes harm to ourselves or others.

There is an old expression that goes something like, "Do not open mouth before brain is in gear." Many times we find ourselves saying things, particularly to people close to us, that we regret even before they have left our lips. Unfortunately, once they are out there, they are out there.

Next time you find yourself in a situation at home in which you are about to lose it, be aware of the accompanying body sensations—the heat and flush of anger, maybe a knot in the stomach. Ask yourself if what you are about to say will be harmful. If your answer is yes, don't say it. This application of meditation in action ensures that your brain is in gear and nobody gets hurt.

## *MINDING YOUR WORDS*

The best way to be mindful of your words is to stay calm. The following exercise will help you do exactly that. It is inspired by an exercise by Linda DeVillers, Ph.D.

Use it to calm yourself down anytime something you hear upsets you. Remember, staying calm and paying attention are key to resolving differences and misunderstandings.

1. During discussions of charged or touchy issues, be mindful of the words you are using for signs of defensiveness, argumentiveness, and the urge to get away.

2. Call for a time-out whenever you sense your pulse or heartbeat is increasing.

3. During a time-out, take slow, deep breaths and do whatever else helps you calm down—whether it's a hot shower, listening to soothing music, or a walk around the block. (Alcohol is not recommended here.)

4. Replace thoughts that reinforce distress and physiologic arousal, such as, "Why is s/he doing this to me?" or, "Things will never get better," with distress-reducing thoughts such as, "Somehow, we'll figure this out."

5. Don't resume the discussion until at least twenty minutes have passed. And be mindful of your words when you do. (If you're like most people, you'll think you've calmed down before you actually have. It typically takes twenty minutes or so for your body to return to normal and your pulse and heart rate are the surest gauge.)

## *MINDFULNESS AND CHILDREN*

More than anything else in the home, you should be mindful of your children. Their world is unique, valuable, fragile, and easily injured or destroyed. They can be draining, annoying, infuriating. Yet they are also your greatest treasure.

Meditation centered on your children can be one way of reconnecting with your love for them and their importance to you. If you have children, devote an upcoming session to each. Let whatever associations and memories arise, good and bad, come to mind. You may find one session is not enough for you to contemplate all the thoughts and images meditating on a child stirs up.

## The meditative child

Parents should invite their children to share their meditative experiences—if the child wants to, says Frances Vaughan. You will be doing both of you a favor, this transpersonal psychologist insists. Not only will you be able to share an important part of your life with them, but you may well be helping to validate your child's inner realm at the same time.

> "The world of the preschool child is analogous to that of the mystic—alive, and without the concept of space and time as we know it.... There is enough overlap so that our children can help us enter into 'beginner's mind'—that state before defenses, concepts, and conditioning insulate us from experiencing directly. What we can do for their spiritual life in the first five years is to allow their joyfulness to inspire us, and encourage them to continue to expand their love and wonder even as they enter the age of reason."
>
> ANNETTE HOLLANDER
> *How to Help Your Child Have a Spiritual Life*

• • •

> "A child's world is fresh and new and beautiful, full of wonder and excitement. It is our misfortune that for most of us that clear-eyed vision, that true instinct for what is beautiful and awe-inspiring, is dimmed and even lost before we reach adulthood."
>
> RACHEL CARSON

"Many adults," Vaughan writes in *Awakening Intuition*, "have said that they felt they were more intuitive as children, and that they learned to keep their intuitive perceptions to themselves after encountering skepticism or ridicule from adults." After receiving rejection, discouragement, and ridicule, "We tend to keep silent about these things, not only because we are afraid others will think us crazy—we ourselves wonder if we are crazy. We have internalized society's judgment."

Meditating with a child, being receptive to what they may say about their inner worlds, is one way to encourage this side of them. Though children, with all their fidgets and energy, might not seem likely candidates for mediation, "children are natural contemplatives" according to Theresa Schoning, a family therapist who teaches Christian meditation to children. "What continues to overwhelm me as I prepare children for meditation and contemplation," writes Schoning, in *Our Treasured Heritage*, "is the undeniable fact that many of them are already familiar with the contemplative."

*In the East, children are taught to meditate as soon as they can sit upright.*

In the East, children are taught to meditate as soon as they can sit upright (one or two years old). In *How to Help Your Child Have a Spiritual Life*, Soto Zen Buddhist abbess Rev. Roshi Jiyu-Kennett describes this process. The family sits quietly in front of the family shrine. The child is allowed to do what it will. Typically, a child will either sit in imitation of its family for a while or roll about on the floor. Those meditating, however, take no notice. "The parents," Kennett writes, "thus express their knowledge of the child's latent understanding and do not treat it like less than themselves." Usually, after a while, the child will again try to sit still like the rest of the family. "Thus," Kennett concludes, "if the parents meditate, the child will meditate too."

## INTIMATE RELATIONSHIPS AS A SPIRITUAL PATH

That your intimate relationship with spouse, partner or lover should be an object of mindfulness and the center of your meditations seems obvious. Seen correctly, say Harrison and Olivia Hoblitzelle, therapists and meditators, your relationship with your loved one is a spiritual path. It is usually a spiritual connection that brings us together initially, of which the sexual act was only an expression of our need to be close to each other and merge our individual beings in something larger and more powerful. Of course, it's easy to lose sight of the spiritual side of a domestic partnership, with all the worries and cares of workaday living together. That's one reason so many meditative and religious traditions emphasize the spiritual side of sex. Next time you meditate, let your loved one—or your relationship--be the object of meditation for the session.

> *"Traditional cultures, which do not recognize our modern separation between sacred and profane, have always considered sexuality as an aspect of the great mystery of existence. I believe that these cultures contain many important clues for us. Traditional societies—from the Stone Age to our own era—have integrated sexuality into their religious-spiritual worldviews.*
>
> *"Men and women once embarked with unshakable faith on the great adventure of the spirit, risking everything for a glimpse of the eternal reality beyond appearances. Today, adventurers of the spirit who boldly scale the mountain of self-discipline and self-transcendence are as good as extinct. We have too limited a view of our humanness; hence we also have too limited a view of our own sexuality.*
>
> *"Yet we cannot live fully as sexual-erotic beings without first recovering our spiritual depth. Our sexuality can help us get in touch again with that depth; it can serve as a gateway to the spiritual dimension."*
>
> GEORGE FEUERSTEIN
> *Sacred Sexuality*

## The spiritual in your relationship

The Hoblitzelles found six key attitudes that help us focus on and nurture the spiritual side of intimate relationships.

1. Acknowledge that you have a sense of karmic destiny. It's important that people accept that they are together for a purpose that goes beyond personal satisfactions. They are together to be teachers to each other and to recognize the divinity in one another.

2. Respect the divine longing in one another. Understand the greater meaning of life beyond our limited sense of ourselves.

3. Accept the relationship as a central part of your spiritual path. In India they speak of the *sadhana* or "practice" of relationship as being "hot like a chili pepper."

Don't expect it to be easy.

4. Look at difficulties as a training. Relationships are a perfect learning experience to develop mindfulness and understanding of where we are caught in old models, attachments and identifications.

5. Have faith in the process of growth and change in your partner as well as yourself. You can specifically help your partner by providing support during difficult periods, giving space for developing a spiritual practice even though it may be different from your own, and creating a balance of time alone and time together—of solitude and society.

6. Keep before you the vision of your partner's true self, especially when it's lost to view. And also keep the faith that believing in your partner's true self will cause it to manifest.

## Mindfulness in the bedroom

If you think of your home as your monastery, then your bedroom is the inner sanctum. Making love is a perfect time for mindfulness in both yourself and your partner. There are many guides and manuals on sexual practices, techniques, and other ways to improve your love life. But the simple practice of being awake, alert, and in touch in your bedroom may be worth more than all the sex advice contained in *Cosmopolitan* and *Playboy* combined.

Once again, the simple, overall idea is to bring the fundamental technique of mindfulness to making love. Your object of meditation is simply the different states of body and mind that arise, for both you and your partner, during that experience. It needn't be mechanical or forced.

As the act of lovemaking unfolds, bring total attention and awareness to each moment. Let the process unfold simply and naturally.

*As the act of lovemaking unfolds, bring total attention and awareness to each moment.*

*"Sexual union is an auspicious Yoga which, through involving enjoyment of all the sensual pleasures, gives release. It is a Path to Liberation."*

KAULARHASYA

## Mindful lovemaking

Meditation and lovemaking can make a powerful spiritual combination.

In *The Art Of Sexual Ecstasy,* Margo Anand, who teaches tantric meditation, tells of her own discovery of the spiritual power of mindful sex at the age of eighteen. At the time, she was a beginning student of yoga. Anand says she found sex wildly fulfilling, but began to wonder how its energy and excitement related to serenity of yoga. Neither she or her lover had heard of tantra, said to result in higher states of consciousness, spiritual merging of lovers, and profound sexual ecstasy. Entirely by chance they stumbled on the tantric secret of union through sexual stimulation without orgasmic release.

One evening Anand and her lover were making love in their usual energetic way, when she asked him to slow down and try something new. The couple stopped and simply relaxed, with her lover still inside her. Anand felt excited because, "I had initiated something new, removing his responsibility for making something happen. There was a subtle switch of roles, and I felt him shift into a more feminine, receptive attitude." They remained like that for many minutes, relaxed but at the same time aware of excitement of sexual arousal in their bodies. Soon both became aware of a warm, glowing energy suffusing their whole pelvic area.

### Lovemaking

*Alan Watts defined "contemplative sex" as a way of lovemaking that transforms physical lust into gentleness and true satisfaction:*

*The secret of goalless lovemaking is actually quite simple and natural. As excitement builds, we usually increase our movements to increase tension and force release. But in contemplative sex, you simply relax. You slow down, and breathe deeply and slowly. If your eyes are closed, open them, open your mind and senses too. Notice your breathing, and the radiance of your partner.*

When they felt arousal began to fade, the couple returned to making love energetically. Then, just before the peak of orgasm, they stopped again, relaxed, and became still once more. "We repeated this pattern several times," she writes, "and then something totally unexpected happened. Suddenly we both seemed to be floating in an unbounded space filled with warmth and light.

The boundaries between our bodies dissolved and, along with them, the distinctions between man and woman. We were one. The experience became timeless, and we seemed to remain like this forever. There was no need to have an orgasm. There was no need even to 'make love.' There was nothing to do, nothing to achieve. We were in ecstasy.

## *Maithuna*

Anand's account is very similar to those reported by practitioners of the tantric sexual meditative technique known as *maithuna*. The essence of tantric meditation is use of the senses to transcend sense consciousness and achieve *samadhi*, a state of mystical oneness with god or the divine or the universe. In maithuna, controlled, ritual, sexual intercourse is used to arouse kundalini and channel it to the higher spiritual energy centers (chakras) of both partners, bringing them together in total spiritual union. However, though it involves sexual practices, maithuna, as Omar Garrison says in *Tantra: The Yoga of Sex* is not about intensifying sex ecstasy, as many Westerners seem to think—though that is often a by-product—but a path to spiritual mastery and union with your partner.

"During maithuna itself, the yogi carries out carefully delineated ritual actions—including exactly where and how to touch his partner's body," Garrison writes. "In maithuna, the male is passive, the female active; since the arousal of energy rather than climax is the goal, there is little movement." While physically joined, the lovers meditate on mantras, like "Om, thou goddess resplendent...into the fire of the self, using the mind as a sacrificial ladle, I, who am engaged in harnessing the sense organs, offer this oblation." Key to maithuna is the refraining of both partners, especially the male, from full orgasm for long periods, paving the way for the detachment of samadhi, which "converts the energy of desires into higher forms."

> "In this technique it is common for the individual to experience as many as a dozen or twenty peaks of response,...deliberately avoiding actual orgasm. Persons who practice such techniques commonly insist that they experience orgasm at each and every peak, even though each is held to something below full response and...ejaculation is avoided."
>
> ALFRED KINSEY, PH.D.

## *Beyond sex*

Mindful lovemaking, the art of combining meditation with sex, is said to have many benefits.

For men it is said to:

- ameliorate erectile and ejaculatory problems,

- give greater control of the orgasmic response,

- enhance staying power, and

- create more intense orgasms.

Women report that they:

- become aroused more easily,

- experience arousal in their whole bodies,
  not just the genital area, and

- experience orgasm more frequently.

Both sexes also experience:

- transcendence of what in religion is known as lust,

- awareness is catapulted into the level of ultimate reality,

- genuine spiritual breakthroughs, and

- true intimacy and spiritual union, dissolution of the barriers
  separating them as individuals.

## *MINDFUL LOVEMAKING*

The following is a meditation on lovemaking inspired by the work of Linda DeVillers. You can do it with or without your partner's involvement. Like all meditation, this exercise is all about you—not the other person. It shows you how to become mindful of your partner as a sacred being.

1. Before you begin with your partner, take a moment out. Recall the exciting feeling of him or her being an almost divine figure that you felt when the two of you first became lovers.

2. Meditate on the reality of your partner as an instrument of divine love. After all, the universe/God/Goddess/Allah sent your lover to you, didn't it/he/she/they?

3. Let your partner's connection with the divine shine brighter and brighter, until you feel such awe and reverence and desire to serve that you want to fall down on your knees before them. Think of how fortunate you are to be allowed to make love to a messenger from above.

4. Continue to meditate on this aspect of your lover as you make love. Use what you've learned to surmount distraction. Look, talk, touch, treat and serve them at every moment the way you would a god or goddess or a representative of the divine in your life.

5. Focus on your lover's body as if each square inch of skin and every physical and emotional response were your object of meditation. Lavish it with the attention it deserves. When you are serving the divine, time doesn't matter.

6. Afterward, look at your partner's divine aspect again. Allow yourself to bathe in the glow of having been blessed by being allowed to serve such a wonderful being.

# CHAPTER RECAP

- Our home is our monastery, a place where meditation will benefit every aspect of our lives.

- When done mindfully, any chore around your home, from mowing the lawn to scrubbing a sink is an opportunity for spiritual development.

- The best way to eat healthy is simply to be mindful of what you are eating and how it affects you.

- Meditation is not only about being as mindful as possible, it's about being as compassionate as possible.

- If words start to get tense between you and your partner or kids, take a meditation break, and when you return, be mindful of what you say.

- Meditating on and with your children is a good way to get back in touch with their significance to you, and to support their own inner experiences.

- Meditation on and with your lover can reconnect with the spiritual aspect of your relationship, which is what originally brought you together.

- Lovemaking is also part of the spiritual path.

- Certain tantric meditative approaches to sex can produce profound ecstasy and a sense of mutual oneness with each other—and with God.

# From Pain to Ecstasy

# 11

It has been said that the purpose of life is to be happy. This is a totally legitimate goal. You deserve to be happy. In order to achieve outer peace and happiness, you must first achieve inner peace and happiness. Meditation offers you a way to happiness, enabling you to transform your life and develop the art of opening to each moment of life with calm awareness.

## HAPPINESS AS A GOAL

Think of meditation and you think of fifty monks with shaved heads, sitting silently in the most uncomfortable positions imaginable in the most remote place in the world. They sit in silence, never moving or speaking. It appears painful, purposeless, and boring. And, by the looks on their faces, they aren't very happy. In fact, the monks look totally unhappy.

But looks can be deceiving. The practice of meditation springs from our fundamental desire to be happy in our world. The Buddha said, "I teach only one thing. Suffering and the end of suffering."

### Dissolving barriers to happiness

Yet, much as we desire happiness, few things prove more elusive. Between us and happiness are two obstacles that

- Overcoming barriers to happiness

- Distinguishing between pain and suffering

- Relieving pain and stress

- A new way of experiencing happiness

255

*Often we experience happiness in the midst of suffering, and pain in the midst of joy.*

hold it at bay. These are stress and pain. No one can be happy when they are stressed out or suffering. Or can they? Both seem the very antithesis of happiness.

Experienced meditators might point out that often we experience happiness in the midst of suffering, and pain in the midst of joy. Meditation can make the apparent separation between them disappear, so that we can claim the happiness that we deserve, even in the most difficult circumstances.

But meditation can also alleviate stress and pain themselves so that there are no hindrances between us and happiness. By relaxing and toning the body, meditation releases chemicals that heal us physically and return us to optimum mental well-being. As psychobiology researcher Earnest Rossi, Ph.D. notes, "Meditation, mindfulness...and many rituals of shamanism, spiritualism, and prayer all involve tuning into a natural process of healing."

## REDUCING STRESS

Daniel Goleman, the author of the best-selling book *Emotional Intelligence*, was among the pioneers who did research on meditation as a stress reduction tool. In *The Meditative Mind*, Goleman comments on a 1984 report by the National Institute of Health (NIH). The report on mild hypertension recommended meditation in conjunction with diet rather than prescription drugs in early treatment.

Goleman also recounts that his own research revealed that, "meditation lowered anxiety levels and sped the meditator's recovery from stress arousal."

In earlier work with meditation and heart disease conducted at Harvard University by Dr. Herbert Benson, author of *The Relaxation Response* and *Beyond the Relaxation Response*, results showed that meditators' heart rates responded differently from those of non-meditators upon administration of *norephinephrine*, a stress-reaction induced hormone. Instead of increases in blood pressure, as might be expected, meditators actually experienced pressure decreases, similar to those that occur with the administration of beta-blocking drugs.

In recent years, some of the most thorough and exciting results concerning meditation and stress have come from the Stress Reduction Clinic at the University of Massachusetts Medical School. The clinic's founder/director, Dr. Jon Kabat-Zinn, has had remarkable results with meditation and stress and pain reduction.

Meditation has psychological as well as physiological benefits. It is used by many psychotherapists in conjunction with conventional treatment to lower anxiety and stress levels.

*Meditation has psychological as well as physiological benefits.*

Meditation can be an effective tool in helping patients open up to emotions and feelings as they arise during psychotherapy. Patients learn to defuse the oftimes overwhelming emotional charges that appear with the uncovering of repressed feelings.

Rather than being tossed and hurled by their thoughts, feelings, and emotions, like mariners in a typhoon, meditators learn how to position themselves securely. Calm and alert, they watch these thoughts and feelings pass, like clouds in the sky, without origin or destination. The lowering of identification with what the mind presents allows the patient naturally and gradually to desensitize himself or herself to problem states.

Dr. Mark Epstein, a Harvard-trained psychoanalyst in New York City and a meditator, writes about psychotherapy from a Buddhist perspective in *Thoughts Without a Thinker*. In a chapter entitled "The Psychodynamics of Meditation," Dr. Epstein talks about the therapeutic value of meditation:

> Much of what happens in meditation is therapeutic, in that it promotes the usual therapeutic goals of integration, humility, stability, and self-awareness. Yet there is something in the scope of Buddhist meditation that reaches beyond therapy, toward a farther horizon of self-understanding that is not ordinarily accessible through psychotherapy alone.... In [meditating], one's deeply ingrained sense of self is profoundly and irrevocably transformed.

## MANAGING STRESS

The following meditation is inspired by a guided. meditation found on Shinzen Young's *Break Through Pain* audiotape course.

1. Take a moment to let the body settle. Feel the entire body. Relax and be aware of how your body feels right this moment. Feel the totality of you body as one unified field of feeling: the arms, torso, legs, head, and so forth. Be as relaxed and still as possible, even if you are in some discomfort or stress.

2. Go to the primary location of your stress, the place where you feel the stress most strongly at this moment. Begin to map the shape of that stress. It's as if you are a map-maker, charting the outline of a new territory. What does it look like? What is its shape? Is it symmetric or asymmetric? Is it round or oval? Is it three-dimensional? A sphere?

3. Bring all your awareness to the perimeter of that primary stress location. Follow it closely, as meticulously as you can. Pinpoint the level of the primary stress in your body. Is it on the surface of the skin, just below, or deep inside?

4. Take a close look at the borders of the shape. Are they distinct, blurred? Look at the intensity of the stress within its borders. Is it sharp? Dull? Does it expand and contract between both extremes? Examine the movement of the stress within the confines of its borders. Is it uniform? Or does it oscillate? Perhaps it rises and falls, expands and con-tracts. Examine the "flavor" of the shape. Is it dull, sharp, burning, aching? Does it feel muscular, organic? Continue to flood the stress with awareness.

5. Take a look at the impact of this stress on the rest of your body. Does it send out local waves? Global waves? Does it cause your body to contract in certain areas? How does it do this? Are there visible runners, or is it like an invisible signal?

6. Continue to focus on the shape of your stress. Watch for any changes, particularly subtle ones. Once you have mapped this primary area, go to any other parts of the body where you feel stress. Explore each of them in the same way. Define as clearly as possible the location, shape, size, borders, intensity, flavor, and movement of the stress. Compare its attributes with the primary site. Don't draw parallels or theories. Merely observe.

7. When you have finished mapping the local areas of stress in the body, move back, as if you were a movie camera, slowly pulling away. See your entire body. And really feel it. Take a survey of it—the limbs, the face, the chest. Feel your body as one integrated space.

8. Observe how the body is impacted by both the primary and any secondary stress locations. See how your negative thoughts and sensations distort and exaggerate the localized stress areas, making them more intense and unpleasant than they were when you were examining them by themselves. Be aware of how your beliefs and judgments contribute to the feeling that the stress cannot be handled.

9. With relaxed awareness, drop any resistance to your feelings and body sensations. Try to release thoughts as they arise. When you do this, notice any decrease or increase in stress intensity. If stress prevents you from thinking, look at it as Nature telling you that this is no time for thinking.

10. You may, by this time, have experienced some relief, some diminishing of your stress, either at its primary location or throughout your entire body. If you have not, do not become angry or agitated. Try not to pass judgments on your ability to follow these directions. just let the thoughts come and go, like clouds in the sky. They arise and pass without your doing anything.

11. Accept any stress and confusion, both in your body and mind. In this way, you are letting go of your whole suffering self. Allow your resistance to drop. You will suffer less. How close to zero can you allow it to drop?

12. Rest into the constant change. Become like the sky—vast, spacious, placid, and serene. And let time do the rest.

## REDUCING PAIN

Pain is one of the inevitable facts of life; it visits all sentient beings. A time will come in your life when you will have to face this fact.

Our immediate response to pain, both physical and emotional, is to do something about getting rid of it. Why deal with something that you can avoid? A real problem occurs when your physical or emotional pain is the kind that you can't numb, avoid, or stop.

In addition to all its other benefits, the practice of meditation provides a powerful tool for pain reduction. If you have begun to meditate, you already have the tools for dealing with physical and emotional pain.

*What you call pain is not pain, but your resistance to pain.*

*The more
we open to
the truth
of our
emotional
pain,
the less we
resist it, and
the less
suffering we
have to bear.*

This radically different theory of pain control, is based on the concept that pain reduction can be achieved, not in escaping *from* pain, but in escaping *into* it.

Remember that while meditation may be useful in pain management, there is no guarantee that it will relieve pain all of the time. Meditation is not a substitute for proper medical treatment. The techniques discussed in this chapter are meant to support and complement standard medical practices and protocols. If you experience the kind of pain that you feel requires medical attention, see your health care professional immediately.

## Living with pain

Pain is an unwanted part of life; it interferes with everything from your mood to your movement. The first thing most of us think about when pain arises is how to get it to stop. The less pain we experience, the happier we are. And if a couple of aspirin can do the trick, fine. If aspirin doesn't do it, we'll try anything and everything else to numb, deaden, and kill our pain: stronger analgesics, acupuncture, alcohol, potent prescription medication—even narcotics.

There is, however, one fly in the ointment—the pain you can't avoid.

The pain you can't avoid comes in a variety of guises. It may be a type of physical pain that does not respond to drugs or is of unknown origin or is of known origin but not treatable. Unavoidable pain is the kind where your doctor, after many tests, pills, procedures, and protocols, looks at you helplessly and says, "I'm sorry, but this is something you're just going to have to live with."

There have been various studies on the neurochemical effects of meditation on the body in connection with pain reduction, increased relaxation, and calmness. These states are thought to result from increased neurochemical secretions and the brain's ability to more efficiently utilize these natural "happiness" chemicals, including serotonin and dopamine.

However these effects happen, all you need concern yourself with is meditation; your body will naturally take care of the rest.

## The components of pain

To more fully understand how meditation can play a role in pain management, let us briefly examine several different aspects of physical and emotional pain in order to understand their value in the body.

Pain has several components:

### Flavor

Pain comes in various flavors, or types, including sharp, dull, and pressure; including grinding emotional ones, which include anger, fear, sadness, shame, and frustration.

### Location and Shape

Pain may stay localized or move about the body. It can also change shape.

### Intensity

The intensity of pain is the degree to which the flavor of the pain is experienced. For example, the intensity of a sunburn is low, as opposed to the high intensity of a third degree burn.

## The value of pain

Although you may not realize it, pain plays an important role in your life as both a messenger and a teacher.

Pain is the body's messenger, alerting the nervous system to the fact that some part of you needs immediate attention. Pain informs the brain that homeostasis (the body's equilibrium) has been disturbed and that immediate action is required to attend to the nature of the imbalance.

Physical or emotional pain, when closely examined, can teach an important and powerful distinction: What you call pain is not pain, but your resistance to pain.

Another word for this distinction is suffering. This dis-

*Pain plays an important role in your life as both a messenger and a teacher. Pain is the body's messenger.*

tinction is not an exercise in semantics, but a fundamental breakthrough in your ability to cope with any kind of pain you experience.

## Pain versus suffering

**Pain is inevitable, but suffering is optional.**

In human existence, pain is inevitable. No matter what your belief, philosophy, or religious affinity, you simply cannot avoid pain. But here's the good news: While pain is inevitable, suffering is optional. And therein lies the key to pain reduction.

Let's take a closer look at this critical distinction.

When pain arises, the decision as to whether or not we experience it is out of our control. But suffering, our mental response to pain, is not. A large portion of what you feel when you feel pain is not pain at all but suffering, your mental response to pain, which is characterized by resistance.

Once again, pain is inevitable, but suffering is optional. Let's say you're going to hang a picture on a wall. You raise your hammer, take aim, and...*Pow!* You hit your thumb instead of the nail! You immediately feel physical pain. On a scale of one to ten, this might be at level one.

The first emotion you probably felt after the physical pain was anger at yourself because you hit your thumb. Then you experienced a variety of emotions, judgments, and thoughts. Thus, the primary source of your pain at this moment was not your thumb, but your resistance to accepting the pain. Indeed, actual physical pain has taken a back seat to mental and emotional resistance—which equals suffering.

Now, let's return to the same situation and discover an entirely new way to deal with it, reducing the pain.

## A mindful reaction to pain

Same nail, same hammer. Same thumb. Again, level one on the pain scale.

But see how the pain is reduced when, instead of resisting it, you do just the opposite, and *open* to the pain. What happens is that you experience only the pain of your injury, not the suffering sensation that is a function of your resistance to it. With the suffering component lower, you actually feel less pain. How much less? Let's look at an interesting equation.

Shinzen Young, an Insight meditation teacher with a science background, has worked extensively applying meditation in pain management. He has developed the following simple formula that clarifies the distinction between suffering and pain:

SUFFERING = PAIN x RESISTANCE (to that pain)

What this means is that suffering, which feels the same as pain (but is not), increases and decreases in direct proportion to your resistance to pain. Thus, the less you resist pain, the less you suffer—and the less total pain you experience.

Hurting your thumb is one thing, but is our formula applicable to emotional pain? The answer is yes; the more we open to the truth of our emotional pain, the less we resist it, and the less suffering we have to bear. Meditation can be a gateway to an entirely new way of looking at and dealing with pain.

Again, meditation is the art of opening to each moment of life with calm awareness. When painful thoughts, feelings, or emotions arise, the idea is to treat them with non-critical awareness, acceptance, and equanimity. When they appear, simply label them as thought, feeling, or emotion.

The following techniques are well-suited to working with both physical and emotional pain.

> *The less you resist pain, the less you suffer—and the less total pain you experience.*

## Clinical proof

*The Stress Reduction Clinic at the University of Massachusetts Medical Center pioneers in the use of meditation for stress and pain reduction. Several studies conducted there indicate that meditation practice can result in pain reduction. Here are some of the results reported in* Full Catastrophe Living *(1990), by Jon Kabat-Zinn, director and founder of the clinic:*

- *A dramatic reduction in the average level of pain among the majority of meditators in the eight-week training program.*
- *Thirty-percent perceived their bodies as "less problematic."*
- *A thirty-percent drop in the degree to which pain interfered with daily life.*
- *Reduction in negative mood states.*

### The topography of pain

This technique is designed to help you develop clarity about the basic structure of your pain and your reaction to it. You observe the area or areas where pain is located, the shape and structure of those areas, and their impact on your entire body. As you break the experience down into its basic components, you can view your pain more objectively, so that you are not so overwhelmed and intimidated by it.

If you are suffering physical pain, go back to the Managing Stress exercise a few pages earlier and go through the same steps to localize and get an understanding of your pain.

### Pain as an object of meditation

The expansion-contraction technique (chapter 5) can be used against pain. Take as your object of meditation the phenomenon of your pain. Thus, on your in-breath, open to the contractive, fading aspects of your pain. On your out-breath, bring attention to your pain's spreading, intensifying, or expanding nature.

Just as a masseur kneads your stiff, rigid, tight muscles into soft, pliable, relaxed tissue, let the breath's outward and inward qualities perform a whole body massage, bringing release, relaxation, and warmth to the area of your pain and to your entire body and being.

## EXPANSION AND CONTRACTION

Simply repeat the stress locating steps of the Stress Management Exercise, this time focusing on pain.

Then pick up with step 1 of this exercise.

1. Let the body settle. Note how various kinds of sensations arise from within the body. Feel any overall sensation in the body.

2. Bring your awareness to your breath. Become aware of your breathing. No matter what you think of it, no matter what judgments you make, do not try to control it. Just let it be.

3. Continue settling into your breath. And, at the same time, let go of it. Allow the breath to dance its dance. No judgment, criticism, or identification with it. There is nothing you have to do.

4. Begin to attend to your areas of pain selectively. During the in-breath, confine your attention to those aspects of pain that are contractive. Ignore the expansive aspects, even if they are prominent. Let these thoughts, feelings, and perceptions of pain pull in and collapse on the in-breath. Let them contract down to an effortless nothingness. There is no pressure in the contraction, no feeling of discomfort. But rather, the simple feeling that distance is collapsing. There is a bodily sensation of letting go.

5. Bring your attention to your out-breath or exhalation. During this part of the breath cycle, again bring your attention those feelings and sensations of pain that are expansive. Let your pain expand outward to infinity, becoming weak, diffuse, diluted.

6. As the feelings and sensations and thoughts situated in and around your pain expand and contract, simply observe them. They don't have to be named, conceptualized, or held onto. Watch them intensify and ebb.

7. Let your mind and body be treated to a deep massage as the qualities of expansion and contraction knead and iron out your painful sensations, reducing them to a soft, pliable, warm mass of pure, healing, peaceful energy.

## PATIENCE

A person who appears to us to be an overnight success may in reality be a twenty-year overnight success. It's the same thing with using meditation for pain reduction.

If you have been meditating for a month and suffering from chronic pain for years, it would not be realistic to expect total alleviation right off the bat. But with persistence and discipline, you can make a dent in acute and chronic conditions and eventually manage them.

So be patient, not only with the process of meditation, but with yourself.

### Acceptance is not passivity

Do not confuse acceptance with passivity; this is particularly true when dealing with pain. The meditation techniques we have described for dealing with pain should always be used in conjunction with whatever medical or other treatment is necessary to attend to the pain itself.

Let's say, for example, you fall and hurt your wrist. What do you do first? Well, you certainly don't sit down and meditate. You get immediate medical care: X-rays, a doctor, a cast if necessary, a high-powered pain killer—whatever is needed. But while you are doing all this, you can also be mindful and try to accept, with the least resistance possible, the pain in your wrist.

It's the same with emotional pain. If, for example, you are being abused by a fellow worker, don't just sit there and and take it. Do what you have to do—either respond or extricate yourself from the situation. But at the same time you are taking these necessary actions, you can be aware of the pain that situation is generating. Being mindful can result in your refraining from doing or saying something that you'll regret later on.

You receive an extra bonus when you learn to open to your pain in a mindful, non-resisting, and accepting way. The energy that you were wasting by resisting pain is now free to be channeled into overcoming it.

*Do not try to drive pain away by pretending that it is not real. Pain, if you seek serenity in Oneness, will vanish of its own accord.*

SENGSTAN

## HAPPINESS—FINDING THE WAY

In the late 1950s, Parker Brothers put out a game called *Careers: The Game of Life®*. The object of *Careers* was to earn 60,000 points. At the beginning of the game, each player decided how many points to go for in three categories: Fame, Fortune, and Happiness. For instance, a person who wasn't interested in being famous, just rich, might divide his points this way: Fame: 5,000; Fortune: 50,000; Happiness: 5,000. The first player to score all the points in each of his categories won the game. Along the way, players could trade unwanted points to other players, such as Fame for Fortune. They also made sacrifices in one area, love for instance, to get more points in another, money perhaps.

*Careers* is an excellent metaphor for the way most people pursue happiness. They set up some kind of arbitrary point system and then try to accumulate the right number of points in the right proportion. Unfortunately, most of us find out, all too late, that life does not imitate Parker Brothers' games. Scoring points is not happiness.

Even when we accumulate all the points we think we need in our personal pursuit of fame, fortune, and happiness, there still seems to be a feeling that something's missing somehow; we haven't quite won. We try to hold onto pleasant experiences forever, but they are only transitory. We try to sweep the disagreeable parts of life under the rug. And every so often, we throw up our hands in anger and frustration, wondering aloud, "Is this all there is to life?"

Once we realize the basic truth of the human condition, we begin to see that what we thought was the answer may actually be the problem. Then it becomes time to try another way, a way like meditation.

"There is that in me—I do not know what it is—but I know it is in me...
I do not know it—it is without name—it is a word unsaid,
It is not in any dictionary, utterance, symbol...
Do you see O my brothers and sisters?
It is not chaos or death—it is form, union, plan—it is eternal
life—it is Happiness."
                                              WALT WHITMAN
                                              *Leaves of Grass*

## Just do it!

For your own peace of mind, know that you can enjoy the full benefits of meditation without having a total understanding of its very profound underlying theories. The Buddha himself said that asking too many questions is like being shot with a poisoned arrow and refusing to have it removed until it is known who shot it, where it came from, how fast it was going, and what the poison is. By the time you get the answers to all your questions, the Buddha told his followers, you'll be dead.

## How meditation leads to happiness

Here is an analogy that shows the connection between meditation and happiness.

Border collies spend their entire lives running in circles, nipping at the heels of sheep. They keep the herd contained and bark for the shepherd when wolves threaten.

Imagine that this herd of sheep represents your personality—all of your thoughts, perceptions, and concepts about yourself and the world in general. It's the way you see things, deal with things, and react to life's successes and challenges.

Now imagine that the border collie represents your desire to be in control of all your thoughts and feelings—the sheep. In order to control the flock, this poor dog is going to spend the better part of his life in the exhausting, depleting, and unrewarding task of racing around in circles and snapping at heels. All this just to maintain the status quo.

*"Life has always taken place in a tumult without apparent cohesion, but it only finds its grandeur and its reality in ecstasy and in ecstatic love."*

GEORGES BATAILLE
*The Sacred Conspiracy*

• • •

*"Happiness is the only sanction of life; where happiness fails, existence remains a mad and lamentable experiment."*

GEORGE SANTAYANA
*The Life of Reason*

Meditation is simply giving the border collie a rest and letting the sheep roam where they may. The practice of meditation lets you take yourself off the emotional hook. You begin to gain insight into the truth that this constellation of things you think is you is actually a collection of uncontrollable thoughts, ideas, and sensations that arise by themselves and pass by themselves. You cannot control them. And that is totally okay.

Meditation helps you learn to work skillfully with your sense of self gradually and to stop running around in circles and to allow these thoughts, concepts, and perceptions to come and go as they please.

Freeing the mind to do its dance without interference and control leads to acceptance of what is. Acceptance of what is leads you to distance yourself from what is. This is the freedom that leads to true happiness.

## *LOCATING YOUR INNER ECSTASY*

Finding happiness for ourselves—or even knowing what happiness is—can be problematic. The following will take you on a journey to the true source of your own inner happiness, and introduce you to an ecstatic meditation whose glow can linger far into even the most trying of days.

1. Sit or lie down in a comfortable place where you won't be disturbed. Close your eyes and let yourself relax but remain alert mentally.

2. Meditate on happiness.

3. Just let whatever thoughts and images come to your mind surface as they will. They may be about people or memories or dreams. Some will be more intense. Others only peripheral. They will doubtless be multitudinous. How ever many there are, let them come. (You may never before have realized how much happiness and potential happiness you have inside you.)

4. Eventually, your memories and thoughts of happiness finally run their course and no more will come to mind. When this happens, you may suddenly feel detached from them. This is because they were only a kind of happiness. They were not true happiness, or you would not now be feeling this way.

5. Take a deep breath and let it out slowly.

6. Now, turn your senses within and meditate on what your real happiness is.

7. You will know when you find it, because you will feel a deep, ecstatic inner glow.

8. Slowly relax and return to normal. This inner glow of happiness will continue with you for some time. Take a moment and attune yourself to it, especially during those times in your life when you're in need of a little ecstasy in your life.

## YOUR SUMMATION

Now that you have sampled solo meditation, you may wish to carry things further and get the kind of instruction only a good teacher can provide. The following checklist will help you evaluate what you have gotten out of meditation so far—and whether you are ready for this final step.

____ Have you experienced greater inner happiness and/or peace of mind?

____ Have you experienced relief from high-blood pressure, stress, a heart condition, asthma or other medical condition?

____ Have you had a spiritual experience?

____ Have you experienced self-discovery or greater self-knowledge?

____ Have you discovered a solution to a personal or professional dilemma?

____ Have you experienced creative insights?

____ Have you experienced healing from the stress and pain of traumatic life events, such as the death of a loved one, abuse, war, accident, divorce?

____ Have you experienced relief from anxiety, confusion, depression?

____ Have you found aid in recovery from alcoholism, substance abuse, sex-addiction, or other obsessive-compulsive behaviors?

____ Have you experienced boosted memory and/or intelligence?

____ Have you experienced a reduction or elimination of chronic physical pain?

____ Have you experienced communion with God?

____ Have you developed a better handle on your weight, temper, passivity, anger, or other unbalanced areas of your life?

Meditation can help you achieve these goals in a natural, simple, and permanent way.

Meditation works at a deep, intuitive level and results in real, not superficial or cosmetic, changes. Meditation is not a form of wishing for something. When you meditate, you don't meditate to lose twenty pounds. You simply meditate.

Compare this list with the original list you made in Chapter 1 of what you wanted from meditation. Have you met those goals? Or were you disappointed with the results?

Which has the most check marks? The goals list or the accomplishments list? Did meditation accomplish more or less than you set out to do?

If you feel the pluses outweigh the minuses—and if you have come this far, it is likely they will—you may want to consider deepening your practice through working with a meditation instructor in a group. See the appendix, *Deepening Your Practice,* for pointers to those proceeding on the path in this manner.

> *"The great end of all human industry is the attainment of happiness. For this were arts invented, sciences cultivated, laws ordained, and societies modeled, by the most profound wisdom of patriots and legislators. Even the lonely savage, who lies exposed to the inclemency of the elements and the fury of wild beasts, forgets not, for a moment, this grand object of his being."*
>
> DAVID HUME
> *Essays Moral, Political, and Literary*

## CHAPTER RECAP

- The two barriers between us and happiness are pain and suffering.

- Laboratory research shows meditation can ameliorate both.

- Focusing on and visualizing your stress can actually cause it to dissipate.

- Pain has three components: Flavor, location and shape, and intensity.

- Pain has value as an important messenger in your life.

- Pain is inevitable, suffering is not.

- How to relieve pain with an expansion and contraction meditation.

- True happiness may not be what we think it is, but we can always find it within us.

# Meditation from the Heart— Lovingkindness and Compassion

# 12

There is yet another kind of meditation that comes from the heart—the sending and receiving of lovingkindness and compassion. Simply expressed, lovingkindness, sometimes called *metta* in Eastern meditation traditions, is our innate desire to wish the best possible life for everyone and everything. Compassion, its partner, is the quality that enables one to feel another being's sorrow as one's own. These two branches of meditation, wisdom on the one side, compassion and lovingkindness on the other, work synergistically. In Tibetan Buddhism they are likened to the two wings of a bird: To fly straight and swift, a bird must have two good wings.

Lovingkindness and compassion, along with equanimity and sympathetic joy, comprise what are called in Buddhism the *brahma-viharas*, or heavenly abodes. The extent to which we can express lovingkindness and compassion is directly proportional to the happiness we enjoy in our own lives. While mindfulness meditation usually gets the airplay, lovingkindness and compassion are equally important, if not more so, to living a mindful life.

Some of the great spiritual teachers have considered lovingkindness and compassion to be the cornerstones of mindfulness meditation. In fact, some traditions first require students to learn the practice of lovingkindness before they are introduced to the practice of mindfulness.

• *Lovingkindness and compassion in meditation*

• *Lovingkindness and mindfulness*

• *Benefits of lovingkindness*

• *Compassion sent to the ill and dying through an ancient Tibetan tradition*

273

## LOVINGKINDNESS, MEDITATION, AND COMPASSION

If you've just started a meditation practice, you might say you've already got a full plate. Why go out looking for more? Especially something that sounds as touchy-feely as lovingkindness. Besides, you might ask, if the object of mindfulness meditation is to be totally present, non-critical, and nonjudging, doesn't that mean also being totally unemotional?

### Wisdom and compassion

D.T. Suzuki, a great scholar of Buddhism, said, in his book The Essence of Buddhism, that lovingkindness and the wisdom that arises from mindfulness are inseparable; one cannot distinguish where one ends and other begins. Suzuki referred to them as "spiritually coalesced"—lovingkindness without wisdom would be like Abbot without Costello.

In our normal world, there is a great deal of confusion about the meaning of the words "love" and "compassion." Frequently, what we think of as love is nothing more than possessive attachment, a kind of disguised business transaction, a *quid pro quo*: "I'll love you, so long as you love me." As for compassion, this quality is all too often confused with pity for someone less fortunate.

Such mistaken concepts of lovingkindness and compassion, rather than bringing us closer to others, actually increase the distance, creating a vast abyss between the self and others.

On the other hand, real love and true compassion bridge this chasm of separateness. The boundary between "I" and "other" gives way to a feeling of transcendent, universal connectedness. Jung called it the collective unconscious. Scientists call it "the butterfly effect."

"The butterfly effect" is an expression physicists have given to the theory of universal connectedness on a molecular level. Thus, a Monarch butterfly flapping its wings in Carmel, California, would have an effect on the weather patterns in the Persian Gulf.

Through our practice of meditation, we open to each moment of life, jettison delusion, and discover the truth—

that there is no separation, no boundary, between our supposed external and internal worlds. This dissolving of our imaginary boundary reveals the truth that another being's suffering is no more than the reflection of our own pain. This is true compassion.

As we continue to practice, our horizon of good will expands to all human beings, even those from whom we previously withheld it. The "me" is now clearly the "we." And now we naturally want the best for all beings, including ourselves. This is true lovingkindness.

Let's look at how lovingkindness and compassion meditation is related to, enhanced by, and enhances mindfulness meditation.

Lovingkindness and compassion are what Goethe called "The Golden Wedding" or "the two that are one." Lovingkindness and compassion are the flip side of mindfulness meditation.

The ground that lovingkindness and compassion share with mindfulness should be familiar to you: It is the very same ground of calm awareness that you have already begun to explore in your daily meditation practice.

In *Seeking the Heart of Wisdom*, Joseph Goldstein and Jack Kornfeld describe how mindfulness meditation practice opens the heart as well:

> When we realize in our own experience that happiness comes not from reaching out but from letting go, not from seeking pleasurable experience but from opening to the moment to what is true, this transformation of energy frees the compassion within us. Our minds are no longer bound up in pushing away pain or holding on to pleasure. Compassion is the natural response of an open heart. When we settle back and open to what's happening in each moment, without attachment or aversion, we are developing a compassionate attitude toward each experience. From this attitude that we develop in our practice, we can begin to manifest true compassionate action in the world.

*"The rational mind stresses opposites. Compassion and love go beyond pairs of opposites."*

JOSEPH CAMPBELL
*The Joseph Campbell Companion*

## *The goal*

"Charity begins at home." So does the practice of lovingkindness and compassion. Insight meditation teacher Sharon Salzberg tells her students that one of the goals of the practice of lovingkindness and compassion meditation is to enable us to "...become user-friendly—to ourselves."

## Kindness

*"Whether one believes in a religion or not, and whether one believes in rebirth or not, there isn't anyone who doesn't appreciate kindness and compassion.*

*Foolish selfish people are always thinking of themselves, and the result is negative. Wise selfish people think of others, help others as much as they can, and the result is that they too receive benefit.*

*This is my simple religion. There is no need for temples; no need for complicated philosophy. Our own brain, our own heart is our temple; the philosophy is kindness"*

DALAI LAMA
*A Policy of Kindness*

The practice of lovingkindness and compassion is initially directed at one's own self, then expanded outward to the world. As we become skillful in our practice, we spontaneously remember our natural inclination and nature—to be a good friend to the world.

A good friend is not a fair-weather friend. He or she is as solid as the Rock of Gibraltar and does not judge, criticize, or condemn. The good friend's religion is kindness. Becoming a good friend to the world not only confers your intrinsic goodness on the world, it also confers the world's intrinsic goodness on you. It's a spiritual two-way street, with no speed limit.

In *Insight Meditation*, Joseph Goldstein describes that place inside each of us from where lovingkindness and compassion are born as the "soft, open space."

Your own soft space has always been there, just beneath the surface of a lifetime's accumulation of thoughts, emotions, and habits. As your meditation practice develops, mindfulness acts like a spiritual Brillo pad, scouring out the crusty buildup of delusion and revealing underneath your true, shining, stainless nature. Polished and pure, you reconnect with your original soft space. And the world.

## Priceless benefits

The practice of lovingkindness and compassion is not a theoretical exercise in wishful thinking; it is the virtual harnessing of your life energy so as to confer benefits on everyone—including you.

*"Let me live in a house on the side of the road and be a friend to man."*
AN AMERICAN SAMPLER

In *Tibetan Buddhism*, B. Alan Wallace describes why lovingkindness and compassion are so important in today's world:

> The cultivation of lovingkindness is ideally suited for the bustling world we live in. It generates a quality of mind that wishes for the well-being of others, and at the same time it profoundly enhances our ability to attain well-being in our own lives. Instead of focusing on a poised state of mental peace it penetrates deeper into the root causes of our dissatisfactions and transforms them.

You could call the practice of lovingkindness and compassion a form of enlightened self-interest, or as the Dalai Lama says, being a "wise selfish" person. It's true—when we help others, we help ourselves. When we send lovingkindness and compassion to others, we experience increased altruism and less fear, hatred, and suspicion.

## Serenity

*"The mind becomes clear and serene when the qualities of the heart are cultivated. Friendliness towards the joyful, compassion towards the suffering, happiness towards the pure, and impartiality towards the impure."*
PATANJALI, THE HINDU SAGE
*Yoga Sutras*

Even if you look at it from a purely selfish viewpoint, the practice of lovingkindness and compassion make good sense. It is virtually impossible for any of us to fulfill our dreams without the help of the rest of the world.

The indisputable fact is that we are connected to each other, interdependent for our survival, food, clothing, shelter, education, friendships, and sense of self. John Donne's line "No man is an island" might be restated today as "No man can afford to be an island."

Lovingkindness and compassion are powerful tools for the world we live in, where interconnectedness of all beings takes place on the worldwide level Marshall McLuhan called "the global village."

*Lovingkindness and compassion make good sense. It is virtually impossible for any of us to fulfill our dreams without the help of the rest of the world.*

## Metta sutra

The literal translation of the word sutta or sutra is thread. These are the discourses collected in the Buddha's teachings known as "Basket of the Teachings."

The Metta Sutra is attributed to the Buddha himself and considered one of the foundations of his teachings on kindness.

The following is part of the sutra that is recited daily around the world, not only by Buddhists, but those who seek unlimited access to the well of their own internal, human kindness.

"This is the work of those who are skilled and peaceful, who seek the good:

"May they be able and upright, straightforward, of gentle speech and not proud.

"May they be content and easily supported, unburdened with their senses calmed.

"May they be wise, not arrogant and without desire for the possessions of others.

"May they do nothing mean or that the wise would reprove.

"May all beings be happy.

"May they live in safety and joy.

"All living beings, whether weak or strong, tall, stout, medium or short, seen or unseen, near or distant, born or to be born, may they all be happy."

SAMUEL BERCHOLZ AND SHERAB CHODZIN KOHN, EDITORS
*Entering the Stream*

On the personal end of the spectrum, lovingkindness and compassion bestow benefits on the deepest relationships in our lives.

The Dalai Lama, in *The World of Tibetan Buddhism,* recounts a meeting he had with a group of scientists, including neurobiologists, in which he was told that there is strong "...scientific evidence to suggest that even in pregnancy a mother's state of mind has a great effect on the physical and mental well-being of the unborn child."

Even after a child is born, the first few weeks are crucial to a child's future development.

> During this time, I was told, one of the most important factors for ensuring rapid and healthy growth of the baby's brain is the mother's constant physical touch. When a child sees someone with an open and affectionate demeanor, someone who is smiling or has a loving and caring expression, the child naturally feels happy and protected.

One need not be a neurobiologist or a Nobel Laureate to understand that parents who have cultivated the benefits of lovingkindness and compassion within themselves are endowed with an even greater blessing—the chance to pass it along to their children.

True lovingkindness and compassion is intrinsic to the practice of prayer and contemplation in Western traditions such as Judaism and Christianity.

To the Trappist monk and writer, Father Thomas Merton, one of the great paradoxes, yet truths, of existence was,

> That a man cannot enter into the deepest center of himself and pass through that center into God, unless he is able to pass entirely out of himself and empty himself and give himself to other people in the purity of a selfless love.

In *Seeking the Path of Life,* Rabbi Ira F. Stone of Temple Beth Zion-Beth Israel in Philadelphia echoes this.

> God's presence in humanity is not limited to one person but

## The best insurance in the world

*The Buddha enumerated on the limitless benefits of lovingkindness to his followers:*

*"One sleeps in comfort, wakes in comfort, and dreams no evil dreams. One is dear to human beings, one is dear to non-human beings, deities guard one, fire and poison and weapons do not affect one. One's mind is easily concentrated, the expression of one's face is serene, one dies unconfused."*

*In tonglen, the meditator becomes a spiritual heart-bypass machine, taking in another's pain and suffering, purifying and transforming it.*

resides equally in each person and awaits acknowledgment by that person. The failure of one person to acknowledge God's presence at any moment means that God's presence in the entire world is diminished by exactly the amount of that disbelief.... We recognize God's presence in the lives and faces of other humans. And we respond to that presence by trying to nurture it in the lives of others.

## TONGLEN—TIBETAN BUDDHIST PRACTICE FOR THE SUFFERING

In Tibetan Buddhism, there is an ancient compassion meditation technique called *tonglen*, which means giving and taking or sending and receiving.

To understand tonglen, imagine a heart-bypass machine in an operating room. During surgery, the patient's blood supply is rerouted through this machine, which cleans, filters, and oxygenates the blood before ultimately returning it to the patient's body.

In tonglen, the meditator becomes a spiritual heart-bypass machine, taking in another's pain and suffering, purifying and transforming it into joy, compassion, and happiness, and then sending it back to help heal the sufferer.

Kyabe Kalu Rinpoche, one of the leading teachers of Tibetan Buddhism, describes how one begins to cultivate the right attitude for tonglen:

> [W]e first think about the love we have received from our own parents in this life, the manner in which they have raised, educated, helped, and protected us.... We then imagine how we would feel if the person most dear to us—usually our mother—were in a state of intense suffering right in front of us. We couldn't remain unmoved; we would immediately do something to help her.
>
> To become skilled at tonglen practice, it is best to begin by sending and receiving from your core relations: family members, loved ones, close friends, and especially yourself. As you develop this sending and receiving skill, you can gradually expand the arc of your transmission to all beings everywhere who suffer.

A natural question is whether, in doing tonglen practice, the absorption of another's pain and suffering will adversely affect the practitioner by exposing him or her to it.

The answer is no. Centuries of practice by thousands of people show exactly the opposite to be true. One need only bring to mind such figures as Mother Teresa, Albert Schweitzer, Jesus, and the Dalai Lama to see that the development of compassion is a source of strength, fearlessness, and confidence, not weakness, illness, or fear.

This great protection afforded to those who selflessly give to others was called the holy secret by the eighth-century Tibetan sage, Shantideva, who said in *A Guide To Bodhisattva's Way Of Life:*

Whoever wishes to quickly afford protection
To both himself and others
Should practice that holy secret
The exchanging of self for others

### *Tonglen and the ego*

"The one thing you should know for certain is that the only thing that Tonglen could harm is the one thing that has been harming you the most: your own ego, your self-grasping, self-cherishing mind, which is the root of suffering.
SOGYAL RINPOCHE
*The Tibetan Book of Living and Dying*

## *No fear*

*Just as mindfulness can dispel fear, so can lovingkindness and compassion. It is said that the Buddha first taught lovingkindness and compassion to his monks as a tool to help them overcome great fear. Legend has it that these monks went out into the forest and encountered some major demons. They came running back to the Buddha, who urged them to return to the forest, and when they encountered these demons again, to send lovingkindness and compassion to them.*

*The monks heeded the Buddha's advice and returned to the woods. When the monsters appeared again, the monks were able, through the practice of lovingkindness and compassion, to overcome their fear. The monsters then evaporated.*

Tonglen can be an especially powerful practice at times when someone close to us is ill, in the hospital, in great physical pain, or in serious danger. It's also a very appropriate practice for comforting those who are dying. Sogyal Rinpoche says:

At every moment of our lives we need compassion, but what more urgent moment could there be than when we are dying? What more wonderful and consoling gift could you give to the dying than the knowledge that they are being prayed for, and that you are taking on their suffering and purifying their negative karma through your practice for them?

# TONGLEN EXERCISE FOR ONE WHO SUFFERS

Here's a tonglen exercise you can use when someone close is ill, suffering, or dying.

1. Sit comfortably. Visualize, with as much detail as possible, a close friend or relative who is currently in distress or ill or suffering.

2. Imagine, with great detail, every aspect of the affliction or ailment. Do not spare yourself from distaste or aversion.

3. Visualize all of the person's pain and distress congealing into a mass of charcoal grey, acrid smoke.

4. As you inhale, take in this grey ball of smoke as far into your own being as possible. Do not be afraid to do this. Watch as your innate lovingkindness and compassion performs spiritual alchemy, transforming this acrid energy into clear, pure, positive rays of peace, joy, lovingkindness, and compassion.

5. As you exhale, visualize a clear, healing light flowing out of your body and directly into the person who is suffering. Shantideva said that when you do this, your entire being is transformed into a beautiful jewel, capable of bestowing on each individual exactly what is needed at this time.

6. Continue to send and receive energy. When you feel that your stream of lovingkindness and compassion naturally end, sit quietly, and take several deep breaths. You may continue this practice or stop.

# APPROACHES TO LOVINGKINDNESS

There is nothing complex, abstruse, or difficult about the practice of lovingkindness and compassion. If you can care for yourself and others in a sincere, heartfelt way, you are already practicing lovingkindness. In some Eastern meditation traditions, lovingkindness is practiced at the beginning or conclusion of mindfulness practice. But you may also devote an entire sitting session just to lovingkindness. As in your mindfulness practice, begin with five to ten minutes of sending lovingkindness and compassion.

Use the following exercises, which, although based on traditional lovingkindness and compassion practices from the Eastern Buddhist tradition, are nonsectarian.

## SENDING TO A LOVED ONE

You can start practicing lovingkindness and compassion immediately, just as you began to meditate. The following are instructions for a five- to ten-minute lovingkindness meditation session.

1. Sit in a comfortable posture.

2. Close your eyes. Bring to mind a person in your life that you really, truly love.

3. In your own words, silently express your love for that person. Select your own phrases.

4. Start each phrase with "May you..." For example: "May you be free from danger" or "May you have ease of being" or "May you be free from disease."

5. As you enunciate each phrase, become it. You're not just saying words but expressing your true heart. Let each phrase emanate from your soft space.

6. You don't have to chant these phrases or bear down on them. You just have to feel them, gently and genuinely. With sincerity, but without pressure.

7. Feel the phrases coming from your intrinsic source of lovingkindness and compassion.

8. After you are done, rest for several minutes. Feel the warm, gentle, energy of lovingkindness and compassion you have generated.

## All that you can be...

"*I want you to meditate on what's really good about you.... Don't just think about it; try to feel it. If you can do this in a simple way for even a few minutes, then practice feeling it more strongly. Do this each day. If you'll think about this and meditate on it every day, you will grow tremendously as a person, and your whole understanding of yourself, of your life, and of the creative power that binds these two together will change completely. Then, whatever the form in which you live your life, whatever the form in which you express yourself, whatever inconstancies or 'imperfections' there may be, you will find a great sense of peace and a great ability to bring benefit to those people whose lives touch your own.*"

SWAMI CHETANANANDA
*The Breath of God*

# THE LIGHTHOUSE

Just as the beacon of a lighthouse shines its guiding light onto the ocean, in this exercise you will beam the light of your lovingkindness over the entire planet. Then you will gather it back, finding it enhanced and strengthened by lovingkindness returned to you from other beings who have engaged in this practice from time immemorial.

1. As with your mindfulness meditation practice, begin by taking your place on your chair or cushion. Feel your entire body. Be aware of it. Close your eyes. Relax your body. Think about something that made you feel good recently. Allow that feeling to grow.

2. Visualize yourself as you are right now, sitting in your posture. Begin by visualizing all the loving people on this planet, including the departed. Such people could include historical figures like Gandhi or Martin Luther King or Jesus Christ, as well as great friends, teachers, parents.

3. Become a lighthouse of lovingkindness and compassion. As the beacon of your mind sweeps slowly, it illuminates these and all enlightened beings—past, present, and future. Feel the light of lovingkindness that emanates from each and every one of them. It is a clear, transparent light that penetrates through everything, even time itself.

4. Bring your attention to the crown of your head. Picture an opening, an energy center, there. Allow the accumulated light of lovingkindness to enter through this opening and flow down, permeating your entire body. It is as if you were a bottomless vessel being filled with liquid lovingkindness. Feel this accumulation of lovingkindness spreading throughout the body. It flows through you like warm, amber light.

5. Add your own lovingkindness to this flow. Watch as it exponentially enhances the lovingkindness sent to you. Slowly, gather the lovingkindness within you and return it to the crown of your head.

6. Again, imagine your sweeping beacon. This time, instead of using your panoramic sweep to gather in lovingkindness, shine it out into the world. As your beacon revolves, the powerful, clear light of lovingkindness pervades the entire world. It cuts through the fog of hostility, doubt, and fear.

7. Continue to shine your beacon on all people and beings everywhere—without reservation. When your beacon has gone full circle, stop.

8. Sit quietly for several minutes. Allow the good feelings you have generated to wash through your body and mind. Enjoy these feelings.

9. Retaining this lovingkindness, slowly arise and continue on with your day, bringing these qualities to everything you do or say.

## How to practice lovingkindness

Much can be gained by sending lovingkindness to yourself and three other people in your life who represent your fundamental relationships. Altogether, they are:

- yourself,
- someone you look up to: a mentor, teacher, or close friend,
- a neutral person: someone you do not know that well, and/or
- a difficult person: someone you do not like or may even hate.

You may change your selection of people (other than yourself) each time you do the exercise. Sometimes yesterday's difficult person is today's mentor.

The phrases you repeat should come from your heart. They are connected with the best in you, the things you want for yourself. What follows is a list of suggested phrases; they are by no means the only ones. Any phrase, wish or thought of lovingkindness that resonates for you is the right one. Repeat each phrase twice.

May I be happy.

May I be healthy.

May I be safe.

May I be free from anger.

May I be secure.

May I be carefree.

May I be free from pain.

May I be free from suffering.

May I be liberated.

May I have ease of being.

*Sometimes yesterday's difficult person is today's mentor.*

Traditionally, three or four phrases are grouped together, and then sent sequentially. The set of phrases you use is the same for all four people. For instance, you might chose the following three phrases:

May I be happy.

May I be healthy.

May I be safe.

Don't use more than four phrases, or the exercise may become confusing.

Remember to keep it simple. This is not an exercise in wishing for things. While there is nothing wrong with the phrase "May I get that new Lexus," the time and place for it is not during your lovingkindness meditation.

## LOVINGKINDNESS

1. As with your mindfulness meditation practice, begin by taking your place on your chair or cushion. Feel your entire body. Be aware of it. Close your eyes. Allow the body to relax. Think about something that made you feel good recently. Allow that feeling to grow.

2. Visualize yourself as you are right now. Begin to send lovingkindness to yourself by repeating the following phrases, slowly and silently: "May I be happy. May I be safe. May I be carefree." As you repeat the phrases, try to really let them soak into your awareness. Try to be accepting and relaxed. If you find discomfort or tension arising, let them do their dance, and, as with all phenomena, float away like clouds in the sky.

3. Picture someone in your life whom you really look up to. It could be a teacher, or a mentor at work—someone you respect and admire. Visualize situations or events where this person really helped you.

4. Repeat the phrases, changing "I" to "you," sending your best wishes to him or her as you repeat: "May you be happy. May you be safe. May you be carefree." Let your phrases envelope this person in lovingkindness After you have done this, pause for a moment.

5. Turn the object of your attention to a neutral person. This can be someone you may not know very well, even a total stranger, a person who represents the quintessential human being. Picture this neutral person in your mind. Send him or her lovingkindness and repeat the following: "May you be happy. May you be safe. May you be carefree." Sit softly with the feelings that arise. You may be surprised at how connected you feel with a complete stranger. Don't be surprised. Don't be anything. Just continue to send your lovingkindness.

6. Turn your attention to a difficult person in your life. With as much sincerity as possible, envelope this adversary, this tough person, in your lovingkindness. And repeat the following phrases: "May you be happy. May you be safe. May you be carefree."

7. When you're done sending lovingkindness to these four people, sit quietly for several minutes. Allow the good feelings you have generated to wash through your body and mind. Enjoy these feelings.

8. Slowly rise and continue on with your day, trying to bring these qualities with you in everything you do or say.

## Send lovingkindness to enemies

There is no doubt that sending lovingkindness to people we don't like is a huge challenge. Why bother to do it? The answer is simple: because it's very important. And we know it. There are several strategies for sending lovingkindness to someone you don't like. Here are three.

### Overcoming Anger

You're not doing it for them. You're doing it for yourself. That may sound a bit crass, and not nearly as elegant as "I love the world," but it is honest, which is what really counts. Along this line, Sharon Salzberg, in her book

*Lovingkindness, The Revolutionary Art of Happiness*, suggests asking yourself :

> Who is the one suffering from this anger? The person who has harmed me has gone on to live their life (or perhaps has died), while I am the one sitting here feeling the persecution, burning, and constriction of anger. Out of compassion for myself, to ease my own heart, may I let go.

During your next lovingkindness session, when you reach the difficult person, take a moment to reflect on, "Who is the one suffering from this anger?" And when you realize it is you, send yourself strong lovingkindness—and then send the same to that difficult person.

### Approach Your Enemies
Pick someone you dislike, then build up to the real stinkers.

This is as simple as it sounds. Instead of selecting your boss, start out with someone easier—perhaps that bus driver who splashed you at 38th Street today.

Once you've succeeded in sending lovingkindness to the splashing bus driver, you can begin slowly working your way up the ladder of the loathsome. At some point you'll be ready to accept the challenge of sending lovingkindness and compassion to your boss—or whomever you thought you'd never send lovingkindness to.

Some people report miraculous transformations in their relationships with difficult people as a result of their lovingkindness practice. Who changed? Them? You? Both of you? Does it matter?

### Forgiveness
Another way to deal with the person you don't like is to see what you don't like about them in yourself.

Realize that everyone, even you, has been guilty of the same transgression. And when you were, didn't you want to be forgiven? Of course you did. Anybody would, including the person from whom you're now withholding that same forgiveness. Why not forgive and move on?

## SENDING LOVINGKINDNESS TO YOUR OBJECT OF HATRED

Consider the following exercise as a mindfulness meditation with the person you hate as your object of meditation.

1. Sit in a comfortable posture. Close your eyes. Bring to mind a person in your life for whom you have intense dislike or hatred—your object of hatred.

2. Ask yourself what exactly it is that you hate about this person. Is it the person's mind? Where is this so-called mind? Can you show it to anyone? Is it the person's body? Probably not. How can you possibly feel hatred for a collection of chemicals and energy?

3. Ask yourself, "Where is the person I hate so much?" Is there such a person, after all? Or do you hate a collection of thoughts, feelings, and emotions that not only make up the object of hatred, but that also make up your own self? Where then is this person you hate?

4. After you are done, rest for several minutes. Picture that person now. Compare how you feel now with how you felt before you started.

## Sending to yourself

The directions for the following exercise are exactly the same as the directions above. Only this time, the person you really, truly love is—you. Don't feel bashful, guilty, or unentitled. It is perfectly legitimate, even encouraged, to send feelings of lovingkindness and compassion to yourself.

Many meditators initially have a problem with sending lovingkindness to themselves. That's because society keeps sending us the wrong message: that to care for yourself and wish yourself the best is selfish, egotistical, narcissistic, and a sure sign that you are on a major ego trip. Nothing could be further from the truth.

Remember what the Buddha told his followers: "You can search throughout the entire universe for someone who is more deserving of your love than you are yourself, and that person will not be found."

If you are having difficulty loving yourself, try the following exercise.

## LOVING YOURSELF

1. Take a comfortable posture. Close your eyes.

2. Remember and visualize the times in your life when you have done good things for others. It doesn't have to be Nobel Peace Prize caliber stuff. Maybe you helped a lost child at the beach, or an elderly neighbor carry her groceries into her house. These are the moments when, objectively and undoubtedly, you were a giving, kind, compassionate person who certainly deserved lovingkindness.

3. As you go through this process you are sure to find an episode that seems to glow with unencumbered, total lovingkindness on your part.

4. Feel it as vividly as possible. The time of day, the color of the sky—make it very real. Remember the thanks bestowed on you. Remember how your body felt, glad all over.

5. Cultivate the sensations of lovingkindness that arise. Direct them toward yourself.

In the world we live in, there seems to be less and less encouragement for compassion and lovingkindness. For every "Practice Random Acts of Kindness" bumper sticker, there are fifty that say, "The one with the most toys wins," or, "My kid can beat up your honor student." Compassion, lovingkindness, and goodwill have become seasonal products, trotted out annually for the hours between Thanksgiving Day and New Year's Eve. Then it's back to business as usual—"Take no prisoners."

We have come to think that the qualities of lovingkindness and compassion are luxuries, not necessities. After all, does compassion pay the rent? Does lovingkindness get you a DeBeers diamond? When most of our waking hours are filled with images reinforcing the idea that "nice guys finish last," lovingkindness and compassion are associated with being soft—not the stuff that role models are made of.

To the contrary, lovingkindness and compassion are a profound manifestation of tremendous inner strength. Sharon Salzberg says, "Compassion is not at all weak. It is the strength that arises out of seeing the true nature of suffering in the world.... It allows us to name injustice without hesitation, and to act strongly with all the skill at our disposal."

You know what's right and wrong. If someone cuts ahead of you in the bank line, that's wrong. And you can tell him, in a kind, compassionate way, to go to the end of the line.

True practice of lovingkindness allows no room for self-deprivation, guilt, or being a victim. The only requirement of true lovingkindness and compassion is that you be you—not Saint You.

## CHAPTER RECAP

- Lovingkindness, sometimes called metta in the Eastern meditation traditions, is our innate desire to want the best possible life for everyone and everything.

- Compassion is the strength to see the sorrow that is part of the human condition in ourselves and others, and the capacity to feel that sorrow as our own.

- The practice of lovingkindness and compassion is first directed at one's own self and then extended outward toward all beings.

- Lovingkindness and compassion are powerful tools for today's world, where the interconnectedness of all beings takes place on the truly global level.

- Parents who have cultivated the benefits of lovingkindness and compassion within themselves are endowed with an even greater blessing—passing it on to their newborn children.

- In tonglen, the meditator acts as a spiritual bypass machine, allowing another's pain and suffering to flow into him, where it is purified by the meditator's feelings of joy, compassion, and happiness, whence it is returned, cleaned and energized, to the sufferer.

- The Buddha told his students, "You can search throughout the entire universe for someone who is more deserving of your love than you are yourself, and that person will not be found."


*This is my simple religion. There is no need for temples; no need for complicated philosophy.*
*Our own brain, our own heart is our temple; the philosophy is kindness.*
**His Holiness the Dalai Lama**

# A P P E N D I X
# *Deepening Your Practice*

Yyou may now be ready to deepen your meditation practice. This section is about finding a teacher and attending a meditation retreat. There is an old saying that goes, "When the student is ready, the teacher appears." Choosing a teacher is a personal decision that depends on many things, including availability of the teacher and his or her personality and teaching methods.

## TEACHERS

When seeking a teacher, be honest about what you want. Are you seeking a master, a guide, or a coach? Perhaps what you seek is called a spiritual friend. As B. Alan Wallace says, in Tibetan Buddhism: From The Ground Up, The questions we pose are important ones, but most of us do not know how to answer them on our own, or how to distinguish between teachers who speak with knowledge and those who are deluded or dishonest.

There are three hallmarks of good teachers:

- They enhance your life. They don't run it.

- They are not on ego trips that can only be satisfied by your dependency.

- They keep you from straying from the path, while at the same time letting you find your own way.

*• What to expect from a teacher*

*• What to expect from a retreat*

*• How retreats are organized*

*• Finding a retreat for you*

**293**

## Your relationship with your teacher

In the two most common student-teacher relationships, the teacher assumes the role of *guru*, or master, or spiritual friend.

## The guru

The guru-student relationship is not one of parity; the guru's authority, rules, and activities are rarely questioned and never challenged by the student, who is subservient to the ideas, opinions, and demands of the guru.

This type of relationship is regarded warily, particularly in the West, where questioning authority is considered appropriate as well as healthy. A guru relationship can be a blessing to a student. It can also be a potential source of abuse. If you choose to go the guru route, be aware of your motivation and intentions and the possible risks.

## Following blindly

An early Buddhist story shows the pitfalls of following a teacher's instructions too closely:

When the king's horse trainer died, the king hired a new one, who, unbeknownst to him, had a pronounced limp. The king's perfect, beautiful, well-bred stallions were brought to the new trainer, who taught them to run, gallop, and pull the king's coach. There was only one problem: Each of the stallions performed its task with a pronounced limp.

When the king saw this, he was puzzled. He summoned the trainer to court. When that man limped before the king, the king understood everything.

## The kalyana mitta

*Kalyana mitta* means spiritual friend in the Insight tradition of Southeast Asian Buddhism. It is also a good way to define teacher-student relationships in many other religious and meditative traditions.

Buddhadasa Bhikkhu (1906-1993) was a Buddhist teacher in Thailand and the author of several books. In *Mindfulness With Breathing, A Manual for Serious Beginners*, he discusses what it means to be a spiritual friend:

In truth, even in the old training systems they did not talk much about an *acariya* [teacher, master]. Such a person was called a good friend (kalyana mitta). It is correct to refer to this person as a friend. A friend is an advisor who can help us with certain matters. We should not forget, however, the basic principle that no one can directly help someone else.... Although he or she is able to answer questions and explain some difficulties, it is not necessary for a friend to sit over us and supervise every breath. A good friend who will answer questions and help us work through certain obstacles is more than enough.

In the spiritual friend-student relationship, you are not subservient to your teacher; you don't place your spiritual friend on a pedestal of power. As you recognize your teacher's innate compassion and wisdom, your respect and deference for him or her increases spontaneously and naturally.

Obviously, the spiritual friend connection is less intimidating and dependent than the master-student relationship. A spiritual friend acts as an experienced guide on your journey into meditation and mindfulness. He or she has walked this road before and can help you steer clear of the pitfalls.

A good spiritual friend wants you to lead your own life and will not allow you to become dependent. He or she will also act as your spiritual coach, someone who won't hesitate to let you know when you could be working harder.

> *A good spiritual friend wants you to lead your own life and will not allow you to become dependent.*

The demands of modern life make the spiritual friend route the most practical one to follow. Modern teachers understand this and have developed materials, including books, audiotapes, and visual aids, that enable students to connect with them across wide geographical distances.

The Resource section in this book provides you with jumping off points for finding a spiritual friend. Of course, this is no substitute for personal contact; you should try to attend retreats, seminars, and other events where he or she teaches, speaks, or is in residence.

## Spiritual friends on tape

*Audiotapes featuring good teachers are the next best thing to being in the same room with them. For example, the following selections represent hour upon hour of fine instruction.*

- *How to Meditate,* Lawrence LeShan, Ph.D.
- *Wherever You Go, There You Are: Mindfulness Meditation in Everyday Life,* Jon Kabat-Zinn
- *The Art of Meditation,* Daniel Goleman, Ph.D.
- *Personal Meditations,* Richard F.X. O'Connor
- *Alan Watts Teaches Meditation* and
- *The Way of Zen,* Alan Watts

## Teachers—spiritual friends or spiritual enemies?

The vast majority of meditation teachers, yogis, clerics, and gurus are well-balanced, well-intentioned people who confer a positive benefit on their students. However, there are exceptions, many well-publicized, where students have been exploited sexually, financially, and emotionally by teachers who acted more like spiritual enemies than friends. The most extreme examples involve turning students into cult-like robots that follow any order—including joining in mass suicide or even murder.

*"He who would reform the world must first reform himself; and that, if he do it honestly, will keep him so employed that he will have no time to criticize his neighbor. Nevertheless, his neighbor will be benefited—even as a man without a candle, who at last discerns another's light."*

TALBOT MUNDY
*The Devil's Guard*

For this reason, many people are afraid of becoming involved with a teacher. They have read about the self-styled gurus, fakirs, hustlers, pie-in-the-sky artists, and hordes of other New Age and spiritual-type charlatans who prey on unwary meditators and those seeking a spiritual path. This thought alone holds many back from seeking a teacher or joining a meditational group.

As Talbot Mundy writes in *Om: The Secret of Arbor Valley,* "The outward semblance of authority is not a necessary symptom of its essence. There are men in high places who have no authority at all beyond what indolence confers because the indolence of many is the opportunity of one. Such men lead multitudes astray."

The thought of joining a meditation circle or class is also problematic for many. One hears all sorts of stories about cult-like groups, politics in groups, and zealots in groups. For the beginner, how to choose wisely among them can be perplexing, to say the least.

Sensible moderation is the surest guide, according to one Tibetan proverb. It goes something like this: "A guru is like a fire. If you get too close, you get burned. If you stay too far away, you don't get enough heat. A sensible moderation is recommended."

"There be many gurus, and some good ones whom it is no great task to differentiate, seeing that those who make the loudest claim are least entitled to respect. They who are the true guides into Knowledge know that nothing can be taught, although the learner easily can be assisted to discover what is in himself. Other than which there is no knowledge of importance except this: that what is in himself is everywhere."

TSIANG SAMDUP
*The Book of the Sayings of Tsiang Samdup*

## CULT OR CONSCIOUSNESS RAISING?

So how is it possible to tell whether a teacher is benign or a group is closer to cult than consciousness-raising? Below, extracted from the work of Daniel Goleman, former human behavior editor of the the *New York Times* and the author of *Varieties of Meditative Experience,* nine key questions you should ask yourself about any group with a meditational or spiritual bent. Consider a yes to any of them a warning flag—and take a closer look. If you answer yes to most, look elsewhere and avoid that group at all costs!

___ Do important questions—about ethics, money, behavior, inconsistency, and other matters—go unanswered, like, "Why does Yogi teach macrobiotics but eat ham and eggs?"

___ Is key information—like how money is spent and who the teacher is sleeping with—confined to a tight, inner circle?

___ Is the group filled with people who dress, groom themselves, and act just like their leader?

___ Does everyone pretend to a narrow range of emotions—always happy or solemn or extremely spiritual—no matter what?

___ Do group members believe they are special, that

theirs is the only truth and the only path to salvation—
and that all others are wrong-headed and perhaps
damned as well?

___ Are members asked to prove they are obedient by
doing what they are told, even when violates their
personal ethics?

___ Is the group's public persona misleading—for instance,
pretending to be a simple public service organization,
when its real purpose is recruiting new members?

___ Is a single metaphysical explanation—"It's Mithra's
will"—used to explain everything that happens to
anyone, whether it's physical illness or alcoholism?

___ Is laughter and friendly joking rare—or absent
altogether?

## MEDITATION RETREATS

People usually picture retreats as remote places, cut off
from the world, where extremely devout monks and
novices pray ceaselessly in solitude. But this image has
nothing whatever to do with a meditation retreat. In meditation practice, the retreat has a special purpose. Before
we discuss what a meditation retreat is, however, let's take
a look at what it is not.

*"Go into the desert not to escape other men but in order to find
them in God....*

*The great temptation of modern man is not physical solitude but
immersion in the mass of other men, not escape into the mountains
or the desert (would that more men were so tempted!) but escape
into the great formless sea of irresponsibility which is the crowd.
There is actually no more dangerous solitude than that of the man
who is lost in a crowd...."*

FATHER THOMAS MERTON
*New Seeds of Contemplation*

# What a meditation retreat is not

### It Is Not Club Med®

Meditation retreats are not vacation destinations. If you are looking for a place to sleep in, be pampered, make your own schedule, feast on surf and turf, and party hearty, head for Aruba.

### It Is Not Luxurious

The people who run retreats make sincere efforts to keep the retreat affordable to those of average means. Some retreats even offer scholarships. This means that many retreat facilities are of the rented, low-cost, no-frills variety. Catholic prayer centers are very popular. If the sponsoring organization has its own facility, you can be sure that it will be simple and utilitarian.

You will almost never have a private room at a retreat and will most likely share a small room with several other fellow participants.

### It Is Not Withdrawal from the World

Although retreats are often held outside of cities, this is no guarantee of babbling brooks and hummingbirds. Some retreat centers are situated on major highways, which means you're not going to be shielded from the traffic noise you thought you were leaving behind.

# A meditation retreat offers

A meditation retreat is first and foremost an opportunity for you to engage in intense meditation practice with a minimum of responsibilities and distractions. Some meditation teachers tell students that one seven-day retreat a year is not a luxury, but a necessity for building and maintaining a strong practice.

### A Setting for Intense Practice

The more you do something, the better you get at it. Just

as a tennis player intent on improvement attends a tennis camp, the meditator who wants to move his or her practice to the next level attends a retreat.

Meditation retreats are designed to provide you with the optimal setting for intense practice.

*A meditation retreat is...an opportunity for you to engage in intense meditation practice.*

### A Controlled Environment

Meditation retreats are no-brainers; at a retreat, you neither think about nor have to provide for your basic needs. You have safe and adequate shelter, your meals are cooked for you, and you are provided with a daily schedule that you must follow. Everybody does the same thing at the same time. This leaves you with nothing to do but what you came to do—meditate.

### Magnification

Constant and intense meditation heightens all your sensations. It's similar to the warning on the sideview mirror of your car: "Objects in this mirror appear closer than they are." At a retreat, everything seems closer than it is. Meditation retreats are the perfect setting for making mountains out of molehills.

Suppose, for example, someone accidentally steps on your meditation cushion. Ordinarily, this would be trivial. After four days of meditation, however, it may seem to you like justifiable grounds for World War III.

The luxury of being able to observe, from a safe vantage point, how your mind blows things out of all proportion is an important benefit of the retreat environment. This is also very apparent in another retreat phenomenon—instant feedback.

### Instant Feedback

In the confined world of a meditation retreat, just as in the secluded world of the monastery, your actions yield clear, instant feedback. If you do something unskillful or inappropriate, you will instantly realize it. No one will have to tell you.

Instant feedback strips away the layer of excuse and subterfuge that ordinarily hides your true motivations. It enables you, in a kind and compassionate way, to observe the effect your thoughts, judgments, and ideas have on your actions. It is invaluable in your quest for personal happiness. Instant feedback shows you where your life does and doesn't work.

### Opportunity to Be with a Teacher

When you are near a good teacher, something positive always seems to rub off. Since good meditation teachers are few and far between, a retreat offers you a special opportunity to spend time, connect, and interact with a teacher through dharma talks, guided meditation instruction, and group and individual meetings.

At most retreats, you will have the opportunity for at least one private meeting (dokusan) with your teacher and additional meetings with his or her assistants. During these private meetings, you are free to ask questions and bring up problems concerning your practice. One brief exchange at the right time in your development can be a wonderful catalyst for your growth.

### Escape into Life

At meditation retreats, as in life, looks can be deceiving. Although meditation retreats may appear to be retreats from life, they are described by many who attend them as the opposite—retreats into life

When you attend a meditation retreat, you may, on a physical level, leave behind your lifestyle and physical environment. But you still carry a lot of unneeded physical and emotional baggage—problems, hang-ups, and interpersonal difficulties.

In the stillness and silence of retreat, your hindrances become your tormentors, unruly children who now have even more space to harass you. They pursue you relentlessly until you have no place to hide.

Look at this not as aggravation, but as a great blessing. The confined world of the retreat allows you to see, perhaps for the first time, where your life does and doesn't

*Instant feedback strips away the layer of excuse and subterfuge that ordinarily hides your true motivations.*

In the stillness and silence of retreat, your hindrances become your tormentors.

work. Continued opening to each moment of life with calm awareness encourages the kind of true, intuitive wisdom that naturally invites your mind to jettison its excess mental baggage. The result is a lessening of pain, delusion, anger, and suffering—and a lightening of spirit. You are happier. And you stay happier. Even after you leave the retreat.

Many people report that when they come back from a retreat, they feel healthier, as if they've lost weight. This incredible lightness of being occurs because they have escaped, not from life, but into it.

## FINDING THE RIGHT RETREAT FOR YOU

Once you decide that it is time for your retreat, you need to find the right one for you. Following are some considerations:

### Who runs the retreat?

Retreats are usually organized and run by private, non-sectarian, non-profit meditation groups, centers, and societies. An upcoming retreat is normally announced several months in advance in advertising that details the sponsor, the purpose, and the schedule.

Although some meditation retreats are held at religious centers, most retreats are non-religious. For example, retreats sponsored by VSI, the Vipassana Support Institute of Los Angeles, are devoid of any religious rites or rituals. On the other hand, retreats sponsored by the Zen Center of Los Angeles will be in the Zen Buddhist tradition, which means that you should expect not only to meditate, but also to participate in religious services and rituals.

Many people prefer non-sectarian retreats. Others relish the prospect of participating in Eastern or Western religious traditions to which they might never otherwise be exposed. If you have any questions regarding a retreat, the time for answers is before you write a deposit check or drive 500 miles. Don't be shy about calling. A contact number for questions is usually included in the announcement.

## Levels of retreat

Meditation retreats vary in duration and intensity. Just as you would not take your first nature walk up Mount Whitney, you should use common sense when choosing a retreat. Pick something that is doable. Find out what will be demanded of you in actual sitting time. Ask questions that will help you determine whether the location is too rustic for your peace of mind or health needs—and whether the proposed retreat sounds more like boot camp than meditating.

Just as English Literature 101 was a prerequisite for English Literature 102, some retreat groups may require that you already have a retreat under your belt. This ensures the best possible outcome for all concerned.

Thus, before you take a ten-day retreat, you may first be required to complete one that lasts four days. A shorter retreat usually does not have to be with the same organization whose ten-day retreat you are now planning to attend.

The most important consideration when searching for your retreat is to pick one that you can finish. This cannot be stressed too strongly.

> *The most important consideration when searching for your retreat is to pick one that you can finish.*

## Where to find out about retreats

There is no central clearing house for meditation retreats. The Resource section of this book contains information about how to contact several organizations and publications that can get you started on your search. Here are several more sources of information.

### Newsletters

Newsletters are treasure troves of knowledge that also contain—besides retreat listings—advertisements for books, sitting equipment, and professional services. Subscriptions to these publications are usually by donation.

Quarterly newsletters and magazines published by meditation organizations and societies include *The Inquiring Mind*, published by IMS in Barre, Massachusetts, and *Ten Directions*, published by the Zen Center of Los Angeles.

### Magazines

A number of commercial magazines devote themselves partially or entirely to meditation. Magazines such as *Tricycle, Yoga Journal,* and *The Shambala Sun* usually carry listings and advertisements for retreats. You can find these publications and more at most large newsstands. They are also available by subscription.

### Bookstores

Your local bookstore—particularly one that specializes in books on spirituality and meditation—is a valuable resource for information on retreats in your area. People who run retreats will usually leave flyers at bookstores.

Your bookstore may also host book signings by meditation masters and teachers. If the store has a mailing list, make sure you are on it.

## *What to bring*

Ordinarily, the retreat announcement will tell you what the facility is providing and what you need to bring. This is the bare minimum. Use your common sense to anticipate and plan for weather, environmental and lodging conditions.

As an example, consider the ten-day retreat for which VSI rented La Casa Maria, a Catholic retreat center in Montecito, California. The facility provided rooms, beds, mattresses, linens and towels, buffet-style vegetarian breakfast and lunch, and an evening snack.

This is the bare-bones list of what meditators were asked to bring:

- meditation cushion and sitting mat, and
- comfortable attire, conducive to meditation environment.

Here's a suggested list of what else you might bring:

- support cushions or other meditation accessories,

- a flashlight, particularly for remote locations,
- slip-on shoes sturdy enough for walking (you always remove your shoes at the door of the meditation hall),
- light blanket (allowed in the meditation hall at some retreats—ask beforehand),
- prescription and non-prescription medications, toiletries, soap, shampoo, glasses,
- a notebook and pen,
- an umbrella or raincoat,
- an alarm clock,
- warm socks,
- parka, gloves, hat, and
- extra blankets.

Remember that, except for emergencies, participants do not leave the retreat grounds. Once you are there, you are there. Since you may be two hundred miles from the nearest K-Mart, take what you need. Don't assume it will be provided.

## What to wear

Some retreats have dress codes. For instance, at a Zen retreat the monks wear traditional black meditation robes, while novices and students wear black tops and pants. No matter how cold it gets, blankets, jackets, hats, sweaters, or gloves are not allowed in the meditation hall.

At other retreats, such as those conducted by Insight groups, there is no dress code; you are asked to wear appropriate, comfortable clothes for meditating. The over-all rule of etiquette for the retreat is: Do not wear, say, smell like, or do anything that would disturb your fellow meditators.

Some retreats have laundry facilities. Even if they do, we suggest that you bring enough extra socks and under-wear. That way, you have one less thing to think about.

## GETTING YOUR FEET WET WITHOUT DROWNING

A retreat lasts for as long as advertised, whether one day, four days, or ninety days. The sponsor of your retreat wants participants to start at the beginning and stay until the end. Finishing what you start is vitally important for two reasons:

1. The act of completion is a vital aspect of meditation, a natural extension of experiencing each moment of life from beginning to end.

2. Completion brings tremendous satisfaction and a genuine feeling of accomplishment.

For your first retreat, choose a duration between one and four days. This way you can get your feet wet, without drowning. Be prepared to stay until the conclusion of the retreat—no matter what. If you feel as if you just can't take it, contact your retreat manager, who can arrange for you to discuss your desire to leave with a teacher.

### Period of adjustment

When you arrive at a retreat, you may initially feel that you are out of your depth. Looking around the meditation hall, you're positive that everybody is calm and serene—except you. Rest easy. You are not alone.

The first several days of a retreat are difficult adjustment periods for everyone—even the teachers. You've asked your mind and body to stop on a dime. And it's going to take a few days for the message to get through.

Once again, stick to your guns. It is common for a meditator to initially regret coming to a retreat, only to experience even greater regret when it is over.

### Daily retreat schedule

Retreats are well organized. A typical day might look like this:

| | |
|---|---|
| 5:45 | wake up |
| 6:15 | sit (all sitting sessions are 25 minutes) |
| 7:00 | breakfast |
| 7:45 | mindful work |
| 8:45 | meditation instruction |
| 9:45 | walking meditation (all periods are 25 minutes) |
| 10:45 | sit |
| 11:30 | walk |
| 12:15 | sit or walk |
| 12:45 | lunch, rest |
| 2:15 | sit |
| 3:00 | walk |
| 3:45 | sit |
| 4:45 | walk |
| 5:15 | tea, light snack |
| 6:15 | sit |
| 7:00 | walk |
| 7:30 | dharma talk |
| 8:30 | walk |
| 9:15 | sit |
| 10:00 | bed |

> *It is common for a meditator to initially regret coming to a retreat, only to experience even greater regret when it is over.*

The orderly schedule, in itself, helps you to develop your meditation practice.

## Roommates

Most retreats do not have private accommodations. Depending on the facility, you will probably share your room and bathroom with more than one person. Generally, quarters will be fairly tight. At some retreats, as many as eight people may share a room.

Should problems with roommates arise, look at the upside; this is a terrific opportunity to practice mindfulness. If your roommate's sleep-shattering snoring sounds like an Aerosmith concert, take a close look at how you let unwanted noise make you angry, or your obsessive need to control people and your environment.

## Problems and emergencies

Your retreat sponsor tries to ensure that the retreat environment is as safe and conducive to meditation as possible. From time to time, though, there will be problems or emergencies. The person who handles emergencies is the retreat manager. He or she is usually a meditator with extensive experience attending, assisting at, and supervising retreats.

Meals, room assignments, and work schedules are all planned by the retreat manager, and it is the manager, not your teacher, who makes sure things run smoothly.

During the retreat, you will probably observe "noble silence", which means that you do not talk to anyone. If you have problems with a roommate, become ill, have a special disability, or encounter any extraordinary situation, don't take things into your own hands—go to the retreat manager.

## Silence at retreats

Silence is particularly golden at a meditation retreat, and all participants observe the noble silence: Once the retreat starts, all talk stops. Noble Silence includes non-verbal communication, such as direct eye contact, which is to be avoided. The only exceptions to maintaining noble silence are emergencies, asking directions when performing mindful work, asking a teacher a question, and interviews.

Noble silence is meant to benefit the development of your own meditation practice. As for your fellow meditators, your silence allows them to work with a minimum of distraction. Keeping silent also curbs everyone's natural propensity to chatter, complain, or shmooze. This affords you a great opportunity to wake up to the reality that much of what you say is meaningless, useless, and perhaps even harmful, both to yourself and others.

*During the retreat, you will probably observe "noble silence", which means that you do not talk to anyone.*

After several days of an intense dialogue with yourself, you may become so bored with it that you actually stop. When this happens, you may find yourself experiencing what many meditators describe as the most profound sense of peace and freedom they have ever felt.

To discourage breaking the silence to deliver messages, most retreats set up bulletin boards near the dining area where you can post urgent messages to and receive replies from the retreat manager, teachers, and other personnel. Unless it is truly an emergency, this is your first line of communication. Simply write a short note explaining the situation and wait for a reply.

*After several days of an intense dialogue with yourself, you may become so bored with it that you actually stop.*

## Noble silence

In 1994, Ron Suskind, a reporter for the Wall Street Journal, attended an Insight meditation retreat at the IMS center in Barre, Massachusetts. He reported his experience in an article (11/16/94) entitled "Silent Treatment: Our Reporter Tries The Meditative Life." Here are excerpts from his account:

"This fall's long silence [87 day retreat] was fully subscribed by early spring. Shorter sessions, three and ten day meditations are even more crowded...."

"Though religious conversion to Buddhism is not high on the menu—guests tend to arrive with some Judeo-Christian background...and leave with it intact—much else may be altered during the long hours of silence...."

"In the darkness, at 5 a.m., a wake-up gong rings. Meditation starts at 5:30.... After 45 minutes...everyone shuffles to break-fast—a hearty, vegetarian buffet.... The absence of conversation [as Noble Silence is observed] without speaking or making eye contact is like taking a meal on a crowded subway car, only quieter...."

"Halfway into the second day of silence...something happens: a lifting, expansive sensation. I feel weightless, aware and very much awake, but completely still...."

"The next two days pass slowly, but I don't mind because I've slowed down too."

Learn to be patient. Time is a funny thing at a retreat. What might seem like an eternity could only be an hour. While you're waiting, take as your object of meditation the process of waiting. Use this time as an opportunity to mindfully explore exactly what arises when you have to wait.

Obviously, if there is a medical or other emergency, do whatever you have to do to seek help for yourself and others.

## Dharma talks—personal and group interviews

Dharma, or teaching, talks are given each day by the head teacher (or on a rotating basis from a group of teachers) on a selected aspect of meditation practice. They are not intended as either lectures or sermons, but as a spontaneous manifestation of the truth of the way things are.

The teacher's aim is the communication that goes beyond words, communication that emanates directly from the teacher's intuitive wisdom and passes directly to you the student. This is one reason that many teachers do not encourage notetaking during these talks. Many talks are taped by retreat sponsors, so that students may obtain them later. If you want to tape dharma talks, you must first have the speaker's permission.

At the conclusion of each talk, the teacher will usually take several questions from the retreat members. You may also save your questions for your personal interview.

At large retreats, interviews are conducted on a daily basis by the head teacher and the assistants on a revolving basis so that each student has the opportunity to interact with all teachers at least once during the retreat. These individual and group interviews present an ideal setting for meditators to explore and define their meditation practices. It is always comforting to hear a fellow meditator asking the same question or expressing the same feelings of doubt that you might have.

You will probably be told at the outset that group and individual interviews are not therapy sessions. Discussions and questions are confined to those arising out of your meditation practice. It is not appropriate to use this time to express your feelings, expound on your philosophy of life, or ask questions that are not questions, but merely your desire to hear your own voice.

## Mindful work

At the retreat, simple tasks and chores, usually involving manual labor, need to be done to keep the facility clean and feed everyone. This mindful work, called samu in Buddhist and Zen traditions, is what we earlier called meditation in action.

Mindful work is usually voluntary. At retreat registration, members consult a list of open positions, including early morning wake-up bell ringers, vegetable peelers, pot scrubber, gardeners, and meditation hall cleaners. Believe it or not, these positions fill rapidly. Doing mindful work is considered by meditators both the privilege of serving their fellow retreat members and the opportunity for additional practice of meditation in action.

It is recommended that you participate in some kind of mindful work. Especially beneficial is choosing a task that you have always felt to be sheer drudgery. For example, if you hate doing dishes, volunteer to wash and dry them every day. The effect on your overall meditation practice can be tremendous. The work is also good exercise.

*If you hate doing dishes, volunteer to wash and dry them every day.*

## ETIQUETTE—THE GOLDEN RULE

There is only one basic rule of etiquette at retreats—Do unto others as you would have others do unto you. Thus, do nothing that would disturb or harm your fellow meditators. If someone is rude or disturbing, do not confront him or her or break the noble silence. Contact the retreat manager.

One of the great virtues of meditation practice is learning restraint. Retreats afford an ideal opportunity for you to develop your restraint muscle. Follow the Zen proverb: "Can you wait until the water settles?" Or at the very least, count to ten.

## COSTS

Retreat costs vary according to the facility and the number of days. Here is where your money goes.

### Registration fee

This is the basic charge you will be asked to pay. It covers only your room and board. Your registration fee does not include any payment to your teachers or to the assistants, retreat manager, and other personnel, such as a cook and assistants.

As a rule of thumb, you can estimate the registration fee for retreats will be between thirty-five and seventy-five dollars per day. Some retreat sponsors offer scholarships for those who need assistance.

### Dana

At meditation retreats, teachers follow the custom set forth by the Buddha himself—the tradition called *dana*, which translates from the ancient Pali, the old Indian dialect of Southern Buddhism, as giving, generosity, or gift.

In the dana tradition, the teachings are freely given by teachers without expectation of return. Historically, followers and students reciprocated by providing the teacher with shelter and sustenance.

In accordance with this tradition, modern students contribute financially to the support of the teacher by making individual monetary donations. Separate dana bowls are placed in the meditation hall at the end of the retreat. Students use these to place their contributions to the teacher and the sponsoring organization, and the retreat staff as well.

Teachers and assistants sustain themselves on dana; there is no suggested amount, and the only guideline we offer is that you should contribute what you feel is appropriate.

### "Can you shut down the airport?"

*Teacher Joseph Goldstein relates that at a retreat he conducted, a woman meditator came to him with a distressed look on her face. She told him that the noise coming from the private planes overhead was distracting and disturbing her meditation. Could Goldstein kindly call the nearby airport and ask them to alter the flight patterns for the remainder of the retreat? He could not and did not.*

The dana is given according to means. If you are of modest means and were attending a political fundraiser, you might leave twenty-five dollars, where your wealthy neighbor might leave a thousand. The idea at a retreat is to leave something, a gift. One example (not a hard and fast rule, because there are none when it comes to dana) would be: If the registration fee for a week-long retreat is four hundred to five hundred dollars, then it would be reasonable to leave twenty-five dollars per day for the teacher and fifteen dollars per day for the support staff and retreat manager.

Dana given to teachers is considered by the IRS to be income, and as such is not tax deductible. As for the sponsoring organization, if it is not-for-profit, you may be able to deduct your registration fee as a charitable contribution.

## Dana and lovingkindness

*The act of giving itself is of immeasurable benefit to the giver; for it opens up the heart, diminishes for a moment one's self-absorption, and places value on the well-being of others.... The size or value of the gift is of almost no importance—the act of giving itself generates a thought-moment devoid of greed and full of lovingkindness.*

INSIGHT
*A joint newsletter of the
Insight Meditation Society and the Barre Center for Buddhist Studies
(Spring 1997)*

## *APPENDIX RECAP*

- An ancient Tibetan proverb says that the teacher is like a fire: Get too close and you get burned. Stand too far away and you miss the heat.

- Three hallmarks of good teachers:

    They enhance your life. They don't run it.

    They are not on ego trips that can only be satisfied by your dependency.

    They keep you from straying from the path, while at the same time letting you find your own way.

- In some meditation traditions, the teacher is thought of as a spiritual friend. A good spiritual friend wants you to be as independent as possible.

- Meditation retreats should provide the optimal setting for intense practice with good teachers.

- When choosing your retreat, pick one you can finish. For your first retreat, choose a duration between one and four days.

- Observing the noble silence means that once the retreat starts, all talk stops.

- The basic retreat rule is: Do nothing that would disturb or harm your fellow meditators.

# Glossary

*acariya.* (Insight tradition) Teacher, master.

*ashram.* Indian monastic community.

*Bhagavad-Gita. The Song of God,* Hindu scripture.

*bodhicitta.* The altruistic aspiration, based on love and compassion, to achieve enlightenment for the benefit of all beings. Bodhicitta is the first rung on the ladder for a *bodhisattva.*

*bodhisattva.* A person on the path to spiritual enlightenment through compassion. A bodhisattva manifests the Eight Precepts and has vowed not to enter nirvana until all other sentient beings have gone before. The Six Perfections comprise the practice of the bodhisattva. They are: generosity, ethical discipline, patience, perseverance, meditation, and wisdom.

*brahma-viharas.* Lovingkindness and compassion, along with equanimity and sympathetic joy, the four "heavenly abodes," (supreme virtues) in Buddhism. These states are aroused or achieved by meditation.

*brujo.* Male witch in Mexican and Native American traditions.

*Buddha.* The great teacher, founder of Buddhism.

*c'hi or chi.* (Chinese) Energy flow in the body.

*ch'an.* Chinese for Zen.

*Chakras.* The body's energy centers, wheels of light. Originating in Hinduism, this system views the human body as a constellation of energy fields. The chakra centers in the body are the nexus between the spiritual and physical aspects. There are seven major chakras—the root of the spine, the sacral plexus, the solar plexus, the heart, the throat, the center of the head, and the top of the head—each of which contains a unique energy that contributes to the overall energy flow of the body (see *c'hi*). In Sanskrit, the centers are called, respectively, *muladhara, svadhishthana, manipura, anahata, vishuddha, ajna,* and *sashasrara.*

*Dalai Lama.* Reincarnated spiritual and political leader of Tibet.

*dana.* (Pali) Gift, generosity. An ancient Buddhist tradition in which followers and students contribute to the teacher's sustenance and survival. At retreats, dana is usually a monetary donation from students to teacher and other personnel.

*Dhammapada.* Collection of the Buddha's teachings.

*dharma.* (Sanskrit) Literally, "holding." The main pillar of Buddhist teachings. (1) The impermanent state of existence. (2) The immutable universal laws. Cosmic order, right action, truth. (3) The teachings of the Buddha. *Dharma pain.* Pain from experience stored in the body.

*dhyana.* (Sanskrit) Meditation.

*dikenga.* Cross within a circle. Basic symbol of the Kongo religion.

*dokusan.* Private meeting between Zen teacher and student.

*ein sof.* In the *kabbalah,* the highest meditative state.

*fakir.* (Originally Egyptian, then Hindu) Beggar and holy man.

*fetish.* Sacred or magical object.

*Gehennah.* Valley where refuse was buried near Jerusalem. Figuratively, a place of torment.

*gnosis.* (Greek) Knowledge, wisdom.

*gomden.* Tibetan cushion.

*guru.* (Sanskrit) A teacher or master. Some gurus require unconditional obedience from students. Compare with *kalyana mitta.*

*hara.* Energy center of the body, lower abdomen, genitals.

*Hinayana Buddhism.* Literally, "the lesser vehicle." One of the main branches of Buddhism.

*Hindi.* Modern Indian language.

*hitbodidut.* Kabbalistic meditation practice. As described by the eighteenth-century Hasidic master Rabbi Nachman of Breslov. "The height of hitbodidut meditation is when, because of your great longing to unite with God, you feel your soul bound to your body by no more than a single strand. Is there anything better to strive for in this life?" *See Maggid.*

*hoja.* (Sufi) Meditation teacher. Nasrudin was one.

*I Ching.* (Chinese) *Book of Changes,* contains fundamentals of *Tao.* The first versions of this ancient classic were believed to have been written as far back as 3000 B.C. The book is considered to contain the fundamental principles of the *dharma.* Practitioners traditionally cast yarrow sticks (now coins) and matched them with a collection of sixty-four hexagrams, which were then interpreted through the book and the practitioner's intuition. The I Ching became popular in the West with philosophers, mathematicians, and psychiatrists, including Carl Jung, who was a major proponent of its veracity.

*kabbalah.* Jewish sacred mystical teachings based on the scriptures. There are several systems of kabbalist teachings. One, called the Tree of Life, is based on the story that there were two trees in the Garden of Eden, the tree of knowledge of good and evil and the tree of life. Kabbalists believe that before Adam and Eve were cast out of the perfection of Eden for eating the fruit of the tree of knowledge, they were given a glimpse of the tree of life. It is the knowledge this glimpse afforded them that is said to be the basis for Jewish mystical traditions.

*kalyana mitta.* (Spiritual friend). The teacher-student relationship In the *Theravadan* tradition, preferred among meditators in the West. In this relationship, the student does not subordinate his or her own will to that of the *guru.* Instead, he or she recognizes the teacher's intrinsic authority, wisdom, and compassion and naturally comes into a respectful relationship with it.

*karma.* Totality of a person's actions. Fate.

*karma yoga*. Meditation in action. The practice of mindfulness in daily activity. *See samu.*

*kensho. See satori.*

**kether**. Highest level of the kabbalists' tree of life.

*kinhin*. Zen walking meditation.

*koan*. Zen riddle leading to enlightenment. In *Rinzai* practice, koans are the core of the teaching method. Koans cannot be solved with logical, deductive reasoning methods. Thus, in order to "pass" (solve) a koan, the student must go beyond normal discursive thinking.

*kriya*. Powerful tantra meditation technique.

*kundalini*. The spiritual/physical power center at the base of the spine.

*lama*. (Tibetan Buddhist) Master or guru.

*maggid*. Among Jewish mystics, a spiritual teacher who is qualified to give the secret teachings. The Maggid directs the student in different techniques, among them *hitbodidut* meditation, a form of unstructured, wordless self-expression.

*Mahayana Buddhism*. Literally, "the greater vehicle." One of the main branches of Buddhism.

*maithuna*. Tantric sexual meditation techniques.

*makosi*. Zulu spirit master.

*mandala*. A circular design containing images and forms representing the total universe.

*mantra.* Repetition of a sound, word or phrase, used in many meditation traditions. Some schools, such as Tibetan Buddhism, believe the sounds generate protective forces.

*marker.* Object of meditation. An anchor device used in meditation to prevent the mind from wandering.

*maya.* Illusion.

*meditation.* The art of opening to each moment of life with calm awareness. The cultivation of mindfulness both while at rest and in action.

*metta.* Lovingkindness in Eastern meditation traditions.

*metta sutra.* Discourses of the Buddha.

*middle way.* A path to enlightenment which balances searching and surrender. Mindful living in moderation. Followers of the middle way do not dwell in extreme behavior or conduct, whether overindulgence or deprivation. This leads to the cessation of attachment and aversion, which is the cornerstone of the release from suffering.

*minkisi.* Kongo medicine fetishes.

*mudra.* (Sanskrit) Gesture or hand position. In meditation practice, the way the hands are held. Certain mudras are thought to embody particular energies. For instance, the cosmic egg expresses the desire to overcome delusion and ignorance and achieve enlightenment.

*nirvana.* A state of soul in which all suffering has ceased.

*noble silence.* Silence observed on retreat.

*norepinephrine.* A stress-reduction hormone.

*noting.* A mindfulness technique allowing the meditator to note temporary *objects of meditation* that take over the field of awareness. Noting allows you to view feelings, emotions, and thoughts in the context of your meditation.

*object of meditation.* An activity used as the focal point of meditation. In the breathing technique, for example, the object of meditation is the breath.

*Om.* (Hindu) Symbolic, mystical utterance of affirmation.

*orisha.* African god.

*Pali.* Old Indian dialect of Southern Buddhism, the religious language of Buddhism.

*pantheon.* All of the gods in a religious tradition.

*prana.* Breath, intuitive wisdom. *Pranic.* Having to do with prana.

*quies.* (Early Christian) Rest, peace of the highest state.

*rinpoche.* Same as *lama.*

*Rinzai.* Zen school which uses koans in teaching.

*roshi.* (Japanese) Honorific title for a Zen master, teacher or elder who shows students the way to enlightenment.

*ruah.* (Hebrew) Breath, translated as the "spirit of God."

*sadhana.* Meditation practice.

*samadhi.* Oneness with God and the universe.

*samatha.* Mindfulness.

*Samu.* Work-practice. in contrast with *zazen,* sitting practice. Mindful work. Samu can be anything from washing dishes to writing software applications.

*Sanskrit.* The classic Indian language, dating back to the third century B.C. The language in which Buddha taught and in which many Hindu scriptures are written.

*sashasrara.* (Hindu) Highest *chakra,* just above the crown of the head.

*satori.* In Zen practice, the state of awakening to one's true nature, and thus becoming enlightened.

*sephiroth.* Levels of the kabbalists' tree of life.

*shaman.* A human mediator between the spiritual and natural worlds.

*shema.* A Jewish meditation focusing on several aspects of God.

*shikantaza.* The core of *Soto* Zen meditation practice, loosely translated as "just sitting." Shikantaza does not rely on breath techniques, *koans,* or use an *object of meditation.* This practice is based in the belief that the practitioner, by assuming on a mental and physical level the posture that the Buddha took, manifests by definition the state of enlightenment. Shikantaza has no object of meditation, no technique. It is empty, devoid of everything.

*Six Perfections.* See *bodhisattva.*

*Soto.* Zen sect.

*stillpoint.* Pause or gap between inhalation and exhalation.

*sutras.* The recorded transcripts of the original teachings of the Buddha as recorded verbatim by his student Ananda. Both major schools of Buddhism, the Hinayana and the Mahayana, have their own versions of these sutras.

*tai-chi.* A system of postures and exercises for self-defense and to aid in meditation. The Great Wisdom.

*tai-pei.* The Great Compassion. Related to *tai-chi.* Also *Daihi.*

*tantra.* Higher esoteric teachings and literature of Vajrayana meditational practice. *Tantric.* Having to do with tantra.

*Tao.* (Chinese) "the way of life and death," the Universal Truth. Similar to the concept of *dharma.* Expounded in the Tao Te Ching (Book of the Way), by Lao-Tzu.

*Theraveda Buddhism.* The school that predominates in Southeast Asia. It is a part of the Hinayana school, one of the two major belief systems, or "vehicles" of Buddhism.

*tokusan.* Bamboo stick used to wake napping meditators.

*tonglen.* Tibetan compassion meditation. Literally, giving and taking. A form of meditation in which the meditator assimilates another's pain and suffering purifies it and returns it to the sufferer, cleansed and energized.

*Torah.* The body of Jewish scripture, more narrowly, the five books of Moses.

*Vajrayana.* Also called the *tantric* school or the Diamond

Vehicle. A tradition, part of the *Mahayana* school considered to be the pinnacle of aspiration in Buddhist practice. At this level, the practitioner is empowered to perform a kind of "spiritual alchemy," transforming the hindrances of worldly thought and sorrow into blissful states of enlightenment and realization. These insights are achieved through a sophisticated combination of mental and physical techniques that seek to open the body's energy centers, the *chakras*.

*Vipassana.* Insight tradition of *Theravadan Buddhism*. A school of meditation.

*Wicca.* Contemporary religion based on witchcraft.

*yoga.* A general term for a variety of Indian meditation traditions.

*yogi.* A person who practices yoga.

*zabuton.* In Japanese, a small meditation futon upon which the *zafu* sits.

*zafu.* In Japanese, a meditation cushion, usually round.

*zazen.* In the Zen tradition, the practice of sitting meditation, including *koan* practice.

*Zen.* Japanese form of *dhyana,* the Sanskrit word for meditation, related to the Chinese *ch'an.* A branch of Buddhism.

*zendo.* Zen meditation hall.

*zikr.* (Sufi) Remembrance. Among dervishes, a *mantra* used while dancing.

# Resource Section

## BOOKS

Adler, Margot. *Drawing Down the Moon*. Beacon, 1979.

Anand, Margo. *The Art of Sexual Ecstasy*. Jeremy P. Tarcher, 1988.

Andrews, Lynn V. *Teachings Around the Sacred Wheel*. Harper & Row, 1990.

Anderson, Margaret, *The Unknowable Gurdjieff*. Routledge and Kegan Paul, 1962.

Artress, Lauren, *Walking A Sacred Path*.

Beck, Charlotte Joko, *Nothing Special*. San Francisco: Harper, 1994.

Bercholz, S. and Kohn, S.C. eds. *Entering the Stream: An Introduction to The Buddha and His Teachings*.

Bhikku, Buddhadasa, *Mindfulness with Breathing*. Wisdom Publications, 1996.

Blakesee, Thomas. *The Right Brain*. PEI Books, 1980.

Bolen, Jean Shinoda. *Goddesses in Every Woman*. Harper and Row, 1985.

Boorstein, Sylvia, *It's Easier than You Think: The Buddhist Way to Happiness*. San Francisco: Harper.

Bradbury, Ray, *Zen in the Art of Writing.* Joshua Odell Editions, 1993.

Cavendish, Richard. *The Tarot.* Crescent Books, 1986.

Chetanananda, Swami, *The Breath of God.* Rudra Press, 1988.

Chodron, Pema, *When Things Fall Apart. . . .* Shambhala, 1997.

Coomaraswamy, Ananda K. and Nivedita (Sister). *Myths of the Hindus and Buddhists.* Dover, 1967.

Copleston, Frederick, S. J. *A History of Philosophy, Vol. 2,* Doubleday, 1962.

The Dalai Lama, *Healing Anger.* Snow Lion, 1997.

Daraul, Arkon. *Secret Societies.* Octagon, 1983.

Davies, Hunter. *The Beatles.* McGraw-Hill, 1978.

Durant, Will. *The Story of Civilization Vol. I: Our Oriental Heritage.* Simon and Schuster, 1936.

Engler, R. and Hayashi, Y., *The Way of No Thinking: The Prophecies of Japan's Kunihiro Yamate.* Council Oaks Books, 1995.

Epstein, Dr. Mark, *Thoughts without a Thinker.* Basic Books, 1996.

Feuerstein, George. *Sacred Sexuality.* Jeremy Tarcher, 1992.

Fields, Rick; Taylor, Peggy; Weyler, Rex; and Ingrasci, Rick. *Chop Wood Carry Water: A Guide to Finding Spiritual Fulfillment in Everyday Life.* Jeremy P. Tarcher, 1984.

Gaer, Joseph. *How the Great Religions Began.* New American Library, 1956

Gallwey, W. Timothy. *The Inner Game of Tennis.* Random House, 1974.

Garrison, Omar. *Tantra: the Yoga of Sex.* Julian Press.

Gersi, Douchan. *Faces in the Smoke.* Jeremy P. Tarcher, 1991.

Glassman, B. and Fields, R., *Instructions to the Cook: A Zen Master's Lessons in Living a Life That Matters.*

Goldstein, Joseph, *Insight Meditation: The Practice of Freedom.*

Goldstein, J. and Kornfield, J., *Seeking the Heart of Wisdom: The Path of Enlightenment Meditation.*

Goleman, Daniel. *The Meditative Mind.* Jeremy P. Tarcher, 1988.

Goldstein, Joseph, *Insight Meditation: The Practice of Freedom.* Shambhala.

Griffin, Susan. *Woman and Nature.* Harper and Row, 1978.

Gunaratana, Ven. H., *Mindfulness in Plain English.* Wisdom Publications, 1994.

Gyatrol Rinpoche, Ven., *Ancient Wisdom.* Snow Lion, 1993.

Hanh, Thich Nhat, *The Miracle of Mindfulness.* Beacon Press, 1996

Harner, Michael. *The Way of the Shaman.* San Francisco: Harper, 1990.

Harman, Willis, and Rheingold, Howard. *Higher Creativity.* Jeremy P. Tarcher, 1984.

Hixon, Lex, *Coming Home.* Larson Publications, 1995.

Hooper, Judith, and Teresi, Dick. *The Three Pound Brain.* Jeremy P. Tarcher, 1986.

Huber, Cheri, *Being Present in the Darkness: Depression as an Opportunity for Self-Discovery.* Berkeley, 1996.

Humphreys, Christmas, *Zen Buddhism.* Routledge, Chapman & Hall.

Huxley, Aldous, *The Perennial Philosophy.* Borgo Press, 1990.

Jackson, Phil, *Sacred Hoops: Spiritual Lessons of a Hardwood Warrior.* Hyperion.

Johnson, Will, *The Posture of Meditation.* Shambhala, 1996

Kabat-Zinn, Jon, *Full Catastrophe Living.* Bell, 1990.

Kapleau, Roshi Philip, *The Three Pillars of Zen.* Audio Products, 1995.

Kelly, Marcia and Jack, *Sanctuaries,* Crown, 1996.

Klein, Allen. *The Healing Power of Humor.* Jeremy P. Tarcher, 1987.

Kohn, Michael. *The Shambhala Dictionary of Buddhism and Zen.* Shambhala, 1991.

Kopp, Wolfgang, *Free Yourself of Everything,* Tuttle, 1994.

_____, *Zen: Beyond All Words.* Tuttle, 1996.

Kornfield, J. and Breiter, P. *A Still Forest Pool.* Theosophical Publishing, 1985.

Kornfield, Jack, *Living Dharma.* Shambhala, 1995.

LeShan, Lawrence, *How to Meditate.* Little Brown, 1974.

MacKenzie, Norman, ed. *Secret Societies.* Collier 1967.

Maharshi, Ramana, *The Spiritual Teaching of Ramana Maharshi.* Shambhala, 1989.

Marthaler, Dennis. *Picture Me Perfect.* Newcastle, 1985.

McDonald, Kathleen. *How To Meditate.* Wisdom Publications 1994.

Meadows, Kenneth. *The Medicine Way.* Element Books, 1990.

Medicine Hawk (Dr. Douglas Wilburn) and Grey Cat. *The Medicine Way.* Inner Light, 1990.

Merton, Thomas. *New Seeds of Contemplation.* New Directions, 1972.

Miler, Ronald S. and Editors of *New Age Journal. As Above, So Below.* Jeremy P. Tarcher, 1992.

Mitchell, John. *The View Over Atlantis.* Ballentine Books, 1972.

Mitchell, Stephen, trans., *Tao te Ching.* HarperCollins, 1991.

Mizundo, Kogen. *Basic Buddhist Concepts.* Kosei, 1987.

Moore, Thomas, *Meditations.* HarperCollins, 1995.

Moyers, Bill D. et al., *Healing and the Mind.* Doubleday.

Mundy, Talbot. *The Devil's Guard.* Appleton Century, 1936.

Mundy, Talbot. *OM: the Secret of Arbor Valley.* Little Brown, 1938.

Murphy, Michael. *The Future of the Body.* Jeremy P. Tarcher, 1991.

Mykoff, Moshe, ed., *The Empty Chair.* Jewish Lights, 1996.

O'Neal, D. ed., *Meister Eckhart, from Whom God Hid Nothing.*

Osbon, Diane K., ed., *A Joseph Campbell Companion.* HarperCollins, 1995.

Ouspensky, P. D. *Tertium Organum.* New York: Vintage Books, div. of Random House, 1982.

Pagels, Elaine. *The Gnostic Gospels.* Random House. 1979.

Papus. *The Kabbala.* Samuel Weiseer, 1978.

Prabhavananda, Swami and Isherwood, Christopher. *The Song of God* (Bhagavad-Gita). New American Library 1992.

Rinpoche, Kalu, *Luminous Mind.* Wisdom Publications.

Rolek, Michiko J., *Mental Fitness.* Weatherill, 1996.

Rossi, Ernest. *The 20-Minute Break.* Jeremy P. Tarcher, 1991.

Salzberg, Sharon, *Lovingkindness: The Revolutionary Art of Happiness.* Shambhala, 1995.

Sepharial. *A Manual of Occultism.* Newcastle, 1979.

Shainberg, Lawrence, *Ambivalent Zen.* Knopf.

Sjoor, Monica and Mor, Barbara. *The Great Cosmic Mother.* Harper and Row, 1987.

Sogyal, Rinpoche, *The Tibetan Book of Living and Dying.* San Francisco: Harper, 1994.

Stine, Jean Marie and Benares, Camden. *It's All In Your Head.* Prentice Hall, 1984.

Stone, Ira F., *Seeking the Path to Life.* Jewish Lights, 1993.

Sugrue, Thomas. *The Story of Edgar Cayce.* Holt, Rinehart and Winston, 1945.

Sun Bear; Wabun Wind; and Mulligan, *Chrysalis. The Medicine Wheel Workbook.* Simon & Schuster, 1982.

Suzuki, Roshi Shunryu, *Zen Mind, Beginner's Mind.* Weatherill, 1990.

Suzuki, Daisetz Teitaro, *The Essentials of Buddhism.* Greenwood, 1973.

Time-Life Books, eds. of *The Spirit World.* Time-Life, 1992.

Thompson, Robert Farris. *Face of the Gods.* Museum of African Art, 1996.

Thondup, Tulku, *The Healing Power of Mind.* Shambhala, 1998.

Ueshiba, Morihei, *The Art of Peace.* Shambhala, 1992.

Walker, Benjamin. *Gnosticism.* Aquarian Press, 1985.

Wallace, B. Alan, *Tibetan Buddhism: From the Ground Up.*

Wallace, Black Elk and Lyon, William S. Black Elk: *The Sacred Ways of a Lakota.* San Francisco: Harper, 1991.

Wallbank, Taylor, ed. *Civilization Past and Present.* Scott, Foresman and Co., 1962.

Walsh, Roger. *The Spirit of Shamanism,* Jeremy P. Tarcher, 1990.

Waters, Frank; with Oswald White Bear Fredericks. *Book of the Hopi.* Penguin, 1977.

Watts, Alan, *The Wisdom of Insecurity.* Random, 1961.

Wilber, Ken, *No Boundary.* Shambhala, 1981.

Winokur, Jon, ed. *Zen to Go.* NAL Dutton, 1990.

White, John, ed. *Frontiers of Consciousness.* Julian Press, 1974.

Woudhuysen, Jan. *Tarot Therapy.* Jeremy P. Tarcher, 1988.

Yamada, Koun. *Gateless Gate.* Univ. of Arizona Press, 1991.

# NEW AGE PERIODICALS

*Better World*
17211 Orozco
Granada Hills, CA 91344

*Body, Mind & Soul*
4386 Westheimer
Houston, TX 77027

*Body, Mind, Spirit*
15 W. 24th St.,
10th Floor
New York, NY 10010

*Body, Mind, Spirit*
255 Hope St.
Providence, RI 02906

*Brain & Strategy*
2290 East Prospect
Road, #2
Fort Collins, CO 80535

*Branches of Light*
2671 W. Broadway
Vancouver, BC
CANADA V6K2G2

*Catalyst*
362 E. Broadway
Salt Lake City, UT 84102

*Common Boundary*
515 Rockdale Dr.
San Francisco, CA 94127

*Common Ground*
305 San Anselmo Ave.,
#313
San Anselmo, CA 94960

*Connecting Link*
9392 Whitneyville Road
Alto, MI 49302

*Connexions*
4037 Stone Way N.
Seattle, WA 98103

*Country Connections*
14431 Ventura Blvd., #407
Sherman Oaks, CA 91423

*Creation Spirituality*
P.O. Box 20369
Oakland, CA 94623

*Discovery Center Magazine*
2940 N. Lincoln Ave.
Chicago, IL 60657

*Earthstar/Whole Life New England*
208 High Street, #4
Portland, ME 04101

*Free Spirit Magazine*
107 Sterling Place
Brooklyn, NY 11217

*Gnosis*
401 Terry A. Francois
Blvd., Suite 110
San Francisco, CA 94107

*Health & News Reviews*
27 Pine Street
New Canaan, CT 06840

*Health & Spirit*
410 State Street
Bridgeport, CT 06604

*Heldref Publications*
1319 18th St. NW
Washington, DC
20036-1802

*High Times Magazine*
235 Park Ave. South,
5th Floor
New York, NY 10003

*Holistic Education Review*
P.O. Box 328
Brandon, VT 05733-0328

*Holistic Living*
360 Nassau St.
Princeton, NJ 08540

*Inner Self*
915 S. 21st Ave., #2A
Hollywood, FL 33020

*Inner Views*
P.O. Box 999
Eastsound, WA 98245

*Inquiring Mind*
P.O. Box 9999
North Berkeley Station
Berkeley, CA 94709

*Insight*
Insight Meditation
1230 Pleasant St.
Barre, MA 01005

*Institute of Noetic Sciences*
475 Gate Five Road,
#300
Sausalito, CA 94965

*Integral Publishing*
P.O. Box 1030
Lower Lake, CA 95457

*Intuition*
275 Brannan St.,
3rd Floor
San Francisco, CA 94107

*Lapis*
83 Spring Street
New York, NY 10012

*Let's Live*
444 N. Larchmont Blvd.
Los Angeles, CA 90004

*Lightship of Santa Fe*
P.O. Box 23315
Santa Fe, NM 87502

*Longevity*
277 Park Ave.
New York, NY 10172

*Magical Blend*
133 1/2 Broadway
Chico, CA 95928

*Many Hands*
191 Main Street
Northampton,
MA 01060-3147

*Maplestone*
RR#1, Owen Sound, ON
CANADA N4K5N3

*The Monthly Aspectarian*
P.O. Box 1342
Morton Grove, IL 60053

*Napra Review*
P.O. Box 9
Eastsound, WA 98245

*Natural Alternatives*
P.O. Box 525
Oyster Bay, NY 11771

*Natural Foods
Merchandiser*
1301 Spruce St.
Boulder, CO 80302

*Natural Health*
P.O. Box 1200
Brookline, MA 02147

*New Age Journal*
42 Pleasant St.
Watertown, MA 02172

*New Age Retailer*
208 High Street, #4
Portland, ME 04101

*New Perspectives*
P.O. Box 3208
Hemet, CA 95246

*New Thought Journal*
P.O. Box 700754
Tulsa, OK 74170

*New Times*
P.O. Box 2510
Phoenix, AZ 85002

*New Visions*
10 Taconic Street
Pittsfield, MA 01201

*Nexus*
1680 6th Street, #6
Boulder, CO 80302

*Nexus New Times Magazine*
P.O. Box 22034
Tulsa, OK 74121

Open Exchange
P.O. Box 7880
Berkeley, CA 94707

Parabola
656 Broadway
New York, NY 10012

Personal Transformation
Lotus Publishing, Inc.
4421 W. Okmulgee, #157
Muskogee, OK 74401

The Phoenix
477 Marshall Avenue, #4
St. Paul, MN 55102

The Quest
P.O. Box 270
Wheaton, IL 60189

Revision
1319 18th Street NW
Washington, DC 20036

Science of Mind
3251 West Sixth Street
Los Angeles, CA 90020

Shaman's Drum
P.O. Box 79
Ashland, OR 97520

Shambhala Sun
P.O. Box 399,
Halifax Central
Halifax, NS
CANADA B3J1Z8

Spectrum Magazine
3519 Hamstead Court
Durham, NC 27707-5136

Spectrum Review
P.O. Box 1030
Lower Lake, CA 95457

Spiritual Studies SSC
Booknews
97010 Fields Road,
Apt. 2501
Gaithersburg, MD
20878-2737

Sun
107 N. Roberson
Chapel Hill, NC 27516

Transitions
1000 W. North Avenue
Chicago, IL 60622

Transpersonal Review
21900 Marylee St., #274
Woodland Hills,
CA 91367

Tricycle,
The Buddhist Review
92 Van Dam St., #3
New York, NY 10013

Tripod, Inc.
191 Water St.
Williamstown,
MA 02167

Unity Magazine
5200 NW 43rd Street
Gainesville, FL 32606

Utne Reader
1624 Harmon Place
Minneapolis, MN 55403

Visions
24 Kern Dr.
Perkasie, PA 18944

Whole Earth Review
27 Gate Five Road
Sausalito, CA 94965

Whole Life Times
P.O. Box 1187
Malibu, CA 90265

Words'Worth
30 Brattle St.
Cambridge, MA 02138

World Times
1851 Forest Circle
Santa Fe, NM 87501

Yes
P.O. Box 10818
Bainbridge Island,
WA 98110

Yoga Journal
2054 University Avenue
Berkeley, CA 94704

## SUPPLIERS OF AUDIO AND VIDEO TAPES

Audio Renaissance Tapes
5858 Wilshire Blvd.
Suite 200
Los Angeles, CA 90036
213-939-1840
audiobooks@earthlink.net
(includes Alan Watts Library)

Dharma Seed Tape Library
Box 66
Wendell Depot, MA 01380
(features extensive selection of talks, series, and guided meditations by IMS teachers)

Sounds True
800-333-9185
303-665-5292 (fax)
(eclectic offerings from highly regarded meditation teachers from Eastern and Western traditions)

Stress Reduction Tapes
PO Box 547
Lexington, MA 02173
(mindfulness meditation practice tapes).

Vipassana Support Institute
4070 Albright Ave.
Los Angeles, CA 90066
310-915-1943
310-391-7969 (fax)
(features selection of talks, series, and guided meditations by the Vipassana teacher, Shinzen Young)

## *MAIL-ORDER MEDITATION SUPPLIES*

The following mail-order companies can be contacted for meditation cushions and supplies.

Bodhi Tree Bookstore
8585 Melrose Ave.
West Hollywood, CA 90069-5199
800-825-9798
310-659-1733 (local)
310-659-0178 (fax)
e-mail: bodhitree@bodhitree.com

Carolina Morning Designs
Rt. 67, Box 61
Cullowhee, NC 28723
704-293-5906
Linsi Deyo, Owner
www.Digi-All.com/231/Carolina-Morning-Designs

Samadhi Cushions
RR 1, Box 1
Church St.
Barnet, VT 05821
800-331-7751
e-mail: samadhi@plainfield.bypass.com

# MEDITATION ORGANIZATIONS AND SOCIETIES

The following groups conduct retreats, workshops, and other meditation related events, sometimes outside their geographical areas. Check with group directly for more information.

Cambridge Insight Meditation Society
331 Broadway
Cambridge, MA 02139
617-441-9038
617-491-5070 (fax and information line)

Dhamma Dena
HC-1 Box 250
Joshua Tree, CA 92252
619-362-4815

Green Gulch Farm Zen Center
1601 Shoreline Hwy.
Muir Beach, CA 94965
415-383-3134

Insight Meditation Society
1230 Pleasant St.
Barre, MA 01005
508-355-4378
508-355-6398 (fax)

Lama Foundation
P.O. Box 240
San Cristobal, NM 87564

The Naropa Institute
2130 Arapahoe Ave.
Boulder, CO 80302
800-411-5229   303-546-3578
303-546-5295 (fax)
www.naropa.edu

Northwest Dharma Association
1910 24th Ave.
Seattle, WA 98144
206-324-5373

Southern Dharma Retreat Center
1661 West Road
Hot Springs, NC 28743
704-622-7112

Spirit Rock Meditation Center
PO Box 909
Woodacre, CA 94973
415-488-0164
415-488-0170

Tassajara Zen Mountain Center
39171 Tassajara Rd.
Carmel Valley, CA 93924
415-431-3771
or write: Zen Center
300 Page St.
San Francisco, CA 94102

Transcendental Meditation (TM)
888-LEARNTM

Vajrapani Institute
P.O. Box 2130
Boulder Creek, CA 95006
408-338-6654/7916

Vipassana Support Institute (VSI)
4070 Albright Ave.
Culver City, CA 90066
310-915-1943
310-391-7969 (fax)

## MAIL-ORDER CATALOGS

Audio Renaissance Tapes
5858 Wilshire Blvd.
Suite 200
Los Angeles, CA 90036
213-939-1840
audiobooks@earthlink.net
(includes Alan Watts Library)

Bodhi Tree Bookstore
8585 Melrose Ave.
West Hollywood, CA 90069-5199
800-825-9798
310-659-1733 (local)
310-659-0178 (fax)
e-mail: bodhitree@bodhitree.com

Jewish Lights Publishing
PO Box 237, Sunset Farm Offices, Route 4
Woodstock, VT 05091
802-962-4544
802-457-4004 (fax)

Parallax Press
P.O. Box 7355
Berkeley, CA 94707
(emphasis on Buddhist books and tapes)

Shambhala Publications, Inc.
Order Dept.
P.O. box 308
Boston, MA 02117-0308
617-424-0030
617-236-1563
www.shambhala.com
(mail order division of a major spiritual and meditation book publishers)

## INTERNET

The following are sites where meditation-related pages can be accessed. Several of the sites listed here include hypertext links to others. All web pages were active at the time this book went to press.

http://www. spiritweb.org.
Self-described as "A dedicated worldwide spiritual web site that views spirituality in a modern context in review of current teachings and religious belief-systems.... [T]ries to give an overview of manifold forms of spirituality, independent of any specific...belief system or movement."

http://www.dharmanet.org
DharmaNet International is a website-cum-"clearing house" with many links to organizations, retreats, practice groups, and Buddhist studies.

http://www.yahoo.com/Health/Alternative_Medicine
Massive site with links to everything from Applied Kinesiology to Yoga that relates to "health/alternative/medicine."

http://www.dharma.org/
General and specific information relating to Dharma philosophy as well as sales sites for related information can be found.

http://www.dhammakaya.org
Offers a wide range of information on Dhammakaya meditation; its source, techniques, and results.

http://www.creativity.co.uk/creativity/guhen/meditat.html
An approach to meditation that seeks to combine "Eastern spirituality and Western communicational psychology."

http://www.globe.com.ph/~unicorn/mth.html
A meditation guide that calls itself "Meditation on Twin Hearts."

http://www.hawaiian.net/~innerself/archives/sum95/nukkera.htm
Inner Self, an on-line magazine, offers access to its archives and current articles for information on spirituality and selfhood.

http://www.serenityseating.com/
An online catalog offering a selection of meditation cushions and other products.

http://www.jwdavies.com/chakras.htm
An online catalog.

http://www.seventhray.com/
An online catalog that offers holistic products and self-help tools.

http://www.teleport.com/ ~symbol/
An online catalog that offers meditation pillows.

http://www.gate.net/ ~breath/
From the Transformational Breath Foundation, this page describes transformational breathing and offers products for purchase.

http://www.sivananda.org/meditati.htm
From the Sivananda Yoga and Vedanta Centers, this site describes the benefits and techniques of meditation.

http://www.samadhicushions.com/
An online catalog that offers meditation cushions, gongs, books, and incense.

http://www.meditation.com/
From the Meditation Group Inc., this site provides information on its purpose

http://www.mindspring,com/ ~iquest/
An online catalog that offers "Instant Meditation Goggles."

http://www.catizone.com/sculptor/
An online catalog of self-assembly furniture such as benches, desks, and altars.

http://www.shambhala.org/
A worldwide network of meditation centers that provide instructions, classes and programs in the Shambhala and Tibetan Buddhist traditions.

http://www.he.net/ ~naam/
Provides considerable information on a meditation called Inner Light and Sound.

http://www.indosoft.net.id/personal/anand/
From the Anand Ashram, this site offers information on programs in stress management, meditations, self-exploration and transformation, and other yoga and self-development programs.

http://www.fisu.org/
From the Foundation for International Spiritual Unfoldment, this site promotes meditation through the teachings of Gururaj Ananda Yogi.

http://www.minet.org/
The Meditation Information Network offers online articles that critically examine programs associated with Maharishi Mahesh Yogi.

http://www.sonic.net/~jotokuji/Shugyo.html
Site that offers spiritual therapy and information about the Association for Humanistic Psychology.

http://www.geocities.com/Athens/8612/
This site offers information on Bhaktivedanta meditation.

http://www.haribol.org/
An online magazine with articles on meditation, yoga, health and nutrition, vegetarianism, social issues, and spiritual insights.

http://www.mum.edu/TM.html
From the Maharishi University of Management, this site offers extensive information about the university, its programs, classes and more.

http://www.lisco.com/wuebben/TM/Transcendental_Meditation.html
Site of the Transcendental Meditation-Sidhi program. Offers information about TM, programs, international TM organizations and more.

http://www.osho.org/
"The World of Osho" offers information about "multiversity" programs, stays at the Osho commune and corporate seminars.

# *Index*

**A**

Aboriginal peoples, 175

Acariya, 294, 315

Affirmation, 209

African meditation, 176–81

Akashic Record, 206

Alters, 179–81

Anahata, 118

Anger, 287–88

Anja, 118

Area.
  *see* Environment for
  meditation

Arms, 83

Ashram, 315

Attention, 33, 134

Augustine, St., 48

Awake, 31, 32, 134

Awakening.
  *see* Satori

Awareness, 75–76, 97, 132,
135–37.
  *see also* Meditation object;
  Mindfulness;
  Self awareness

**B**

Back, 79–80, 81

Balance.
  *see* Middle way

Barriers, 59–72, 66, 97–102,
302

Benches, 77, 79–81

Benefits, xviii, 23, 26–29,
201–204, 222, 255–71,
277–78

Berra, Yogi, 126

Bhagavad-Gita, 34, 315

Bhakti, 107, 116

Bliss.
  *see* Ecstasy

Bodhicitta, 140, 315

Bodhisattva, 64, 140, 315

Body scanning, 137–39

Body sensations, 98–100.
see also Discomfort;
in communication,
243–244;
while eating, 239–242;
while meditating, 135–37,
163–64;
and sexuality, 249–251;
at work, 224, 227–228

Bone meditation, 177–179

Boredom, 99, 231

Brahma-viharas, 273, 315

Breath metaphors, 47–48

Breathing, 44, 49–50, 61–62,
119.
see also Exhalation;
Inhalation

Breathing meditation, 45–46,
120–21, 131, 217

Brujo, 176, 315

Buddha, 21, 31, 71, 122–25,
316

Buddhism, 122–42.
see also Religious traditions;
specific sects of Buddhism

Burmese posture, 87–88

Business, 203–04

Butterfly effect, 274

**C**

Calm awareness.
see Awareness

Canonical hours, 166–68

Cayce, Edgar, 205–09

Center.
see Middle way

Centering, 155, 160

Chair, 83, 86

Chakras, 117–18, 140, 208,
250, 316

Ch'an, 125, 316

Chant, 165–68

C'hi, 81, 316

Children, 244–46, 279

Chores, 237–38

Christianity, 143–45, 155–60.
see also Religious traditions

Collective unconscious, 274

Communication, 242–44

Compassion, 70, 243,
273–85, 290–92

Completing a retreat, 303,
306

Concentration, 55, 99.
see also Distractions

Connectedness, 274, 277–78

Consciousness, 106–107

Consistency, 94, 217

Contemplation, 156, 279;
in children, 246;
and sexuality, 249

Control, 47, 268

Correctness, 65, 96, 98

Cosmic egg, 85

Cost of retreats, 312–13

Counting, 54–55, 217

Creative energy, 209

Cross-legged, 87

Cults, 296–98

Cushions, 77–79, 83, 86

## D

Dalai Lama, 35, 140, 316

Dana, 312–13, 316

Dance, 174, 175

Death, 281–82

Deity yoga, 113

Denial, 62, 191

Dervishes, 174

Desert fathers, 155–58

Dhammapada, 102, 316

Dharma, 316;
  pain, 77, 98, 316;
  teaching, 310

Dhyana, 125, 317

Difficulty, 61

Dikenga, 317

Disabilities, 76–77

Discomfort, 73, 77, 83, 98

Distractions, 50–55, 93, 134, 156–57

Divine offices, 166–68

Divinity, partner's, 247–48, 252

Dokusan, 128, 301, 317

Doubt, 59–61, 97

Dreaming, 233–34

Dreamtime, 175

Dress at retreats, 305–06

Driving, 229–31

## E

Earth Goddess, 214–16

Eating, 239–42

Ecstasy, 101, 155, 173, 250, 269

Ego, 69, 151, 281

Ein sof, 150, 317

Emotional pain, 136, 263, 266

Emotions, 224, 243–44, 257, 300–301.
  *see also* Body sensations; specific emotions

Enemies, 288–89, 296

Energy, 37

Enlightenment, 64, 117, 123–24.
  *see also* Satori

Environment, 191;
  for meditation, 98–99, 107–108, 157, 300

Equipment, 92–93, 304–05

Escape, 63, 299

Etiquette at retreats, 306, 311

Exercise, 231–32

Exhalation, 55–57

Expanding breath, 121

Expectations, 25–26

Exploitation, 296

Eyes, 83

# F

Fakir, 191, 317

Family, 242–46

Fear, 60, 101, 281

Feedback, 301

Feel of meditation, 37

Fees, 312–13

Feet, 83

Fetish, 180, 317

Fist, 85

Flexibility, 87, 91

Flow, 221

Flower posture, 75

Focus, 32, 38, 50–55.
  see also Awareness

Food, 239–42

Forgiveness, 288

Fourth way, 191

Free association, 52

Frequency, 39

Friend to the world, 276

Frustration, 52

Full lotus, 91

# G

Gaia, 214–16

Gehennah, 317

Gnosis, 145, 317

Gnosticism, 145–48

God, 113–14, 144–47,
169–70, 225;
  names of, 34, 152–55

Goddess, 210–16

Gomden, 79, 317

Great Spirit, 182–83

Gregorian Chant, 165–68

Groups, 93, 165–66.
  see also Retreat

Guided meditation, 197, 231

Gurdjieff, G. I., 190–93

Guru, 67, 294, 297, 317

# H

Half lotus, 90

Hands, 84–85

Happiness, 53, 255–56,
267–69

Hara, 84, 85, 317

Hare Krishna, 110

Hatred, 288–89

Head, 82

Heart, 68–69, 155, 275

Hegira, 170

Hesychasm, 156

High, being, 31, 67

Hinayana Buddhism, 317

Hindi, 317

Hindrances.
  *see* Barriers

Hinduism, 115–22.
  *see also* Religious traditions

Hitbodidut, 151, 317

Hoja, 173, 318

Home life, 237–54

Humor, 69–70, 172–73

Hunting, 176

Hurrying, 67

Hypnotism, 31, 63, 206

**I**

I Ching, 131, 318

Illness, 206, 256–57, 281

Illusion, 70

Insight, 100

Insight Meditation, 50, 76, 107, 132–33

Interconnectedness, 274, 277–78

Interviews, 310

Intimate relationships, 246–54

Intuition, 101, 127, 146, 194; in children, 245–46

Islam, 169–74.
  *see also* Religious traditions

**J**

Jaw, 82

Judaism, 148–55

**K**

Kabbalah, 149–54, 318

Kalyana mitta, 294–96, 318

Karma, 67, 69, 247, 318

Karma Yoga, 117, 225

Kensho.
  *see* Satori

Kether, 150

Kindness.
  *see* Lovingkindness

Kinhin, 161, 319

Kneeling, 91–92

Knees, 79–80, 81

Koan, 127–29, 319

Kongo, 179–80

Koran, 172

Kriya, 199–200, 319

Kundalini, 116–17, 319

**L**

Labor, 238–39

Labyrinths, 161

Lama, 319

Landmark, 47

Leaders.
  *see* Teachers

Learning, 36

Left-brain/right brain, 60, 101, 187

Levitation, 204–205

Life, 66, 97, 161; mindful, 223–225

Life force, 47, 81

Life Readings, 207

Lion breath, 121

Lord's Prayer, 208–209

Lotus positions, 89–91

Loved ones.
  see Children;
  Family;
  Partner

Lovemaking.
  see Sexuality

Lovingkindness, 273–79,
283–92

Luxury, 299

# M

Maggid, 151, 319

Magic, 177

Maharishi Mahesh Yogi,
200–202

Mahayana Buddhism, xx,
140–41

Maithuna, 250, 319

Makosi, 179, 319

Mandala, 108, 319

Manipura, 118

Mantra, 29, 95, 108–11, 158,
202, 320

Markers, 54–55, 320

Mastering meditation, 36

Mats, 81

Maya, 67, 320

Medical care, 266

Meditation defined, xv, xvii,
xix, 30–33, 114, 142, 320

Meditation objects, 50, 77,
110, 162, 177–78, 320

Meetings, 228–29

Merging, 113–14

Merton, Thomas, 144

Metta, 273, 320

Metta Sutra, 278, 320

Middle way, 65, 70–71, 127,
320

Mind wandering.
  see Distractions

Mindfulness, 132, 221–35.
  see also Awareness;
  while eating, 239–42;
  and pain, 262–65

Minkisi, 180, 320

Miracles, 68

Monasteries, 64, 129

Monk, 191

Moon breath, 119

Mother Goddess, 211–12

Mudra, 84, 320

Muhammad, 169–71

Muladhara, 118

Music, 165–68, 175

Mysticism, 172

# N

Namibian bone meditation,

177–79

Native American, 181–86

New Age, 188

Nirvana, 53, 320

Noble silence, 309–10, 320

Noise.
  *see* Quiet

Norepinephrine, 256, 321

Noting, 134–35, 321

# O

Object of meditation.
  *see* Meditation object

Observation, 133

Occult, 68

Om, 34, 109, 321

Om breath, 120

Oneness, 208, 250.
  *see also* Samadhi

Oracle, 179

Orgasm, 250–51

Orisha, 180, 321

Ouspensky, P. D., 194

Out loud, 95

Over-meditating, 37

# P

Pain, 73–74, 77, 98.
  *see also* Dharma pain;
  Suffering;
  components of, 261;
  as meditation object, 264–65;

reduction of, 137, 259–65

Pali, 321

Pantheon, 321

Partner, 246–54

Passivity, 265–66

Past and future, 48–49, 67

Path of the Sly Man, 192

Patience, 62, 265

Peace of Mind, 167, 303

Peak experiences, 38, 221

Perils.
  *see* Barriers

Personal salvation, 190

Personality, 192–93, 268

Pilgrimage, 170–71

Pillows, 77

Pitfalls.
  *see* Barriers

Plainsong.
  *see* Gregorian Chant

Play, 231

Popularity of meditation,
126, 188–89, 201

Power, 120, 141, 146

Practice, 62, 74, 97, 223;
  at retreats, 300

Prana, 321

Pranic breathing.
  *see* Breathing meditation

Prayer, 34, 109, 143–45, 148,
172.
  *see also* Lord's Prayer;

of Jesus, 157–59

Preconceptions.
see Expectations

Preparation for meditation, 29, 40, 92, 107

Present moment, 132, 221–24, 221–35, 275

Privacy, 308

Prophecy, 207–08

Psychotherapy, 257–58

Publicity, 304

Purification, 107, 133, 174, 184, 277

**Q**

Quarter lotus, 89

Quies, 158, 321

Quiet.
see Silence

**R**

Reactions, 38–39, 51–52, 96

Relaxation, 30, 33, 97

Religion, 62, 177

Religious traditions, 33–36, 105–106

Research, 27–29, 188, 203, 263

Resistance, 60, 262

Retreat, 76, 299–313;
Manager, 308

Right brain.
see Left brain/right brain

Rinzai, 127, 321

Ritual, 108, 133

Roshi, 25, 321

Ruah, 321

**S**

Sashasrara, 117, 118, 322

Sacred geometry, 160

Sadhana, 247

Saliva, 83

Samadhi, 250, 321

Samatha, 321
see also Mindfulness

Samu, 227, 238–39, 311, 322

Sanskrit, 109, 322

Satori, 126, 128, 322

Schedule, 94–95;
at retreats, 300, 307

Self: inner, 192–93;
lovingkindness to, 285–86, 289–91;
observation, 27, 133, 192–93;
in driving, 231;
at work, 226–29;
partner's, 248;
realization, 125

Sephiroth, 152–53, 322

Serenity, 277

Serpent breath, 121

Sexuality, 247, 248–54

Shaman, 113–14, 182, 322

Shango, 180–81

Shema, 149, 322

Shikantaza, 127, 130, 322

Siddhartha.
  *see* Buddha

Silence, 63, 146–47.
  *see also* Noble silence

Sitting, 44, 73–76, 81–92, 303.
  *see also* Shikantaza

Skepticism, 59–61, 97

Sleeping, 44, 63, 233–34

Sleeping Prophet, 205206

Soto, 127, 130–31, 322

Sound, 95.
  *see also* Silence

Spine.
  *see* Back

Spirits, 177, 182

Spiritual: development, 225;
  first aid, 37;
  friend, 294–96;
  intoxication, 173–74;
  materialism, 66–67;
  in relationships, 246–54

Spoon breath, 121

Sports, 232–33

Stillness strategy, 54

Stress reduction, 203–04,
256–59

Study, 133

Suffering, 192, 255, 262–63.
  *see also* Pain;
  and Tonglen, 280–82

Sufism, 172–73

Sun breath, 119

Support.
  *see* Cushions

Sushuma breath, 119

Sutras, xxi, 124, 140

Suzuki Roshi, Shunryu, 25,
31, 53, 74, 126

Svadisthana, 118

Swinging Door strategy,
53–54

Synergy, 74, 273

**T**

Tai-chi, 323

Tai-pei, 323

Tantra, 117, 140, 249–50,
254, 323

Tao, 34, 323

Tarot, 194–95

Teachers, 48, 65, 128, 133,
151, 177, 293–98;
  at retreats, 301, 312–13

Techniques, 217

Theories of meditation, 267

Theravada, 107, 132, 137, 323

Thinking, 33, 52, 99, 136

Third eye, 185

Thought(s).
  *see* Thinking

Three levels, 208

Thumbs, 85

Tibetan Buddhism, 140, 273.

*see also* Vajrayana

Tibetan visualization, 141–42

Time, 39, 93–94, 248;
  as meditation object, 310

Timing tape, 95

Tokusan, 130, 217, 323
  *see also* Meditation object; Mindfulness

Tonglen, 280–82, 323

Tongue, 82–83

Torah, 323

Totem, 184–85

Traditional peoples, 175–86

Training, 248

Transcendental Meditation, 200–204

Transducers, 208

Transition, 40–41, 229

Tree of Life, 150–54

Trust, 47

**U**

Unconscious, 198–99

Unhappiness, 48, 267

Upanishads, 109

**V**

Vacation, 299

Vajrayana, 35, 140, 323

Vipassana, 132–33, 324

Vishuddha, 118

Vision, 111–12

Visitor, 48

Visualization, 111–14, 141–42;
  of the positive, 196–200

**W**

Walking meditation, 160–64

Weakness, 281, 290–81

Western traditions, 143–74

Wheelchairs, 76, 77

Whistle breath, 121

Wicca, 324

Wisdom, 101, 127, 198–99, 274

Withdrawal, 63, 299

Work at retreats, 311

Workplace, 203–204, 224–29

**Y**

Yoga, 116, 324

Yogi, 113–14, 191, 324

Yogic flying, 204–205

**Z**

Zabuton, 81, 324

Zafu, 77, 324

Zazen, 34, 54, 130, 324

Zen, 53, 55, 64, 124–31, 324;
  stink of, 67

Zendo, 64, 76, 108, 324

Zikr, 174, 324

Zone, 74, 221

## ABOUT THE AUTHOR

Victor N. Davich has studied for more than twenty-five years with several of the West's foremost meditation teachers. He has also been a business affairs attorney, creative consultant, and producer for Paramount Pictures, Fox Broadcasting, and Universal-TV. He resides in Venice, California and may be contacted via e-mail at sitstill98@aol.com.